The GACHÍ

My Gypsy Flamenco Quest

Susan Salguero

HICKEY'S BOOKS

Original Design, Photo Imagery, Layout: Ben Skirven

Final Layout, Design & Publication Management by:
Lamp Post Inc.
619.589.1400
www.lamppostpubs.com

Published by:

Hickey's Books
8749 La Mesa Boulevard, PMB 21
La Mesa, CA 91941
www.hickeybooks.com
hickeybooks@juno.com

To Frank,

my brave son.

Introduction

My cousin asked if I'd read a story her friend wrote about her life as a flamenco dancer. Spain was a favorite place of mine, I'd bought a flamenco guitar there and meant to learn how to play that style one day. So I agreed.

The story enchanted me. It gave me the chance to know intimately a culture and people I wouldn't have otherwise met. It helped me to better understand the plight of women in a mans' world. Its insights and graceful language informed and charmed me. So when I learned the author had no clue about submitting to agents or editors, I offered to help her.

All who read the manuscript praised it. But once again commerce trumped art. Agents and editors doubted the story of a flamenco dancer would attract a legion of readers.

Hickey's Books isn't about money. It's about helping valuable works find their readers. So we're proud and delighted to offer *The Gachí*.

We invite you to savor many rich layers of this true story about a young woman who discovers her place in a strange and far-off land.

Ken Kuhlken, author and publisher
www.kenkuhlken.net

Foreword

Susan Salguero paints an accurate and poignant portrait of Flamenco life with vivid sights and delights of a Spanish world. All the bustle of family life and strife within the whitewashed walls of a Spanish household are offered faithfully and without varnish.

For those of us who have actually sat in Antonio Pulpón's office waiting for work, across the room from such notables as Antonio Montoya "El Faruco" and Antonio Nuñes "El Chocolate", these passages bring back heartfelt memories of joy and pain. Foreign artists, struggling to comprehend a complex art form with at best a limited comprehension of the language and the intricacies of the music, were used to fill in for legitimate flamencos at the worst possible venues.

We worked and waited for that moment of acceptance into the flamenco world with a simple gesture or comment of approval that we did it right. Those moments were few and far between.

This book provides all of the excitement of flamenco, and all of the pain that follows that life. The opportunity to see it again from a woman's perspective opens wounds on the soul.

All of the memories are in the book waiting, to be discovered by the reader. The food, the wine, the street, the tablao, the music, the dance, and always the song. Beneath everything is the rhythm. The counter-time and the pulse of *palmas*, some matching the very rhythm of life in the heart, infects you with fascination. Flamenco has a way of captivating the soul and the imagination. This book gives you a clear glimpse into flamenco and why it can hold you captive.

Russ Baggerly, Flamenco Guitarist

Preface

I was not the only angry woman at Cal Berkeley. And I was unaware of the gender disdain and family guilt that smothered me. I only knew I had to flee. Somehow I could not save the world on a freedom train, until I had first saved myself.

My resistance impelled me on a jagged journey over a quarter of the earth's circumference to Spain. I was a foreigner in Spain, a *Gachí* amongst Gypsies. But the isolation I felt there, I had brought with me.

I chose Seville, a provincial city fertile with the art of Flamenco. Drawn by the cry of guitar, I sought indomitability, that arch of spine, that wild and perfect audacity. Coveting gypsy power, driven to dance, I staked my life on Flamenco.

Susan Salguero

Prologue

Lights are low. Center stage is bare, spot-lit to an expectant amber glow. Three men wait in the dusk. The guitarist sits cradling his guitar; strands of black hair straying across its blond wood. He picks out a melody with bare fingers and percussive slaps as if he were abusing the guitar. And it cries.

Flanking him like sentinels, two men stand clapping to his somber beat. One begins to hum, warming into the *Soleá*, flamenco song of solitude.

The room hushes. A dancer paces on stage. The lament draws her into the diluted light and cigarette haze. Smooth as liquid cat she stalks. Chest arching high, head lowered, arms restrained -- a wild thing on an invisible leash. Her dark hair swings long, gathered behind her back with flaming roses. Ready to pounce, the woman pauses in the light of center stage, facing the crowd.

The music raves and pleads.

Her eyes glisten fierce in the lights. Swathed to the throat in black, with a large oval hole cut out of front and back; white woman's breast and soul shine forth through the black frame. With slow arrogance, her body uncurls to unfurl her arms and raise her head.

Against her will, she submits to the urgent music. Her movements undulate, flow seamless as a shadow over uneven ground. Black swinging skirts dip and bob with the lift of her knee, cresting in waves of fuchsia under-ruffles. She prances, spoiling for a fight, daring with a turn, citing with a sudden stance. Bare back to the audience, she peers over her shoulder. Hair flies to the beat, and she peers over the other shoulder. Neat hips swivel, as the beat insists and throbs. Her arms, sheathed in black, reach out supplicating, menacing, caressing. Subtle offerings.

Her beauty is tragic. She belongs to everyone and to no one. She dances like someone in the dark impelled toward light. She dances in delight of her lean fluent body. Yet she reaches beyond.

Tempo builds, music surges. Hot pink swirls like a cape around her curved legs. She spins, tosses her hair, and with the music, stops dead.

No one breathes. Her eyes devour them. Her chest heaves and, in the stillness, like heartbeat, her feet begin to drum. She grabs up handfuls of skirts and nails the beat to the floor. Nailing her pain, nailing her fear, nailing her bitterness to that stage. Her mouth opens in ecstatic wrath. Bird of prey, she attacks that rhythm, backs up and attacks again. She recedes, then turns on it again, her intrepid feet drumming.

She exchanges glances of complicity with the guitarist. The pounding pulse accelerates. Their smiles flicker with the intimacy of their musical bond. She flips her skirts like two sidewheels. A mischievous glance over her shoulder hurls a last insult. The shouts and clapping behind her thicken, heighten her ferocity. Music mounts, peaks to unbearable tension. As passion threatens to annihilate, she turns to leave in a blur of fuchsia, a last fling of hair. She launches across the stage and recoils, retreats in mortal doubt then spins and sets out again, stepping high, skirts leaping. Pain recoils her again. She turns in a primal crouch and with grueling tension unwinds herself until at last, her arms imploring on high, she arches back, melting over into the music that is carrying her away as if draped over a lover's arm. Surrendered.

The Flamenco's last wailing plea dies. A last rugged flourish of guitar ends in silence.

In the dark wings, she straightens out of the backbend, careful to avoid pulleys and ropes. She pushes wet strands of hair off her face.

"That was GOOD. God, that was good," she pants to herself. "'Tonight you danced the Soleá.'"

That was what he had said to her, back in another time, another country. Her most cherished praise. Her Gypsy man had told her once, "Tonight you danced the Soleá." Checking for the roses entangled in her hair, she tosses the mess behind her and returns to the light for bows.

A candle-lit supperclub full of people; some on their feet, are applauding. The dancer looks a few in the eye and showers her delight upon them. Something about no longer seeking it makes triumph sweeter. No longer in doubt, no longer in need, she has danced for herself, for her soul. She is free. Laughing, she nods in agreement with their applause. She is DONE, a finished piece.

I
Seville

One

"*Uno dos TRES, cuatro cinco SEIS, siete OCHO, nueve DIEZ.*
That's it. Good. Again. One two THREE, four five SIX,
seven EIGHT, nine TEN. Then turn here ..." My teacher's
boots kicked and swiveled on the scarred wood floor. I
counted and copied.

"That's it. No no, just kick to the left and cross over to
the right. *Así. Eso es,*" he praised. I caught my breath, moistened lips, and launched again.

"Now angle your body like this. *Así, no. ASI.*"

My long, raised arm like a battle pennant, twinned his in
the studio mirror, my strutting body at an angle, parallel to
his.

"Okay, now with castanets. Right arm up first. Good.
Then left. Ree ah, ree ah, pee tah," rolling the r's, his tongue
imitated the castanets' trill, "Ree ah, ree ah, pee tah."

Our arms wreathed our heads, a pair of circles in the
mirror. I watched and adjusted and watched and adjusted.
My body echoed his directly, without intervening thought.
I had that knack. I learned to dance by osmosis.

Caballo, a retired dancer of rosebud lips and dainty
hands, sold his old Flamenco fare to new dancers. A satis-
factory offering for a beginning foreigner. Eagerly, I

absorbed it. I did not savor his style, but he was generous with the basics I needed to get started. Style would come later. Much later.

I glimpsed my own greedy lopsided grin in the mirror, tongue of voluptuary hooking over moist, even teeth, my forehead beaded, and large-lidded eyes intense with concentration. My forearms ached as I drove my whacking castanets in arcs about my head.

Suddenly I dropped my arms. Two people had invaded the studio. An American woman I knew, with a Gypsy man I did not. Embarrassed to be seen here, I blushed. My head lowered, my shoulders rounded. I felt exposed as a novice, as an American "groupy" in Spain, already twenty-four and foolishly attempting this art which locals learned as children. The woman greeted Caballo and seemed to be pressing him for something.

"What's up, Rosa?"

"Caballo, look, I wanted you to meet this gentleman here, he's a..."

Irked at the interruption, I ignored them and approached the mirror.

Watching my coltish image, I struck poses. I tried to turn my elbows up like Flamenco dancers did, like tarantula spider legs. It pained. My shoulder joints complained and the castanets weighted my hands. I rested them on hips and turned to watch my back in the mirror, my long spine stretched into a Flamenco's arch. I looked audacious. Busty. But it hurt to sustain it even for a moment. My elbows were angles instead of curves, my brown hair was short, my skin mottled, and my practice shoes cloddish. Great.

I studied my face. It was no more beautiful than my boney body. But, like my body, this face had movement, life. A disaster at a poker table, I knew, my face revealed my every mood. My poorly turned nose and long upper lip were redeemed only by a high shadowing cheekbone, and huge melting eyes -- imperceptibly irregular -- animated eyes. My father's eyes. My family's English eyes that shed a warm olive light.

I dropped the smile, deciding to dance with somber face and the foreboding hostility I had seen on stages. I scowled now at the people reflected behind me, annoyed that they were wasting my half-hour class. To discourage further talk, I petulantly resumed stomping out my routine.

"*Uno dos TRES, cuatro cinco SEIS, siete OCHO, nueve DIEZ,*" I huffed, pounding out heelwork, shoe metal clattering.

"Susie," the American woman interrupted me. Big, blasé, and drunk, Rose called me over. Just days earlier Rose had appointed herself my guide to Flamenco. Infamous around Seville, with buck teeth and amazing self-assurance, smelling of expensive perfume and expensive liquor, Rose had claimed in nasal confidence that she had personally laid every Flamenco in the province.

"Susie, come here. I want you to meet Curro," Rose commanded. Reluctantly, the dance pupil clacked across the floor. This Curro person, swarthy and stocky, with shiny ringlets at the back of his head, was all smiles. I automatically appraised him and dismissed him as too short, too handsome, and too cocky.

"They call me Curro de Alcalá. I'm a Flamenco singer, *Cantaor Flamenco*, at your service." With a mocking stare, Curro offered a formal handshake.

I tried to ignore the musty warmth of his voice. I shook his hand around my sweat-moistened castanet, rolled out a pat Spanish phrase, then excused myself and returned to my mirror and my footwork. They left. But my class was ruined that day.

Two

Hush prevailed, and the fragrance of orange blossoms. Flaming bougainvillea cascaded over stark white walls. Familiar from the moment I had arrived, Seville soothed me. The fantasy, history, and reality of Seville wove a lovely haven for me.

Toting my dance shoes and castanets, I toured the old Spanish streets by myself. I peered through high wrought iron gates into wealthy mansions of the Santa Cruz neighborhood. Shaded pools and thick potted ferns in tiled patios spilled cool comfort onto the cobbled lanes. Ornate windows were barred for centuries to protect Spanish women from the passions of men. My own eyes reflected back at me between those iron bars.

I turned into a quiet courtyard, where the "Barber of Seville" once cut gentlemen's hair. I had a room in the little *pensión* there.

"*Buenos días, niña,*" greeted Don Andrés. Rocking on the two back legs of his chair in the doorway, he saluted his tenant.

"Been to dance class," I offered.

"*Bien, bien.*"

"Don Andrés, doesn't my rehearsing on the roof bother your family?"

"No, *hija*, as long as it's in the morning. Everybody is up making noises of their own. These houses are *moriscos*, built very thick. Hundreds of years old. No little American girl is going to rattle them." His voice was fatherly. "Why do you want to learn Flamenco, anyway?"

"*No sé*," I shrugged. "I have to dance. I'll learn here, then dance in California."

"Well now, let me give you some advice." Don Andrés cleared his throat. "Stay away from Gypsies. If they don't get you on the way in, they'll get you on the way out. Everyone knows that."

Stung, I edged away. Prejudice always sucked something out of me. And often in Spain would I hear that mean refrain.

"Thanks," I nodded with averted eyes. I went into Pensión Vida to leave my dancewear on my suitcase there. I left Don Andrés clucking to himself, resting his arms across his wide girth like somebody of authority.

ॐॐॐ   ॐॐॐ

Peering into the sudden dusk of the nearby University, I found my class posted. My first job in Spain while I learned to dance, I would teach English Conversation II. My steps reverberated in the endless hallways and salons of this old tobacco factory of Seville. I envisioned the fiery Gypsy Carmen, brawling here a century ago. Flashing knives and eyes, tossing hair, sneering hostility and indomitability. Carmen's protest was mine. Unconscious protests, both.

Born in 1940 into the most privileged culture of the world -- White Middle Class America -- I had been under-privileged. Merely a female. Subtly despised. I had no rights, except three: to cook, to bear children, and to be the power behind a man. That scorn, insidious and pervasive as the smog of Pasadena, was suffocating me.

❧❧❧   ❧❧❧

I paused at the foot of the Giralda, the Moorish tower that pierced the heart of Seville. Squinting up, my eyes scaled the walls to the top observation windows. Fresh air and a view always helped when I felt dejected. No time to climb now, though. I was hungry.

In these lanes surrounding the Giralda, the only traffic noise was human conversation. The center of Seville was quiet brick streets for pedestrians only. I entered Calle Sierpes. Giant canvases, suspended between buildings, filtered the cruel Spanish sun into a billowing twilight. Here clustered the little cafe-bars, the parlors of Andalucía, which provided the gracious, long evening social life of the *Sevillanos*. The streets echoed high heels on bricks, hiss of espresso steamers, gurgle of beer taps, clink of wine glasses, and laughter.

An initiate to the gentle ways of Seville, I was learning. I worked in the morning -- teaching English and studying dancing. I ate dinner at midday, slept in the afternoon, and stayed up late at night. My favorite eateries were El Mesón over the Triana Bridge, and Enrique's Place, behind the cathedral of Seville, just around the corner from the place where I slept alone.

હન્ હન્ હન્   ન્ન ન્ન ન્ન

Savory aromas greeted me at Enrique's Place.

"Heavenly! Give me some of that, Enrique, whatever you're cooking. I'm starving. And *tinto*, please."

"It's beef in sherry. Not quite done." He poured me a glass of red wine. "Rosa was looking for you. And Mr. Vavra, the American photographer."

Food at Enrique's came in the form of *tapas* - home-made morsels on tiny milk glass oblong dishes. Saffron rice, garlic fried spinach, spicy shrimplets, deep-fried squid. A tapa came with each drink. He served only draft beer and house wine, in tiny glasses. After five or six tapas, I had been fed, and my problems had diminished as well.

Someone offered me a cigarette and lit it. I took my glass to a table in the window. I was becoming fond of wine. Although I never bought cigarettes, I smoked anything offered -- the harsh black Celtas, the perfumed Antillanas, mild Marlboros. But I sat alone.

Men were standing two or three deep at the bar, arguing and gesturing and ceremoniously exchanging cigarettes. They recited banalities, knuckling the counter- top with self-importance.

It was the early afternoon crowd: bank employees on

their way home to family dinner and siesta; Flamencos hoping to make lucrative acquaintances; occasional foreigners seeking Flamencos. Enrique slid them drinks, his toothful grin bounced along the counter, an intimate welcome to all his customers. Including Gypsies. Including a foreign white woman. Including world class photographer Robert Vavra, who was seeking someone to housesit his flat for him. The pert tiles and new wood of Enrique's Place lacked the dingy odors and the dignity of the old wine-soaked bodegas. But Enrique's friendliness made it homey.

I sat and sipped and watched the tobacco man ply his friendly trade. Just inside the door, the tobacco man with his cigarettes and matches in a little carrying case on a tripod, ran his post. He nodded and chatted, the center of the Spanish man's world, the source of local gossip and bullfight news. He sold loose cigarettes, one or two at a time, lighting them gallantly. I wondered how his paltry business could feed his family. Everything seemed so simple here.

At the bar, Enrique gathered up used glasses and merely rinsed them in cold water. I swallowed tart tinto and marvelled that I was drinking the germs from a thousand Spanish mouths. I did not mind. I let the wine take care of that.

"Hello there, Susie."

With glass and cigarette in the same hand, Rose pulled out a chair and sat, uninvited and unwelcome. Although bemused by Rose's gall, I was embarrassed to be classed with her. I prided myself on an ability to blend into a culture without offending local sensibilities. My eyes flicked beyond Rose to see if anyone noticed that this Ultimate Ugly American sat with me. Of course, no one noticed us.

"Did you like the Flamenco show at La Cochera, last night?" Rose queried in her intimate tone.

"Lots of stuck-up pouty-mouth girls. Obviously spend more time on their hair than their dancing."

"They're teenagers for godsake. And they're not Gypsies."

"They're not?" I tolerated Rose's company for her Flamenco tips.

"No, silly, they're *Gaché*."

"*Gaché*."

"*Gaché. Gachó. Gachí.* That is the word Gypsies use for people who are not Gypsies. I'm a *Gachí*. So are you, sweetheart, and don't you forget it."

Enrique placed steaming food before me, which I immediately stabbed with my fork. I never did see Rose eat. Draining her glass, my mentor offered,

"The show at the Guajira is better. Try the Guajira."

"Where?"

"It's another Flamenco *tablao*, like La Cochera. In Triana, the Gypsy neighborhood across the river. Actually, the dancers at the Guajira are mostly Gaché too."

"So where do Gypsies dance?" I implored. Sixteen years old when my world had been altered by the famous Gypsy, Carmen Amaya at the Pasadena Civic Auditorium. The greatest living Flamenco danced in my own home town. A tiny tornado of fringes and heelwork, with the wrath of God pursing her brown face, and unpredictable as sabotage. She was revolution!

"Where are all the Gypsy dancers?"

"Dunno. I haven't seen much dancing. I'm more interested in the singing." She took a drag on her cigarette.

"You mean, you are more interested in the singer."

"Right." Rose inhaled deeply and committedly.

"Is that Curro your boyfriend?" inquired the aspiring dancer who had no interest in him whatsoever.

"I told you," slurred Rose, "I am an independent operator." Her eyes blinked in slow motion. "How's your class with Caballo coming along?"

"Well, I'm sure that I've got that special something. But I can see that same secret conviction glowing in the eyes of each crummy fellow pupil. So I have no clue." I filled my mouth with food, which did not deter me from further speech. "My first teacher was 'Henry the Cripple.' Fat and fruity. And infinitely bored."

"Well, he has taught some famous dancers."

"He was hellbent on not teaching me a thing. He walked like a hobby horse, sat on his fat butt my whole class. I thought he couldn't dance until I caught him with a Spanish pupil. He was clicking away on those mismatched legs! Throughout my lessons, he plunked out the rhythm on a listless guitar, making faces at himself in the mirror." I drank my wine. "At least Caballo shows interest, and dances along with me. I learn fast that way."

I returned to the bar for more food and wine, thinking about my dancing. Caballo only taught the steps. Latino students in America had taught my body. Mambo, merengue, cha cha, rumba. Dancing close as skin, my body received its dance from each man's body. Each limb and muscle directly followed his sustained pull, his resistance, his fluidity. A virgin in chronic arousal, my controlled desire empowered my movements with a subtle fire. Modern dance classes in college gave me the workouts to strengthen and stretch. Here in Seville, my body was ready to dance. Now to learn the feet and arms from Caballo. Good enough. Then style. Gypsies for style.

"Listen," Rose interrupted my thoughts. "Meet me here tonight at ten." She glimpsed someone outside and stood up. "We'll grab a cab and I'll show you the best place in Triana for after-hours Flamenco."

"Sure," I agreed, controlling my glee. Rose left, her stride studious, as if there were treacherous terrain to cover.

So I remained, alone again with my fork. I ate thoughtfully. I felt at home in this soft city. Seville charmed me with its mellow customs and fragrant evening air. But I was not happy. The determination to finish out the school year teaching English, the anticipation of the famous Spring bullfights, and my persistent seven-year ambition to become a wild Flamenco dancer, kept me in Seville. And I had closed other doors behind me. I really had nowhere else to go, nothing else to pursue.

Waiting for my sixth tapa, I did not notice Curro until

he approached a table near me. He was slowly working his way among the crowd, "raffling" a pair of socks he had on credit from a nearby shop. Men hardly paused in their bombastic banter as they dug for a nickel and took a number. He smiled and agreed his quiet way through the bar. After he had sold all his numbers, he simply disappeared.

Conversation coursed, soda bottles hissed. As I squeezed lemon on my squid, I suddenly realized that the raffle had never taken place. I was stunned. Virtuous Anglo, I was righteously amazed at the man's audacity. Curro, a Gypsy, hailing from exotic ethics, from centuries of hoaxes, was pursuing ancient custom as he left with a new, free, pair of socks and a day's grocery money in his pocket.

And I knew even then, that perhaps Curro's honest lies were better than my dishonest truths. The difference between his world and mine was appealing.

Three

I climbed the Giralda. I needed to think. A fresh view. Arabian horsemen had clopped up these inner ramps without dismounting, seven centuries ago. I hiked it alone, imagining the echoes of their hooves, their sparks on stones. At the top of the tower, I caught my breath. I surveyed the history of Seville in one sweeping gaze.

Through filigreed arches, I gazed wistfully down upon the deserted Alcazar palace, where Sephardic sages had translated all the known books on surgery and philosophy; where Eastern melodies in ancient modes caressed strings; where a Moorish princess once cavorted in a private inner patio in a mudbath of cinnamon and rosewater. Cherished.

I hadn't been so cherished in America, my head dented all night by curlers, my round breasts and square feet insulted all day by pointy bras and pointier shoes. Improved by shaved legs and greased red lips, a commodity, I had been humiliated when men whistled, humiliated when they did not.

The silent streets of Seville, tangled and ancient, were my refuge. These houses so matted in clumps that from directly above I could not pick out mine, harbored me somehow. Springtime, the cobbled streets of this old rich

Jewish quarter would blossom with bright polka-dot 'gypsy' dresses. Nearby, rows of orange trees and flying buttresses flanked the massive cathedral where Spanish austerity had its renaissance. In the personal chapel of King Ferdinand and Queen Isabella, Columbus prayed before embarking, and the brutalities of the Inquisition were baptized.

Beyond flowed the idle River Guadalquivir, once a teeming port that sucked all the gold from the Americas. Plunder was recorded at the countinghouse, the stubby "Tower of Gold," now abandoned on empty docks.

The bullring, upriver, a disk of golden sand, radiated the magic of ancient male fertility rites. Power. Power. Where was my power?

Distant suburbs called Los Remedios - squared paved streets with apartments like stacked cubes - had accumulated outside this gnarled ancient capital of the province of Seville. From there emerged a haunting call, the mouth organ of the Gypsy knife-sharpener, a sad hungry tootle carried on the wind that tossed my cropped hair and blew strands across my lips while I ached with the lust and the loneliness of an adventurer needed by no one.

Checking my tourist map, I picked out the parish Church of the Macarena, the Virgin whom bullfighters implored as they dressed in satin to meet their death. The Macarena's photo adorned more postcards than they did. Arrayed in diamond heirlooms by rich Sevillanos for the Holy Week procession, the Macarena would be cheered by the passionate poor while paraded through the streets on the shoulders of sweating stevedores, her robes jiggling, her glass tears glittering on her dolly face.

Near the Church of the Macarena sprawled the Virgin's county hospital for the poor. People flocked to the Macarena Hospital to spawn and die, sometimes simultaneously. As I surveyed its ominous grid of wings and corridors fenced in like a palace, I did not know that one day I would sleep in a bed there.

Across the river, in the Gypsy ghetto of Triana, nomads had exchanged their migratory freedom for urban misery, while assimilating Spain's forgotten Moorish and Jewish music. Only their singing, Flamenco cante, released their captured souls. Precision staccato of clapping hands, rhythmic cry of guitar, and the unforgettable Gypsies' lament, rose from wine taverns to the apathetic skies. Like sirens' songs, which lured mariners to their destruction, those sounds had mysteriously drawn me across the sea. Groping toward Flamenco, I was grappling for myself. Gypsies were also lonely human beings, also despised. But undaunted. Flamencos knew something ...

I drew a deep sigh, clutched my shoulder bag, folded my map, and spiraled down the tower ramp. I had no place to go but I was in a terrific hurry.

On Sierpes Street, I passed a lottery vendor, a cripple from the Spanish Civil War, stationed at a street corner with his strips of numbers and his carnival mouth dangling a yellowed cigarette butt. I, a casualty of American peacetime, stared at him.

࿔࿔࿔ ࿔࿔࿔

I saw Curro next on one of my late night Flamenco quests, in a lowlife tavern in the seamy Pañoleta, beyond the Triana neighborhood where the Flamencos and streetwalkers both waited for rich customers. I hoped to unearth a Flamenco songfest in session and imbibe its raw urban blues. I risked being alone after midnight out in lawless Triana, gambling at finding real Flamenco, desperate as I was for its key to my liberation.

Nervously clutching my glass of cheap red wine, I stood at the bar, sniffed the pungency of old wine barrels, of strong coffee, and wondered what the dirt in the corners of the floor was hiding. I timidly cast my eyes about, then returned them to my glass. I sipped and tried to blend in. Obviously not a big spender, I was safely ignored by the few people around.

But, there was no Flamenco here tonight. I decided to leave, emptied my glass, and turned to the door. And there appeared Curro standing before me. A dark proud bantam, chest bulging under his open suit jacket, immaculate white shirt showing brown chunk of throat. He stood too close and beamed as though he had something to offer me. His mouth lush and silent, his eyes in mine languorous, a dark conceit, a nameless power. Curro stood in total fearlessness.

No words came to me. Drawn to him and alarmed by that fascination, I muddled. When a cab emptied at the door I bolted for it. Rich *señoritos* were arriving, Flamenco seemed imminent, but I fled.

$\mathcal{F}our$

My room in Pensión Vida could provoke nightmares. A high-ceilinged hallway had been walled off and furnished. No outside windows, it faced the inner courtyard in a claustrophobic, tilted way. An end-of-the-line room, it gave a caged feeling. A good place to drink directly from a bottle, or a gun. Or at least to diddle myself goofy under the covers.

Instead, I wrote my heart out to my friend Jessica. My lifeline, ironically, because later she died of loneliness.

After being out all night chasing down Flamenco, the real stuff, in the ventas outside of Triana, I have an 8:00 a.m. English class. A shot of cognac, lots of sugar and hot milk in my morning coffee keep the damp out of my bones in that tiled Andalusían classroom, which is cold as a butcher's walk-in.

The Moors came from Africa's deserts to build cool homes with no heating systems. Surprise! Seville has "nine months of winter and three months of hell." It rhymes in Spanish - "nueve meses de invierno y tres meses de infierno." They got the hell down pat, but in seven hundred years those Moors never figured out what to do with winter. I did. Cognac in my coffee.

With churros to dunk -- very eggy dough in huge spirals like steering wheels, deep fried in a huge vat of oil by the man in a tiny hole-in-the-wall shop. At the counter in the doorway, his wife breaks off six-inch sticks, thick as a finger, wraps them in coarse brown paper which is getting oil-blotched. I take it next door to the bar, stand at the counter asking for milk coffee with cognac, and they give me a heavy white plate for my churros. It simply warms one's gizzard. It's the bar directly across from the entrance to the orange court of the Seville cathedral. Beauty. History. Churros. And cognac in my coffee. Life's little pleasures.

Well, Jessica, there's a big convention in town now. They call it a mission. Three hundred ninety-eight priests from northern Spain have inundated Seville for a unique reanimation of Sevillian religion. The "boys" seem to be having a good time. Rich priests, beaming and as well-fed as a convention of back-slapping liquor salesmen, buy expensive almonds from street vendors and loiter in laughing groups. They eat churros and coffee for breakfast at 11:00 a.m., no later!

The mission for my soul? They pipe sermons every few evenings over LOUD speakers strung up in streets all over the city. The sermon is delivered about Jesus and such things at high dramatic pitch by a good orator. Although, no better oratory than that delivered by fat Don Andrés, about absolutely nothing, sitting pompously in his little Pensión Vida patio. No better orator than any little Spanish man in any café, talking trivia with great national verve.

I'm beginning to enjoy my English students. My remedial classes, at the private school, are very small and all for young males who have failed their English requirements to qualify for *universities. Ages 16 to 20, precious unspoiled things. There are a couple of petulant succulent specimens that I am beginning to lust after. I condone their 'she have' and 'we doesn't' with a gentle smile, or worse, a giggle.*

Jessica, you ask if I could live a whole lifetime in Seville. God, no! Nor anywhere. Temporary hunks, please, or this lifetime is intolerable.

For three days I contemplated going home to marry Floyd at Christmas. I'd surprise him and say here I am, take me, and Mommy'd be so happy creating my white bride's dress and I'd love it any way she'd make it, and I'd live happily ever after in a huge house --- one-third of which is a deliciously smelly kitchen -- with a yard full of dogs and little boys and tree houses.

Then I got hold of myself and resumed my preparation of lectures on grammar. So, yes, Jessica, you're right, we want to be old maids. If only it weren't a social stigma, and if only I weren't so fascinated with breasts and eager to suckle a baby at mine.

I received from Floyd an empty candy box, with a bitter pretentious poem entitled, 'In Lieu of Candy,' telling me metaphorically to go to hell. Which I am. The mission priests are just in the nick of time ... My left eye is twitching badly, and I'm discovering the Comfort of Mother Alcohol ...

Lost in memories of Floyd, I left off writing, my pen producing a growing black blotch on the aerogram. My first love affair had fully occupied my last year at Berkeley, nearly preventing me from graduation. After twenty-one years of steaming virginity, I had found something more important to do than study.

Floyd had needed a place to stay, could share my rented room. Generously, I borrowed a sleeping bag and allowed him to sleep on my small floor. Generously, he never used it. The corn-fresh smell of him, his urgent blue eyes, edible mouth, and his mastery, drove me wild. Floyd relieved me of all scholastic ambition, all remaining inhibition, and my worthless innocence.

Floyd.

Remembering him, I could hear once again, papers rustled and snapped, bookcovers crackled open and thumped closed. Belly to rumpled bed, I toiled over three dictionaries, deciphering a contemporary Spanish novel. Soon I quit. I stretched my confined and restless bare legs. Snuffing bed lamp, I dropped my head upon dreary pages, sniffed their library must, and gazed beyond my books. Floyd sat at my desk. I had promised not to interrupt his study. His bare shoulders and muscled arms were haloed by the glow of the desk lamp, his head bent over his text. He struggled with "gravel", "perk tests", geological lore which once had interested him. I watched him gaze at a diagram, sigh, then turn back a page to re-read. Abandoning my books, I padded across the worn carpet and paused behind him, my belly an inch from his bare back. My heat bridged air molecules. His breathing deepened. With a moan he removed his glasses, dropped head to hands, turned off his desk lamp and turned on to me. My lips dipped to drink thirstily the spring water of his young geological mouth. Our smiles entwined around caressing tongues and catching breaths. His hands cupped my head as he grew earnest. He stood, our mouths feeding upon each other, as I backed towards the bed. Books lay about us, pages crimped disrespectfully, abused amongst the sheets. The blue flame of the wall heater echoed our whispered urges, and shaded with blue the young curves of our gliding white bodies. Oh, the gift of a good education.

❧❧❧ ❧❧❧

With a deep sigh, I returned to myself in Seville and arose to mail my blotched letter. At American Express I was disappointed not to encounter a new friend I had met there. But I found him at the usual cheap restaurant that American backpack tourists find in every country.

Bob had the scruffy new beard, intelligent eyes, and precise speech of an American grad student on a fellowship in Spain - which he was. His wife was elsewhere studying something. I liked him. He had sufficient candor to cast aspersions on my Flamenco ambition, and the grace to get away with it, by admitting to a few self-delusions of his own.

"Well, isn't this the school marm from Des Moines who's transforming into a Flamenco dancer?" was his greeting when I sat down near him. "What was it now. . ? Ethel? Gertrude? Come sit over here, Hortense."

"Not until you're civil, son." I parked my purse, sat, grabbed a bollo bread, broke open the craggy crust, and gnawed. El Mesón did great business. Cheap meals, good stews, wine in carafes, all of two waiters in dirty tablecloths tied around their torsos with string, and priced for Spaniards, not tourists. Daily special today being salt cod and garbanzos stewed in tomato, I was a happy diner.

"Good food," slurped Bob.

"Be grateful Dr. Flemming's not here."

"Who's he?"

"The guy who discovered penicillin," I informed him. "Haven't you noticed his photo over bars wherever bullfighters or whores hang out? Touching."

"Why do you hang out in those bars?"

"Because there's Flamencos, as well as bullfighters and whores."

"Which are you?"

"I'm not telling," I grinned into my lifted wine glass.

સ્ટ્ર સ્ટ્ર સ્ટ્ર   સ્ટ્ર સ્ટ્ર સ્ટ્ર

Together we walked back from Triana towards the center of Seville. We crossed the Guadalquivir, scanning its riverbank along the edge of the city. I leaned on my forearms over the curlicued wrought iron hand rail of the bridge. Fall chill made the sun feel good on my back. I smelled the moist river air. A lazy river now, only small boats moored. Did Spanish galleons actually tie up at the Torre del Oro here? I admired the pristine white arches of the bullring across the water. Ancient little city, close to the ground, the only skyscraper was the Giralda, seven hundred years old.

I told Bob my home state was all prefabricated novelties, overnight developments, corporate conglomerates, roaring

freeway labyrinths; disassociation and alienation and imper-
manence. There was solace here in solid ancient Seville.

We sat in the park at the edge of the river, looking back
at the bridge we just crossed, the arabesqued metal girders
fanning beneath it. I gave Bob the briefest account of my
travels through Europe. Dancing in Mykonos taverns,
exploring the Roman catacombs with Jessica, wintering as a
cook in Zurich. I had kept Spain for last, my fantasy of
warm winds and tatters and Eastern melodies luring me,
awaiting me.

But first, I had gleaned one last stay in Floyd's arms.
He had maneuvered an exchange student's job for a
summer in London, where I joined him. I was his errant
erotic woman gratefully returned to the bed of my good
man. So good. I had exchanged that heady traveler's
freedom for Floyd's mastery; to be once again guided by
his powerful hands into ecstasy, into the sweet sleep of the
temporarily satiated...

Bob abruptly halted my revery, bringing me back to my
struggle as a rookie dancer in Sevilla.

"So how are the Flamenco classes progressing?"

"Mmm ... let's see ... I've got *Fandangos* -- two short
dances. And Caballo is starting to set an *Alegrías* for me."

"Forget it, Susie," Bob's sidelong glance was merry, as he
shook his head. "You will never look like a Flamenco
dancer."

"Never mind. I feel like a Flamenco dancer. Looks
come later. You have never seen me move to mambo music."

"You do walk nicely," he conceded.

I stretched out my hands, palms down, fingers splayed. "Yep, still here," I sighed. "Ugliest hands I have ever seen. Fingers as stumpy and wrinkled as the limbs of a rhino."

One day, these same hands would curl and shift, float like plumes at the end of my undulating arms. I would become known for my beautiful armwork. Arms like tapers, with fingers for flickering flames. Yes, there was a God. But back then, I did not know that, either.

"Who notices a hand wrapped around a castanet, anyway? Besides, I'm not referring to your hands. It's your face. Too perky. Face of a Virgo idealist do-gooder. Admit it, Susie. You were born to be a librarian."

He enjoyed teasing me. I think it masked that he also found me severely sensuous. Made him glad he was safely married, actually. A woman so complex must seem a handful. Voracious, urgent; and pissed, to boot.

"However ..." I confessed, "I am making a strange discovery." I waited. His silence gave me courage to divulge. "Maybe my ambition was not to be a woman Flamenco dancer. Maybe, all this time, I've been wanting to be a MALE Flamenco dancer! Or," I wondered, "maybe I want to have him. To eat him, or give birth to him."

"Nope. I just want to be him. Commanding, unfettered, yet self-contained. That belligerent arch of chest and back leg, his arrogant head, and totally dauntless rhythm. It thrills me so! The power. Could a human be so free, so fearless? Whence comes that wildness, that timing? What is there inside a man, that he could be that way ...? God, what blind bitter yearning ..."

We resumed walking in silence, turned away from the river into quieter back streets, approaching Calle Sierpes.

"Susie. Are you ... in crisis?"

I whooped with laughter. "Man, I AM Crisis. Walking crisis, like walking pneumonia."

What rare luxury. To be understood. "It's good to talk, Bob. Thanks. Nice walking with you, too. Keeps the stupid Spanish men away."

"Do they bother you?"

"Me? Any woman." My voice was throaty with conviction. "Spaniards don't entertain in their homes. They meet their friends in their favorite hangouts. They keep their womenfolk at home. Where they belong, of course," I sneered. "So a foreign woman, living alone in a pensión and eating out, finds herself out in a man's world. And the Spaniards think I am an easy mark."

"Not flattering ...?"

"I cannot begin to express to you how not interested I am in these jerks."

Amused by my vehemence, Bob nodded, like a corrected pupil. He patted my squared shoulder, and my hackles subsided.

"I dress frumpy to make life easier," I complained. "But that makes me depressed, and makes you say I look like a spinster." I was born for the stage. I could look any part I chose. And believe it myself ...

When Bob branched off toward his pensión, I continued through side streets with no sidewalks, listening to my steps echo, leaning against a building to let an occasional car pass. The uneven cobbles knocked my shoe off, and I paused to toe it back on. I heard the plastic mouth organ of a knife grinder. It sounded like a child's toy, fluting through the streets. Dozens of knife grinders in this city, their toot the theme of Seville, like the smell of burnt toast was the signature of Bruges, or lapping water the sound of Venice, drizzle the feel of London.

I passed him and his bicycle loaded with all his equipment. He had set the wheels out of commission to sharpen a pair of scissors. He was pedaling like mad to turn the grinding stone.

A Gypsy's way to make a living, I thought. Metal work. Fresh air. Nobody your boss. No place to call your own. Nothing to sweep. No neighbor you have to abide.

His music resumed behind me, as close to real music as the flailing of a damaged bird is to real flight. Too depressed to play a tune? He just ran his mouth down and up the scale. Waited, then up again. No melodic resolution. No finish. No closure. Just an endless chromatic question. Unanswered.

"Toodle oodle oo?"

❧❧❧ ❧❧❧

Instead of sleeping during Seville's siesta hours, I lay reviewing my plight. One of the disadvantages of traveling alone, you look at yourself. You weigh the causes of this elected loneliness. Back in America with Floyd, I had rejected wifehood. Then in London with Floyd, I refused marriage again. Why did I swerve from that well-beaten track. . ?

Serving Floyd that wifely ritual morning grapefruit, kissing his bare shoulder as he sat up in bed eating it, desire left my lips. In rainy London, I dutifully chatted with the Irish landlady, joked with the milkman, opened umbrella and shopped for a lean bit of bacon. Sweeping and broiling chops, I was cranky; making love, I was unresponsive. Plunking a coin in the meter to draw Floyd's bath, I felt revulsion. That last summer became a sample of urban marital life - and intolerable. I lamented in letters to Jessica.

I am repulsed by the threat of becoming imprisoned like my mother. Imprisoned by rage, frenzy, migraine headaches. Imprisoned by the common assumption that she liked to cook. Her crime? Womanhood.

Yet an unmarried woman is despised. My father considers spinsterhood a subtle form of perversion. It is a failure to be unmarried. Being a woman is scornable. With a man in tow she is somewhat vindicated. That stinks. That insult always hovers about me. I see no remedy other than escape.

I adore the man. I would hate being his wife. My whole body and soul craves to bear a child, to feel it suck life from my breast. My intellect reels at the boredom of child-rearing.

Damned either way. A lonely unloved woman was a bitter human being. Suicidal. Like my friend, Jessica, in fact. Yet an unappreciated married woman was a bitter human, too, with children to resent. Like my mother. My beautiful, unhappy, patronized mother.

Was there no other choice?

Floyd was innocent. Floyd had the succulent mouth of a fruit, but the wooden mind of an engineer. He had no idea what troubled me. He could not help me. So I had said farewell and fled to Spain... the last outpost.

Five

The day I heard Curro sing, my life veered on its axis. I was sitting alone as usual. Enrique's Place was full of the smoke and gab of men. Through the cigarette haze I saw him enter, and the rest of the room faded.

He was quietly drunk. He leaned against the wall just inside the door, to get his bearings. Still erect, he wore his same suit, his hair oiled neat. But his coat was ajar, his eyes were wheeling blind, and he moved as if under water. He stayed propped against the wall for a while, zombie-like amidst the boisterous crowd.

Then, without warning, Curro put his head back, drew his mouth over to one side and issued a primal cry, a wail so piercing and forlorn that it silenced the room.

Heads turned. His cry continued down through a melisma of half-tones, issuing from some other mystical age, from far occult regions. His call would have been unbearably painful, were it not so perfectly melodious. Then he silenced. His eyes focused on nothing.

I glanced around the room. No one moved. Curro cleared his throat, wiped his mouth, and pushed away from the wall to take in a great breath. He strained and drew from his gut the saddest song I ever heard. A song accompanied only by his own loneliness. A song echoing mine.

He sang a *Taranto*. His nasal voice lashed like a whip, burned and seared, then shifted into a smoky, balming plea. It pulled into a guttural gargle, then shattered into a whimper. With a cry like, 'oh ow, ... oh ai, ... oh how, ... ah why', his voice tumbled through evenly pulsated sobs. His lips dilated and ejected the cascade of syllables, as if he were disgorging his soul. His voice tightened into a thin whine of pity, then bestowed loving sweetness. His eyes squeezed shut as he emitted his music. His face turned heavenward. His mouth opened in desperation, lips reaching as if to drink from an invisible cup. His arms were bent, tense hands flattened and vibrating like weapons shielding him from invisible blows. One palm posed upwards near his mouth, ready to catch his life in case he inadvertently spit it out. His voice cracked like a bawling child, then crooned like its mother. His mossy Gypsy voice was more pungent than the most urgent Flamenco, more beautiful than any. The *Taranto* had an eerie beauty. This man spewed a sorrow so exquisite, that I shattered.

You are the jewel and I am the jeweller
You are the river and I am the current
You are the flame and I am the splendor
Ah, you are the fire and I am the burning.

It was a song of love, learned from his forefathers,

offered to no one, steeped in the mislaid devotion of an irreverent race, the dark prayer of a man with no God. The melody was crystalline enigma -- the entreaty and the bequest, the quest and the light. Its rhythm beat quietly like a heart, like constant hope and perpetual resignation, like the passing of time, the fall of fruit. Like eternal dusk, his last, 'aw ... aw ... aw' tunneled through lugubrious tones, each burrowing deeper until it died down in the darkness. Then on the last somber note, he whispered a final, ' ...and so what.' My heart echoed, 'and so what.'

People had resumed talking. Many hadn't heard the end of his cante. No one seemed aware of what had occurred, but I watched as he methodically shouldered his loneliness and mine and swayed out the door.

Curro sang as if he were born to die and the wait was not much fun. His cante, a formulary for my despair, reached me and released me ... somewhere beyond suicide.

❦❦❦ ❧❧❧

"You're from where?" Curro's husky voice unnerved me.

"California." I blushed and looked away.

"Where's that? America?" he asked with no interest. He led us along an unpaved Triana street.

"Yes. Where they make all the movies." My little geography lesson stimulated no further thirst for knowledge from this unlettered villager. I nearly tripped as we approached the Guajira, the Flamenco night club. "And you?"

"I'm from Cuenca," he twinkled, giving me a cynical

34

Gypsy's non-answer. He held open the door for Rose and another fellow, and me.

Dancers were gathering on the stage, beckoning to others. Preened for a party, eyes glinting, laughing and tossing hair, these were Gypsies. This huge tent-like place we entered was full of renowned Flamencos! Guitars were tuning, running scales, and testing chords down squeaky frets. A giant "WOW" roared in my head. JACKPOT. We were at the best tablao in Triana, at a private Gypsy wedding party for Rafael Negro and Matilde Coral, famous dancers for whom Curro had often sung. It would be an all-night juerga, a Gypsy jam session. At last I would see real dancing.

The event was just warming up, wine bottles thunking onto tables, people milling and greeting -- Flamencos – professional, genuine. Matilde, Gachí of sherry-gold tresses, danced a few steps with her coffee Gitano husband, then welcomed guests, then danced a bit more. I did not care that there was no place to sit. I accepted a glass of sherry and exulted at the sight of so many Gypsies.

But Curro complained of being ignored and slighted. No one called him up on stage. No one found him a seat. He got quickly drunk and started a scuffle. Shoves followed insults, and within minutes, I found myself outside the door of the Guajira with Curro and his friends. We had been ejected before the party began. I stood by, heartsick and incredulous as Curro insulted the big bouncer who, with a crack, gave him a head-to-head blow that could have killed him. Our companions disappeared. Curro and I were left alone in the dark.

I followed him home as he bled and sobbed. Mopping and blowing on his handkerchief, Curro was as indignant as an innocent kid who had gotten inexplicably pushed around. It was a sad little trek through the deserted night streets. He was rather ludicrous, but I knew his anguish. Candidate for any addiction that might have been available, I bonded with Curro.

He discarded the filthy handkerchief in the gutter. The next time I saw him, instead of apologizing to me for ruining my evening, Curro actually berated me for not retrieving his handkerchief. That was a cue I chose to ignore.

Six

Gamely courting Flamenco, I scouted, sometimes tolerating Rose's company, sometimes alone, night after night in Seville, with occasional forays out of town. I met a few Flamencos, but none impressed me as Curro had, except perhaps old Manolito de María.

The old Gypsy's home was a cave, but you would not know it from inside -- squared-off whitewashed walls, tidy bed and table, and a disapproving wife with arms crossed as he washed and jacketed to go out.

"Don't worry, woman, I'll be back in an hour." She accepted that with a fishy look at Curro and me. Carefully placing his fedora hat above his cherubic cheek and round innocent eyes, Manolito came out on the town with us. How new I was, and excited, following Curro and Manolito along the hillside footpath beneath castle walls. Gypsy women were taking in clothes at sunset. They eyed this American woman with subtle contempt as I gingerly followed their men back to the stone streets of Alcalá.

An ancient town outside of Seville, Alcalá de Guadaira was renowned for Flamencos. Curro had grown up there, and Manolito de María before him. Benevolent old Gypsy with scrawny neck and just a few long yellow teeth left in his mouth, Manolito charmed me with his angelic look and simple good humor. I did not yet know he was one of the greatest living Flamenco singers in Andalucía.

"There you are, *Rosa de mi vida*," Manolito greeted Rose who was waiting with her drink and her money at Bar España, in the center of town.

"*Qué hay, Manuel, tómate algo*," gushed Rose, offering him a drink.

"That's the girl. Say, how's the family?"

Rose grinned. It was his joke. She had no family, of course. Her breed sprang spontaneously out of bar stools.

"Susie, Curro, what'll you have?" she asked as she turned her back on us and drew Manolito under lanky arm to the bar.

We four scoured the town that night, seeking other Flamencos, searching out a juerga. At least that was what Rose and I sought. Perhaps Curro and Manolito, bored and broke, just came along for the drinks. I don't remember much of that evening ... Rose had a fit of generosity and we all found too much to drink, but we never found a señorito nor even a guitar. Nor a cab home. Well-inebriated, leaning on one another, we trudged along the country highway, heading nowhere. The moonlight was skimpy and Rose stumbled.

"Look here. Let's sleep here." Curro effected a command decision, and led us onto an open field. He began gathering straw in the dark. He scratched and stacked like a mother hen.

"You lie down here," he instructed me, "and ..."

"Over here. Curro. You and I are sleeping over here," Rose slurred. They argued, but Rose, the reeling big spender, was adamant. Without protest, Manolito and I curled up together like grandfather and child. Curro carefully covered us with hay. I dozed before my head hit my arm.

The chill of dawn awakened me to the smells of mown earth. My companions already on foot, smoothing hair and picking at sleepy eyes, I scrambled up.

"Here, daughter, you cannot go socializing like that." Manolito brushed me off. Lisping through gaps in his teeth, he scolded my coat for its untidiness. *"Hombre, me no. No me seas así. Pórtate bien. `Allí`. Eso es. Mejó,"* he chided with quaint Gypsy humor and clicking tongue, "No, man. Don't be like that. Behave yourself. There, that's it. That's better."

Giggling, I picked straw off the back of Manolito's jacket.

ॐॐॐ ॐॐॐ

Then one day it happened. Quite simply. At first I did not even realize it. I found myself at a *juerga*. The fountainhead of Gypsy Flamenco, the Carnegie Hall of Flamenco - a true village juerga -- was germinating.

Picture the dirt floor outside a village tavern on a Sunday afternoon. I sat under an awning on a folding wooden slat chair, at a rickety wooden table, with Curro and a few other

Gypsies. A head of lettuce had been placed there, washed, salted, and vinegared. Picture the simplicity. Dry sherry was poured. Wearing lumpy, wool-tailored jackets and frayed white shirts, these *Gitanos* had survived the hunger during the Spanish Civil War, and all the hunger since then. They sat in dignity.

Manolito de María approached. "Hello, daughter! Curro, let's sing a bit."

"Manolito, sit down, man, have a little wine," the men urged him, handing him a glass. Someone gave up his chair and went to retrieve another. They showed Manolito the special deference reserved for a Gypsy of great nobility and simplicity and total mastery.

"*Hombre!*" he greeted his wine, "when did you get here?" Manolito emptied his glass.

He cleared his throat and began to beat out a slow *Sequidillas* rhythm on the tabletop. His five-beat knuckle taps caused the wine to ripple in the glasses. The other men paid careful attention. Manolito, with tremorous head, began to hum, then wailed out a rhythmic phrase. He stopped, his knuckles still knocking that heartbeat on the table. Then he sang. His whispered voice was cracked and craggy. The words, wrenched from his phlegmy innards, were few and only half-pronounced, in the Flamenco way. But a new phrase brought joy to his companions, or thrill, or relief. "That's it." "That's it," they would say to his rhythm, nodding and imbibing his song. I watched their earnest pleasure. This was it. This was the Flamenco I had traveled so far to find.

"*Ole*, Manuel," one man gently praised him between verses. His eyes squeezed shut, and he chanted the sorrows of his race, in broken, repeated phrases. Then he stopped singing abruptly as though something had been wrung from him.

More dry sherry was poured. Others joined the table, among them an old guitarist with wide brown hands and face, thick snowy hair, and an air of solemn authority. Antonio Sanlucar briefly tuned his guitar. It was a beat-up old box, but how it spoke. Raunchy and sweet, how it pierced the heart. Manolito de María sang many Soleás, sang the style from this very town of Alcalá, where he had lived all his life, and learned to sing at such a table as this, from an old Gypsy before him.

Someone else sang some *Bulerías*, then they broke for more wine; subdued, but jolly. A beefy woman, very self-assured, named La Burra, joined them, and they bestowed upon her the same brotherhood, the same courtesy. The guitar rasped out another intro and La Burra sang with astonishing grit and conviction. Curro sang a few. All were intent upon the songs, knuckling the table, nodding occasional "oles".

Some sang, some did not. All listened. Really listened. Each song was being sung through them. None sang like this alone; it was the group's work. Their palmas, clapped precision, their praise words in rhythm, and their utter attention - fed the song, drew it out of each singer, midwifed it into existence. The guitar empowered, founded the creation. Songs crescendoed in energy, broke into joviality, and crescendoed again. Wine poured, more bottles came, a plate of aged amber cheese. The lettuce disappeared leaf by leaf, and the music grew until, sometime before dawn when the group had woven the energy field, had empowered the critical, sacred moment - the music reached its climax. Manolito's cante, miraculous, illumined, brought tears of exaltation to those leathered faces. Like lovers, they called out endearments, their hands' palmas pounding out their passion and their powerful restraint. Compás was a tangible living bond, and out of their reunion came the purest truth, the deepest soul.

So they were satisfied. The juerga wound down, and they got ready to break it up, and to endure their rugged lives a few more days.

Remembering back, years later, I can appreciate what I witnessed at that juerga. Perfect kinship. Distilled human spirit.

But at the time, I was still disappointed that a juerga seldom included dancing.

ॐॐॐ   ॐॐॐ

"*Angelita. Baila un poquito, niña.* Dance a bit, girl." Angelita was an excruciatingly ugly twelve-year-old, just somebody's sister, doing laundry down by the stream beyond the olive trees. Gypsy men were stewing a rabbit in wine over an open fire, a spontaneous Sunday picnic brewing in a grove outside of Seville. People were sitting on the ground drinking fino. I inhaled the aroma of wine broth and woodsmoke, my blood rushing as more Gypsies gathered. A guitar arrived and Flamenco began with a guitar whining and moaning in the shade of the olives, the sherry cooking in my veins. Someone called to Angelita.

"Angelita, ven aquí, niña."

The guitar fretted softly. Down at the water, Angelita's head angled away. Then she shrugged, left the clothes in a wad on a rock, and came up, drying her hands on her skirts. Her shy grin involved a multitude of huge, crowded teeth. She looked as though she might need to spit out half those teeth just to close her lips. Her eyes small, her hair poor, skin sunburnt to a dull brown, she was a scrawny, backward, very ugly kid.

Then Angelita began to dance. As she raised her arms against the sky, all her lines clicked into place. She stopped the world. She became the queen of mankind. A goddess. *Una Gitana.* A Gypsy's Gypsy.

Angelita was "*a'ge,*" the Gypsies' word for their own untamable, unpredictable art. Like "soul" once belonged to American Blacks, "*a'ge*" belonged to Spanish Gypsies. Her profile had *a'ge.* Her every gesture had *a'ge.* Wild creature, her dance was *a'ge.* Angelita was born like that -- it was nothing she learned. Never was anyone more alluring. She never doubted her beauty, had never even considered it. Unconcerned, her beauty came from a realm that could not be invaded by orthodontia and nose jobs, by affluence and comfort. She danced a cante or two. Then she simply returned to her laundry, while they went on singing and clapping in the dust under the silvery olives.

Dazed, I drank and ate. Forgetting to dunk bread in my stew, hardly tasting the rabbit, I barely noticed the Flamenco that had become pale and zestless without Angelita.

Ah, to dance like that...

❦❦❦ ❧❧❧

Throughout Seville's cold winter I browsed the city at indecent hours, seeking that illusive treasure, authentic Flamenco. By springtime, I found that even after good Gypsy music, if I had not glimpsed Curro, I was still restless. That was how I noticed I loved him.

I hardly knew him. I had never been alone with him. Yet my childhood fantasies of heroically lonesome humans settled on this man. From a history of cave-hidden outlaws, from the mystery of Gypsies, from the rich lure of Seville's hallowed centuries, and the utter simplicity and charm of Andalucían life, emerged this stranger, with whom I had no intention of pairing, and yet who consistently triggered some essential pull in me. Curro was Flamenco.

I had affluence, education, talent. Everything except Flamenco. Curro had nothing. Nothing but Flamenco. It was as if I owned all the land, but the only tree on it was his. A plum tree. And how I coveted those dark tart plums of Flamenco.

Seven

The Spring Fair of Seville promised plenty: seven afternoons of the best bullfights in Spain; seven nights of the best Flamenco in Andalucía. This Fair of 1965 was going to be mine. All seven days and nights of it.

Trumpets screamed *paso doubles*. Waves of olés pulsated across the crowd. The afternoon sun blazed upon the circus pageantry. Archaic costumes, satin and slippered, seemed to have shrunk considerably since they were donned. The bullfighters paraded with old scarred horses, flashy capes, and singular smugness. The cruelty in that arena was unforgivable; yet the courageous beast reigned magnificent amongst the fatuous humans, and stole the show with his utter splendor.

In the intimacy of the pretty Seville bullring, something important, something mystical, was taking place. Sitting alone in the stands, amidst well-to-do Sevillanos, I watched it.

A young bull, sleek and fresh and eager, headed out of the gate beneath me. He swerved, planted his powerful chest, and looked up at me as his narrow hips wheeled behind him. Water streamed from his nostrils, his muzzle, his belly. His black sheen rippled in the Andalucían sun.

ﻬﻬﻬ   ﻬﻬﻬ

"Señorita, buy my pretty little carnation. So fragrant!"

The proud Gypsy woman with fringed shawl was the same height as the hesitant American girl with cropped hair and drip-dry travel dress.

"It's fiesta time and you're not wearing flowers," with winning smile, she cupped my cheek.

I looked into darting eyes, reading distance in them.

"No thanks," shaking my hair loose about my face, "... no place to put it. Yet." My brown hair would grow very long and hold many flowers, one day.

I meandered on, peering into empty tents with their flaps back. The party was over or had not yet started. Nutty aroma of sherry mingled with the dust of the fairground. In one abandoned tent, I found only scattered folding chairs, a table loaded with used glasses and drained wine bottles. In another, a few grand old men waited quietly. Gypsies, by their leathery faces and utter alertness.

"*Niña*, looking for Curro?"

Startled, I shook my head. Too shy to speak, I backed out. How did they know?

I intended to find Flamenco. Everywhere I could hear the wrenching, inflaming cry of Flamenco guitar. I was searching for the dancers, for the Gitanas to gather here from the four corners of Spain, to dance their wildness for me. But my unruly eye kept scanning for Curro. If I caught a glimpse, I was giddy. If it was not he, I was desolate.

"*Camarones fresquitas, señorita.* Taste my shrimp,"
whined a dark-faced hawker with dirty hands. Hungry
woman, I studied fresh shellfish in his deep basket, neat pink
rows of shrimps and prawns on white linen. His caulked
fingernails dissuaded me.

I glanced up and there was Curro! In his impeccable
black suit, he stood sharing cigarettes with another
Flamenco. I coolly walked by, nodded. Then I sashayed
sideways to avoid collision with a pair of horses and their
hatted Sevillano riders.

Curro left his conversation and caught up with me.

"Good evening." He fell in step with me.

"Oh hello." I pretended indifference. If I smiled with
closed mouth, he would not hear my beating heart.

"Enjoying the Fair?" He patronized me with his ironic
grin. Black curls bounced at the back of his head.

"Not yet. Searching for Flamenco dancing," I dissem-
bled. Being a singer, Curro was no great fan of dancing, like
a surgeon might not live in awe of a nurse. But I preferred
to appear neophyte rather than smitten. I had a mission
here, and it was not Curro. That needed to be established.

"*Baile?* I know where to find it."

I was sure he did. He was a singer out of work. He
would certainly know exactly where he was not working.
Question was, would he divulge.

"Where?" I stopped, and my eyes bored into his. Such
yearning must have perplexed him. People streamed past. A
nut vendor pushed between us with a large shallow basket

over his Gypsy arm -- blanched almonds on one side, Spanish peanuts on the other.

"*Vale, vale,*" Curro consented. "Come with me. We'll look."

Such an offer. We walked together, and together we hunted, Curro for a juerga to make money, I for a dance to watch and learn. Most parties were private, in closed tents, family tents of wealthy Sevillanos entertaining friends. Curro inquired at a few. Wending in and out of throngs, in the cool evening air, he avoided the tents offering commercialized Flamenco shows with costly entrance fees. He was accustomed to being paid to sing in them, and he was unemployed.

I halted. "Look, Curro, *baile!*"

"No, not there. Let's go."

Through an open tent flap, I admired the sumptuous ruffles and I throbbed with desire to be swirling amongst them. I could feel the majesty of ugly Angelita glimmering within me.

"Come on, woman," he growled, and I followed, disappointed that he did not pay nor draw on professional favors to invite me in. I had no idea Curro was broke, and bankrupt in his own way. He looked well-fed beneath his snowy open shirt collar. Jobless all winter, he anticipated making good money at the Spring Fair, but he had none to spend.

I longed to watch the pretty girls, a standard gachí *cuadro* from one of the *tablaos* in Seville. But as Curro moved on,

I opted to tag along with this Gypsy, my only key to Flamenco authenticity. Besides, the man had my heart on fire.

ༀༀༀ ༅༅༅

Curro found a tent where money could be made.

"*Me permito cantar un poquito?* Shall I allow myself a song?" Curro was all smiles.

"Sure, hombre, why not." The blond Sevillano gentle-man was hospitable and gracious, Spanish nobility.

"A few friends here ..." added Curro, indicating fellow Flamencos, the guitar, and the American woman.

"But of course." The señorito nodded and sent for more chairs, more wine and mountain ham. Curro was beaming.

The fiesta began with friendly male banter, pouring of wine, and exquisite guitar interludes more compelling than any other music on earth.

I waited eagerly for the señorito to send for dancers as well as wine. He did not. But I gnawed on ham as durable as bubblegum, and gratefully drank in the music with my sherry. I listened intently to the singing, especially Curro's song that aroused in me a bittersweet craving.

Party over, singing done, a few bills in the pocket of each Flamenco, we resumed our beat around the fairground. Walking with Curro, I tingled whenever he neared me, whenever I recalled that he was spending the entire night at the fairground with me, that he might have no one else.

So every night of the Fair, in the sweet Seville air, we

49

searched, each seeking something grand. All we found was each other.

"You went to the bullfights today?" Curro raised his eyebrows. "Who invited you?"

"I did." I did not admit I had season tickets, knowing it would sound ostentatious. Let him wonder why I disappeared every afternoon.

"Woman, you've got money to spare!"

"Hey, I work for Spanish wages, same as you." I tossed my hair, watched some Gypsy boys leading a string of tasseled horses, adding, "I arrived in Spain without one American cent on me."

"Yes, but you have family."

"In America, an adult is not supported by her family. Does your mother feed you?"

"Yes. If she has food and I'm hungry." Family was the only unemployment check, the only retirement, the only health insurance that existed in Spain for him.

"Not mine. I'm on my own." My grand arm gesture swept into a Gypsy vendor's portable rack, dismantling brassware with a clatter.

"Pardon me!" I squatted to replace the souvenirs on their hooks.

"Niña, buy my little pot with fitted lid." He noticed Curro with me and moved on.

"I'm staying with my mother for now," Curro added to make his point.

"Where?"

"Over there," he said without a gesture, vague as usual. "Gotta find some place else. In the rains last week, the roof fell in on my bed." Curro laughed. I never knew whether that was true or not. He would have laughed either way, genuine down-and-out Gypsy laughter.

"There is a room to rent," Curro said, "near here in Los Remedios neighborhood." He cleared his throat, but the voice remained husky, "I'll go see it after the Fair." He gazed at me, a silent invitation.

Slow to perceive Curro's suggestion, I glanced at him then, swallowing hard, locked into his eyes. I blushed and focused on skipping over a fresh mound of horse manure.

"Ole, *prima*, ole," Curro called as he watched a Gypsy flower vendor across the roadway ply her craft. A woman with a baby on her hip and a handful of carnations. *Prima?* Was she his cousin? The spangled, quick-eyed woman of charm was selling a gentleman a single carnation for the price of a week's groceries.

༺༺༺   ༻༻༻

Curro did not work much at that Spring Fair of Seville. Perhaps he was working me. If so, he did it rather carefully, for I was world-worn and wary. He never pressed me. At his side, I was content. And flowing Spanish sherry kept me from worrying about pending folly. And folly in a foreign land, where I could duck out untraceably in a wink, hardly seemed folly.

"I'm thinking of moving to Barcelona," Curro

announced smugly, his suit jacket over his shoulder.

"Why?" That threw me. I thought of him as a fixture of this fine province.

"Never been there."

"That's no reason." Disappointment engulfed me. Weary of travel, Seville my haven - yet how could I tolerate it without him here?

"Lots of work in Barcelona. Too many Flamencos here in Seville. In Barcelona everybody works." He paused to seek my eyes. "Even beginners."

"No, I'm just learning," I stuttered. As a dancer I had never been seen. I was not ready. I rehearsed secretively in Vavra's living room. "I'm not professional."

"You could be professional in Barcelona." That news left me speechless. Learn to dance and return to L.A. had been my plan, until this very moment.

"As soon as I get some train fare, I'm leaving." Curro used his Gypsy mouth shrug, pulling it down at the corners, "You could come." We threaded through a group of laughing revelers.

"I have to work until school is out. Gave my word."

"So what?" He frowned at me, true to Gypsy custom in which a man's word is a mask for truth, not a revelation of it.

"So, I'll keep my word," I retorted. "Besides, Seville is my home now."

He turned away, "Suit yourself."

Eight

Every dawn, after a night of music and crowds, Curro treated me to breakfast, along the amusement fairway. Groggy and silly from wine and sleeplessness, we would find a *churro* stall.

Burning our throats with coffee and cognac, we relished the fried dough sticks and licked sugar grains from greasy fingers.

One morning in the crystal light, waiting sleepily for our *churros*, Curro stood leaning against a pole, with his head thrown back as if asleep. Curious and ready for mischief, I approached and stood belly to belly with him. His head fell forward on my shoulder. Like a horse, Curro was sound asleep on his feet, in public. Astonished into a spell of clarity, I wondered what the hell I was doing here, in this land, with this man. I questioned my very sanity. Embarrassed, I looked to see if anyone had noticed. The churro vendor was busy dropping more dough into the hot oil, and no one else was about. The place was as deserted as my life. So my doubts lasted only a moment, then my laughter awakened Curro, and with half-closed eyes, he laughed heartily. Perhaps that was Curro's virtue. He could laugh at himself. And at me.

He wanted to show off his marksmanship at a carnival shooting booth. Dark suit flapping, collar loosened, he leaned against the booth's counter, squinted along a rifle barrel and hit the bull's eye, which triggered a camera to snap a photo of the three of us: me and him and the rifle.

Jubilant, Curro confessed that he had learned to shoot in the Spanish Foreign Legion. At seventeen, he had inadvertently caused a stepsister to become surprisingly pregnant. He ran away to Madrid, fleeing the righteous Gypsy knives of his stepbrothers, and joined the Spanish Foreign Legion.

Each dawn Curro walked me home from the fair, so that I could sleep away the morning and be rested for the afternoon bullfight. As we threaded our drowsy way past the chortling children of Seville who castaneted and spun "flamenco" flounces through the deserted back lanes, Curro told tales.

"The first time I meet my superior officer, he calls me *Calé*. Even though I am, I resented being called "Gypsy". He's a big man with an ugly, yellow beard halfway down his chest. Which means he's been in that desert a long time, like a very bad bug. '*Calé*, come here. What's my name?' 'How the hell should I know,' I snarl at him and turn away. Bam! The Captain hits me in the face with his fist and I black out. As I come to, he's pulling me to my feet, saying very patiently, 'Now, *Calé*, my name is José María Martínez Castellano.' I am regaining my balance when he asks again, 'What's my name, *Calé*?' Dazed, I can't think of it, and Bam! he hits me again. This time he props me up and asks

54

me nicely and I say, 'Your name is José María Martínez Castellano, my Captain, SIR!' Whew! And I never forgot his name again," laughed Curro, "no matter how loaded I was."

I could barely attend to his story. The hoarse intimate tones of his Gypsy voice confused me, stirred in me such a longing, it ached in the back of my throat.

"The Captain liked Flamenco. He'd given me the money to leave camp and go into the nearby Moorish village for wine. Sometimes I'd bring it and he'd have me drink and sing for him in his tent all evening. Sometimes I'd go, get drunk on his money, come back to camp two days later for another beating. I would have deserted, but a beating from my Captain was better than life amongst Moors in the Sahara. Oh, those unwashed women, how they stank. Besides, I was the Captain's favorite, so I got breaks. He loved to hear me sing."

I laughed as Curro tattled on himself, laughed with his oppressed people, laughed because I had felt oppressed too. Our bitter laughter went unnoticed by the socialites around us.

 crcrcr crcrcr

Curro was the Gypsy, but I had wandered as much as he. I too had been forlorn. The day after the Seville Fair, he came with his suitcase from the tents of the Sahara, and I came with my suitcase from the castles of Europe, and we joined on a mattress on a bare cement floor in Seville. We joined in a rented room furnished only with a mattress, two suitcases, orange blossom air, and moonlight. Curro had not yet kissed me.

That first night I gazed upon him, I was on the mattress under the first clean sheet we shared. He stood naked, compact brave bull, power-chested, narrow-hipped. Freshly washed, his polished face shone golden. I lay startled and watched him incandescent in the moonlight. The glowing copper flesh of Curro seared my senses with wonder.

My weapon had always been my words but, deeply quiet would I lie beside this ignorant villager who owned nothing but a suitcase and a voice.

Would Curro lead me into my own power? Was he the Gypsy priest of my becoming? I would never own Curro, never own his history nor his race, but could I dip into his heritage, be initiated into his mystery? Would I enter his world when he entered me?

Splendid burnished Curro pulled back the sheet and lay down beside me. "Ole-ole-ole." His earthy Gypsy praise dissolved me. "I'd wondered if you were white all the way inside your clothes ..." was his husky murmured caress.

I lay trembling. He was warm honey on my cool cream breast, beaming and blending with me, and beaming at me again. His eyes soft with man urge, his cheeks creased graciously, his glowing body burned me. I became delirious at the touch and sound of my Curro.

Nine

"I could sleep with men for money," I offered brightly, testing him. Curro's life as an urban Flamenco amongst prostitutes and pimps haunted me. Uneasy from the beginning, as the weeks passed in our first room together, my uneasiness increased.

"... and neither of us would have to work ..." Nonchalantly, I brushed my hair.

"Fine, if you'd like," Curro shot me a look and a shrug. He lay shirtless with his back to the floor. His hairless upper body had a smoky finish. A tattoo of a woman's face boasted place of honor over his heart. I hated that woman. Curro never told me who the tattoo was, just laughed at my queries. Probably a random choice of designs available in the Sahara Desert while high on grifa, but no matter, I was jealous of that damned tattoo.

Maybe Curro was testing me, too. His easy response ignited a slow fuse in me. I tossed the hairbrush into my open suitcase, then squatted beside him, chattering about professional prospects, fees.

"That lonely American doctor could launch my career. I could make a pile off him this very night." Smiling, I straddled Curro on the floor. The fuse shortened. Then exploded. Hair flew, arms swung, I slapped that man, pounded on his chest, spat wrath upon him. Caught off-guard, Curro was pinned beneath me.

"Your mother must have shit on you plenty, to give you such an attitude about women!" I screamed and pummeled him.

Somehow he threw me off, rolled out from under me, and stood back, frightened. He stood at a respectful distance, barefoot, in rumpled trousers, until I quieted. And he began to weep.

"My mother loved me very much," Curro protested. The tattooed lady on his chest heaved with his sob. "I was her firstborn, and she loved me very much." He cleared his throat and struggled to speak, "When she was pregnant, carrying me ... that poor pregnant girl they put in prison. The Civil War divided neighbor against neighbor, and my father was an enemy of her townspeople. They killed my father before I was born. They put my mother in prison and shaved her head to shame her." Curro's grief spilled out onto the heavy air between us. His unexpected disclosure melted me, dissolved all my doubts. I moved to comfort him, but he backed away and stood at the window.

"When I was born, she had to go away, and she gave me to her father to raise. My grandfather had a little piece of land and some goats. He called me 'Corrillo' and he raised me. 'Corrillo,' he'd call to me. 'Corrillo,'" Curro sang out the window. "'Corrillo.'"

To himself alone, forgetting me, Curro confessed,

"Some day I want a Corrillo for me too, for my very own."

We were quiet. Then he allowed me to kneel by him and stroke his back.

"Later my mother married and had many children, and I never really belonged in that household. But she always loved me. She gave me her father's last name, as if she were merely my sister, but she always loved me. My mother always loved me," Curro finished, with a double lurching sigh, and wiped his eyes.

I remembered his mother's golden twinkling earrings. I pictured Coral in the Plazuela of Alcalá, where we first met. A small Gitana, with a crooked grin like mine, like my grandma's. Her earrings, and the gold medallion hanging on a long gold chain, were sunlight against her loam brown skin. They were her charge card - she pawned her gold whenever a child got sick. She must have pawned them many a time for Curro, her troubled oldest boy. She resembled Curro, and love visibly tied them. I liked Coral.

"You know what my mother told me, after she met you?" Curro faced his American woman.

My turn to be surprised - I settled back on my knees, wide-eyed and still. Curro stroked hair from my face. Resting his forearms on my shoulders, he said,

"'This one's for you, Curro,' Ma told me. She already knew you were mine from the beginning! 'This one's for you,' my mother said."

59

"Daughter," an old Gypsy man said to Curro's Gachí, "every time I see you, I see the Bank of Spain."

"Ole," laughed Curro.

An American looked like money. I arrived in Spain thirty dollars in debt, with no money for Curro to get, but people always thought he was getting my money. Spanish Gaché warned me with that awful, "Watch out for the Gypsy. If he doesn't get you on the way in, he'll get you on the way out."

My back would stiffen with implacable pride. *"Wives sell it for a home, whores buy it from their pimps."* I wrote to Jessica. *"I won't sell it, and I won't buy it."*

❧ ❧ ❧   ❧ ❧ ❧

"Didn't you get home early last night, Curro?" Saturday housekeeping done, sheets smoothed over the mattress and the floor dusted with a wet rag, we were dressing to go out for morning coffee.

"Yes. I quit at the Guajira. Raphael, the dancer, said something I didn't like so I showed him. I quit. I don't need his damned job."

Disconcerted, I said nothing but pursed my lips and gathered my purse.

"Hey, Lito, how goes it?" Curro had to look up to salute the fellow in the hall - a long and gangly bullfighter I had seen, in a third rate bullfight, mistakenly drawing the bull back into the matador's vicinity, endangering him instead of protecting him. And the jerk was living off a foreign woman in the room next door. I glowered as Curro asked him, "Working?"

"Naw." His shoulders hung, big hands fumbled, long face winked. "The lady wants me to stay close. And you?"

"I quit the Guajira last night ... give the voice a rest."

The scarecrow bullfighter and the Kewpie singer exchanged knowing glances. And my hackles clicked to attention as I left with my man.

Later, back in our room, with the courage that sugared coffee, cognac, and strong thinking can give, I closed our door, sweetened my voice and said,

"Curro, look. There's something you must know." My eyes must have widened like a cat on the pounce. "With my small salary teaching English, which I work hard for, I will gladly pay rent. However, if we eat, the food will be provided by you."

"Sure, woman. Agreed." Curro thought he could out-bluff me. For two days and two nights we went without eating, yet in that bare room, I felt safe. Food did not matter, skipping a meal was no threat. I was not acquainted with hunger and it did not frighten me. But the Gypsy could not take it. Curro grew faint, weak-kneed, dizzy, and convinced he would soon die.

"I've got to eat something. I'll get sick. I'll lose my voice."

"You're right. You should eat," I agreed, but did nothing to provide food.

"Bitch, you're sneaking a meal at work, because you have

money, while I'm starving to death."

"No sir, we'll both eat when you bring the food."

On the third day, Curro returned to the Guajira. With great diplomacy, he retrieved his job. And we ate from then on. Whenever he lacked a singing job, he labored with pick and shovel, or resumed itinerant selling - an ancient respected Gypsy profession - and he always brought food home. Once he got a job working with a jackhammer. For great pay! After one long day on that jackhammer, he spent the whole next day in bed to recuperate, groaning in pain, and never did that again. But he always saw to it that we ate.

I was housebreaking my Gypsy. In exchange, he broke his American woman like a spoiled horse. He taught me to scrub a floor on hands and knees with a rag and a bucket. How I squawked. And to launder by hand, on a washboard. And to smoke lice out of a mattress. And to fry peppers and clean fish. To my utter satisfaction, from then on, we both cooked. And we both earned money. *"Mano a mano,"* Curro used to say, "Hand in hand."

ಶ‍ಶ‍ಶ ‍ಶ‍ಶ‍ಶ

Curro was a very clean man. In Spain, Gaché workers only bathed once a week. They smelled rancid. A week's sweating washed the dust on their backs into rows. After their Saturday night bath, the pearly white shoulders and ruddy neck reappeared. They had a dismal cliché that went: *"Sabado, Sabadete, calzones limpios y polvete."* "Good ole

Satur–Saturday, clean pair of jocks and a lay." I shivered every time I heard it. I was not fond of those people.

But Gypsies generally tried to not work enough to build up a sweat. Gypsies were known for their aversion to water. Unusual in Andalusía was my tobacco-gold Curro, who bathed every day.

"You're never too poor to be clean," he declared. "As a kid, I used to swim in the river of Alcalá, if I had nowhere else to get clean.

"My mother often admonished me. She bathed seldom. She had no odor. She washed her beautiful wavy hair every few months. She implored me, 'Not so much water, Curro, it'll thin your blood.' But I never paid any attention."

Curro was a very clean man. But he and his American roommate had one small disagreement regarding clean. Our first summer together we moved to Barcelona to find work. It was a long trip. We were both far from home in Barcelona. We rented a room with a bed, a wardrobe, a table, and a washbasin. The toilet was down the hall. To avoid that public hallway in the middle of the night, Curro began urinating in our wash basin! This I could not bear. Smell and splatter of urine in the dark, next morning revulsion at having to wash there.

I asked him not to. He persisted. I yelled and threatened, and he persisted. I reasoned and explained carefully, and he understood and agreed, and continued to use the basin next to our bed. I begged. He laughed at me.

One night in the dark, I left the bed, squatted at the

foot, and urinated on our clean brick floor, mortified at the warm splash on my ankles, at the whishing sound. But determined.

"What are you doing?" Curro asked, half asleep.

"Peeing."

"What?"

"Peeing here on the floor."

Lights on, bed torn apart, naked Curro was jumping up and down, enraged as Rumpelstiltskin. Fascinated, I watched his little penis. When he jumped up, it came down. When he landed, it flew up. Then it got out of sync and kind of fibrillated. My cheeks curved with amusement, but my eyes must have been lethal.

"Filthy pig!" He shouted a chain of the worst Gypsy curses. "I shit on your ancestors. You whore's daughter!" He shoved me around, and I was delighted.

"What's wrong?" I hid my triumphant glee behind feigned innocence.

"You clean that up this very moment! Here's the bucket."

Naked under my T-shirt, I dutifully sponged with an artful look of remorse. He supervised with folded arms, the wrath of God on his face, and the tattoo watching me.

"Curro, I don't understand." I quietly spoke my final thrust. "I have to brush my teeth where you pee. You only have to place your feet where I pee. So what's wrong?"

Curro never, ever, urinated in our room again.

II
Barcelona

Ten

Sunday in America meant staying home. It meant loafing in pajamas all day and never combing out the tangles. Sunday was the squeak of the hardwood floors while padding quietly through the house. Sunday was late waffles, the ignition sound of Daddy's throat, smell and whiskers of him, the mirth of the percolator, aroma of coffee, choke of cigarette smoke. It was bricklaying in the backyard, pasting pictures in albums, and arguing at Monopoly. Sunday in America was the funny papers spread out on Mommy's braided rug.

Sunday in Europe was a ceremony of dressing up and going out to greet folks. On Sundays the market place was closed. Instead, the hurried market throng came out for a slow Sunday stroll. Close-shaved, hair slicked, they promenaded the main streets and central parks of towns around the Mediterranean. In Dubrovnik, marriages were made with village courtliness during the Sunday walk. In Mykonos, black clothed strollers slipped quietly among the white dwellings glinting in the Greek sun. In Venetian damp, Sunday coats, like jewels -- ruby and turquoise and emerald -- clustered in a setting of gold ocher buildings.

Barcelona, commercial capital of Spain, its germanic bourgeoisie practical and affluent, had the tall gray buildings and heavy traffic of any big city, but down on the Ramblas of Barcelona, life slowed to the quiet provincial atmosphere of a village plaza on Sunday. The Ramblas was a mile-long, straight pathway cut through the city from somewhere near its center to the edge of the sea. It was a river of pedestrians, each bank lined by giant shade trees. Sunday strollers filled the Ramblas, milled the full length of the Ramblas. Speckled with sun and shade, they mingled, chatted, and sat in wooden slat chairs.

A rambler down the avenue passed groups of kiosks: pet kiosks selling bird songs, whining puppies, and round-eyed monkeys with miniature fingers; flower kiosks offering gladioli, roses, and funeral wreaths on easels out on the walkway; book kiosks swelling into small sidewalk bookstores. Café tables spilled out along the Ramblas. Further down the summer bullfight clique gathered -- pompous men in formal attire congregating to discuss, loud as experts, their favorite bullfighters.

Approaching the bay, the kiosks and trees thinned out. The Ramblas widened, the side streets became narrower and darker, the buildings more grimy, the people more grim. Finally, at Union Street and Conde de Asalto, the Ramblas flowed into the backwaters of urbanity. These side streets housed the city's losers. Drawn to the economic capital from villages all over Spain, they sought money as laborers, waiters, prostitutes, pimps, marijuana dealers, loan sharks, and Flamencos. They took rooms in cheap pensións and ate in cheap restaurants and looked up fellows from back home with slum seniority, who could give them a few tips, a few bucks, or maybe a job.

Union Street was rich in cheap whores. Across the Ramblas the streets harbored better looking whores and slightly classier businesses. Union Street was rock bottom. Whores both lived there and worked there: old whores; crippled, snaggle-toothed, hunchbacked, frazzle-haired, tight-clothed, sloppy-bodied, missing-buttoned whores of a hand job, a weird job, a blow job; relief-for-a-buck-and-a-half whores. Union was a street of run-down four-story balconied buildings, of gutters foul with garbage, green spittle, and dead things.

It was a September Sunday morn. Brats snickered. From Union Street balconies, droplets of filth rained upon the sidewalk. Among the unlucky passersby walked Curro and his Gachí. He wiped his forehead and swore. I stepped more quickly. The lively hem of my skirt danced. He scuffed a bedroom slipper walk in cheap beige loafers, with back arched and chest out, cocky, nearly potbellied. At the end of the street, as we paused to cross over to the Ramblas, an ugly low-slung gutter dog sniffed at us. The Gypsy kicked the creature in the ribs and it retreated with a yelp. My man's lips were a thin line, his eyes pulled taut by tiny transversing tensions. His sudden cruelty startled me.

"Curro!" I entreated, then rushed to catch up with him crossing the street. We walked down the widening lower Ramblas towards the ocean. His hands were fists in his pants pockets, my hand hooked in his elbow. With no sense of myself, I felt invisible, nameless. Back in America I had been Susie, which I thought a silly name. As we walked, my palm rubbed lightly down his forearm. He looked at other strollers, ignoring my touch. I was aware only of his arm.

We approached the statue of Columbus. Centered in the mouth of the cement river, where the Ramblas spread treeless to its widest, the statue of Columbus stood high on a single pillar, the page-boyed bronze gentleman with his robes and his maps and one arm stretched out to sea. Around the base of Columbus' column were benches. A dark-skinned photographer hunkered on one of them, his black equipment perched patiently on its tripod. From another bench, another Gypsy, a slight man with huge eyes and tiny shoulders, approached us. Alejandro, from Alcala', our Barcelona neighbor.

"What's happening, Curro?"

"Not much. We're going to the beach. The lady here says she's going to tan."

"Oh, yeah?"

The men spoke quietly, using few words, as people do who are from the same culture, the same town, the same street, sometimes the same scanty table. Two months earlier, in Alcalá, the featherweight Alejandro had urged Curro to go to Barcelona with his Gachí. There would be lots of work there. Alejandro's woman was already there and Alejandro would be joining her soon. Curro could room in Union Street in the pensión where they always stayed.

Curro and I had rented down the hall from puny Alejandro and his woman, a luscious-fleshed, pig-eyed person of great emptiness. We seldom saw each other in the building; Alejandro's woman worked in some other part of Barcelona.

"And your old lady?" Curro asked.

"Back in the room, snoring."

"Come to the beach with us."

"What for?"

"I don't know. What are you up to?"

"Nothing much." Saucer eyes glanced up at the statue above us. "Thought I'd greet the compatriot here."

"Who?" Curro did not follow him.

"Columbus -- the dude with the arm and the overcoat in summer."

"Friend of yours?" Curro smiled, his eyes nearly shut in a weed-squint left over from last night's grass.

"No friend of mine." Alejandro swallowed a smile, "He's a fool, you know. Look at him up there. He didn't have to go to America. The dummy could have waited. He could have waited a little longer and all the Americans would have come to him."

"Ole ole, cousin, ole." Curro's lips were relaxing out into a fleshy smile with deep vertical creases gathering his cheeks and pulling his eyes down in sleepy mirth. I laughed, too. Country Gypsy humor had a sting that pleased me. And Curro's sensuous grin always felt like a surprise party in my honor.

"Come on to the beach," Curro insisted.

"Naw, I've got to see a guy about something. I've got to see if I can find me a candy or two."

"Candy? Hey, bring me one." Curro was eager to get some good African grifa, sold surreptitiously in candy wrappers. In the privacy of our room, he would crush the seeds carefully between two coins, then roll the two or three joints on my TIME magazine. He might share one with Quino the guitarist tonight after work. Quino probably had shared his last night. They must have had a great time, without me, laughing till dawn, walking and talking ...

"Sure I'll bring you one, no problem." Alejandro glanced at me with total disinterest. "And the 'relative'? What about her?"

"Not much." Curro glanced at me too, shrugged his shoulders in resignation. "Just what you see -- won't leave me for a minute." The two dark men were the same height; I felt much taller and very white. Excluded and awkward, I turned slightly away from them, my hand quiet on Curro's arm while they spoke as though I could not understand, though I followed most of the conversation while gazing at passersby: marching tourists, loitering pimps, sauntering Sunday strollers. I caught myself trying to shrink and I pulled my shoulders back, stacking my vertebrae up neatly, tossing my hair and raising my head. But soon I glanced at Curro and slumped again to his level.

"Is she working?" asked Alejandro as if I weren't present.

"Not a chance. Not only that, she wants some every day.

Imagine, every day! Too much, man. I don't know what to do."

"Yeah?" They laughed. Alejandro's was a dry undernourished laugh, like his body. Curro's laugh came with twinkle and dimple, ripe as he. He laughed best when laughing at himself, deepest when laughing at his own misfortune.

"You bet," he laughed. "Every day."

"Well, you got yourself into it. How's your voice?"

"Okay so far. I'm stronger than a pissed lion so far. But, man, every day. That's too much. What'll I do?"

Alejandro shrugged, "How should I know, man. It's your problem. Take an egg yolk beat up in sweet Málaga wine. How should I know, I'm not a singer. She's bigger than you, too ..."

My head down, amazed at Curro's audacity, I tried to ignore my humiliation. I glanced from his arm to my own, from his satin finish to my pink freckled bundle of bones and knuckles. The hairs on my arm disgusted me. Like always, I believed my ugliness merited such abuse, drew it. My urges, both to envelop him and to flee ashamed, ripped me into a sustained gaze around the lower Ramblas. I studied an empty bench, stood in horrible ambivalence at the foot of Columbus.

"Well, see you later." Curro moved to continue the walk to the waterfront streetcar.

"Where? Back at the room?" Alejandro showed some interest, since he dabbled in drug deliveries.

"No, we might be sleeping. I gotta get my sleep. In Bar Escoba, this evening, before I go to work."

"Okay, Bar Escoba."

Turning to continue up the Ramblas, Alejandro nodded to me politely and added, "Goodbye."

I nodded back, wondering why I did not like him. I would have to see him briefly in Bar Escoba tonight when I accompanied Curro to work. My thoughts drifted back to last night when Curro went to work without me.

It was my twenty-fifth birthday -- a major family holiday in another country. He forgot it. I had taught him to say "Happy Birthday" in readiness for the day, and he had even forgotten to pronounce his "Hepy Borse Youse" for me. It was imbecilic for me to be wretched about it, they didn't even celebrate birthdays here, but I couldn't help myself, I felt so alone. He had told me to set my alarm for 4:00 a.m. He would come get me after work so that we could "dawn" together -- walk the deserted streets smoking and laughing like buddies. He didn't get home until 8:00 in broad daylight, reeling drunk and asking me how old I was. He was so drunk I had to slap him around to undress him and get him to fall correctly on the bed. He was unaware of my abuse and I enjoyed venting my anger on his insensate wine-reeking hulk. He awoke cheerful enough a few hours later, eager for a salty swim to clear his head.

As we passed the Gypsy photographer who had been eyeing us, we heard,

"Cousin. Take your picture? A photo of the handsome couple?"

"Go to hell," Curro snarled.

ھ۔ ھ۔ ھ۔   ھ۔ ھ۔ ھ۔

"Just look at that view!" exclaimed Curro. Shoes in hand, we were plowing through hot sand.

"Where?" My head lifted and scanned. "What view?" I saw an ordinary city beach -- like any in California. Parallel strips of storefronts, gray street, blond sand, ink sea, blue sky, blinding sunblaze.

"Vaya panorama!" Curro repeated, nodding at all the exposed wealthy female Catalan flesh, seldom displayed in the old-fashioned villages of Andalucía.

Beaching with propriety, middle class Barcelona families exposed their fat to the sun. The Gypsy and the American skirted luxuriant towels and blankets. Curro chose his spot, dropped his shoes, pulled off his shirt. He perceived the affluence and its intrinsic disapproval of his dark Gypsy self.

"But can you fart at this beach?" was his loud retribution, as he unzipped.

To cover my embarrassment, and my grin, I began stripping to my bathing suit. My skirt fell around my feet. A shiny cocoa bathing suit rode too high over my rear, exposing two white moons. I pulled my sweater off over my head. My slender long-waisted, well-breasted body lacked Latin plump. I had plenty of ribs, two clavicles, and a pair of obvious elbows. My legs were the color of the sand. My shoulders and arms were freckled on top, milky underneath, like a tropical lizard.

"Great day for a good tan ..." I noted, tugging my suit out of my crotch. I checked my shadow on the sand for the best angle to receive the sun, spread out my clothes and lay down on them. Leaning on my elbows, I watched Curro undress.

"Great day for a swim," Curro said. His threat of belly fell in folds over his bathing suit as he leaned over to pull the pants off his feet. Peeled down to a tight green and black striped bathing suit, he straightened and regained his chunky beauty. His figure exposed not a bone, nor vein, nor tendon. He was one smooth, gently-modulated, hard-packed stack of flawless bronze. His feet were small and neat, his legs full-turned and powered to perfection. His hips were narrow as a bull's and amply buttocked. His chest, barreled full, sported the tacky tattoo. From where I lay, he was not short but a dusky Adonis rising high and magnificent against the insipid sky.

Curro sat down crosslegged beside me and began to talk in that loud voice.

"Listen, you remember the dancer in charge of the show, where I work?"

"Manuel?"

"Yes. Well, last night you should have seen what happened there. I was singing for Amelia to dance."

"Amelia?"

"The Flamenca who plays castanets like mad. I was

singing her a Soleá, very rich and soft-like and right on, and pra pra PRA prarrrrRUMM pa rum pum PUM, she gives me a signal to sing another verse."

"Okay, Okay, so you were singing. So what happened?" I had interrupted because I realized he was not speaking to me but to a family beyond, an overripe woman and her two young daughters who listened as they lotioned each other, adjusted their towels, and doodled in the sand. He was using me as a front to flirt, to establish that he was an "artist." Angry, but wanting to hear the story, I dutifully fed him his cues.

"So, you were singing ..."

"And so Manuel and Trini, his woman, come running out of the back room. She's got a knife and he raises his foot and - Bam! he kicks her until she lets go of the knife. She's on the floor crying and he continues to kick the shit out of her." He shook his head dramatically. "Imagine! ... Oh-hoo! And there was a ripe little American there, brand-new, with her mother. And she got scared and they ran out of the place. Didn't even pay the bill. Imagine!"

"Is Trini ok?" I interrupted.

"I dunno, I suppose so."

"Why did she take out a knife?"

"How should I know," he shrugged. "I guess she was after Manuel. I don't know."

"Why?" I insisted.

"I don't know. He was talking a lot to the brand new American thing..."

79

"Well, no wonder! Will Trini continue to work there?"

"How should I know." His audience had dispersed so Curro lost interest in the conversation. "Guess I'll go swimming." Without uncrossing his legs he tried to jump to his feet in a bound.

I laughed as he tottered. "You're about as graceful as a hippopotamus," I observed. He laughed at himself, too, and stood checking out the ladies in view. He grinned the secret grin of sensual pride that only a man harboring a hard-on can grin.

"What a panorama! What a fine panorama today."

With that parting impudence, he raced to the water and dove and swam smooth and easy, straight out to sea. Unusual Gypsy, he loved the water. As stiffly as he moved on land or stage, so graceful was he in the water. I admired him until my eyes tired.

Beached and bored again, I studied my freckled arm. Back home, all my friends turned brown in the California sun, even my own mother. At six, freckled and quick, I hopped cool stepping-stones, mossed and strewn with fallen Jacaranda blossoms. Pigtails flapped as I cautiously mounted the splintery redwood table. A lost little girl, I dangled my feet on the sunny family patio while a lost mommy in the kitchen scolded and slammed drawers and a lost little sister, olive-skinned and apprehensive, whimpered on the porch. A bluejay nagged from the tree overhead.

That freckled child was a good girl, back in Pasadena, but not good enough. No one ever seemed to want me. I was never abused, only ignored.

At twelve, I had asked, "Mommy, what am I?"

"Why, Susie, you're American." Mommy stopped her sewing machine only to draw the cloth, smooth it, and click back the sewing foot.

"My friends at school are American, too. But Midori is Japanese, and Angie is Mexican, and Judy is Jewish. WHAT AM I?"

"Why, you're American, of course."

"But they're American too. What ELSE am I?"

A scowl ex'd out her beautiful blue eyes; her cheeks hung weighted by chronic displeasure. No answer came but the demanding whir of her incessant sewing machine.

On my own, I concluded, "Nothing. I'm nothing."

Later, sad voices and cigarette smoke filled my dark bedroom. I listened from my bed upstairs while Daddy played his old 78 records, New Orleans jazz and Chicago blues, black people's music. I suckled on the lament, hostility, humor - the driving rhythms - yet blues felt squalid to me. It lacked that audacity of Flamenco...

Sand feathered across my face, halting my reminiscence. I lifted my head and squinted through Barcelona beachlight. Two boys walking by, kicked up sand. They paused to heckle me, then noticed Curro's clothes and moved on.

"Damn," I muttered, "that man has been gone for hours." But the sun had not moved. Its glare blinded me, its ferocity nagged at my eyes even through closed lids. A lump under my clothing irritated me. I smoothed the sand

and replaced the sweater and it was worse. I turned over on my back.

I hated sun. It burned me pink and peeling. I hated the saltwater. It was Curro's escape route. He was swimming way out to sea, would then swim parallel to the beach, and ride back in to ogle freely. I hated sand. He would walk up to a young thing of fourteen or fifteen standing in the sand. Without a word he flirted eloquently. Planted directly in front of a girl, arrogantly, wordlessly, he would offer himself to her, with that grin of the secret hard-on; so inoffensively, he could charm the drawers off a nun.

"Damn him."

I simply hated the beach. But if I endured it long enough I would come out tan enough. At least creamy golden. Maybe all the freckles would unite. Maybe this hot sun would redeem God's mistake: he had not stirred me enough before putting me in the oven to bake. I pulled aside my suit to check my faint tan line. Irritated, I returned to my belly and scanned the horizon.

Not a sight of the sonofabitch in that whole ocean. If he did not return soon I would leave. I did leave the other day. He had been gone over an hour. I had been bored, then worried, then angry, again worried, then hurt, then depressed, then ready to get on the next train to Madrid. I had dressed slowly, tears of frustration from ages of forbearance, stuck in each tear duct. Stony-faced, I had folded his clothes neatly and walked away, looking back at them every few steps. As I walked further and further away, I kept turning and watching the clothes until I couldn't see them amongst the indifferent sunbathers. The sorrow I had felt at the sight of those abandoned clothes I would never forget ... Took him a long time to get back to the room alone. But that didn't cure him, he was out ogling again, today, the lousy ...

Joltlings of dripping water on my back brought my head up. The red-brown splotches behind my sun-soaked lids slowly took the shape of Curro's slender ankles. Laughing, icy-fleshed, he flopped down next to me. Rolling into the sand, he floured himself like a dark fish, powdered ready for the pan. With wet black curls jumping insolently across his forehead, he offered me his best grin. I placed my burning cheek on his cool gritty tattoo and inhaled the sea smell of him. I kissed his wet shoulder and tasted the salt on my lips. I loved the beach.

Eleven

The streetcar back from the beach was crowded. We managed to sit, not together, but both in the wide rear seat, separated by three or four people.

Curro's uncombed ringlets, salted and sandy, still hung in front of his face, which was relaxed and wide-eyed and simpático. His white shirt was tied in a knot over his belly, exposing salty sun-chocolated paunch. His pants showed wet stains at the crotch, from his wet suit underneath. He, of course, did not care. He was most cheerful. Next to him was a solemn gentleman, with a pampered mustache and a very long straight nose, down which he peered at nothing in particular. Curro waved a quiet salute past the row of people to me, which I answered with the same gesture. We sat back for the ride. The streetcar jiggled through traffic noises of the hot Sunday midday.

After a while Curro embarked upon a project involving his nose, which was neatly chiseled and perfectly symmetrical, with the narrow aquiline slope of an authentic Gypsy nose, but with one defect. It was too small. Instead of the massive eagle hook that attested to ages of Gypsy nobility, his nose was more finch. The difference was made up by a long peasant upper lip, useful in enveloping large chunks of food, talking unnecessarily, and smiling erotically. Those with short pug noses, "*chatos*", were considered the height of ugliness in Spain. Although Curro was occasionally called "*chato*" because of the length of his nose, he was never considered ugly because of its fine shape and because the rest of his face redeemed him. His eyebrows were squared off like a leading man's, his eyes intense. But even as his height kept his body from perfect, so his nose kept his face from handsome. He was considered '*gracioso*', a cross between 'cute' and 'charming' -- the face of a Brando with the nose of Tweedy.

Curro's nose seldom misbehaved. It seldom required a handkerchief. When I noticed Curro fingering it, I leaned forward and called across the row of people between us, mimicking a sunny pleasantry of his,

"Hey kid, what are you doing way over there? *Niño, que hace' allí?*"

"Well, pal," he chirped past the man with the mustache who was trying not to notice him, "I'm just pulling hairs out of my nose, one by one. See, I've got this problem, I seem to have caught this teeny cold, see, and a cold is very bad for a singer, know what I mean, pal?"

The man with the mustache brushed off his tie. He tried to ignore the unfortunate seating arrangement of the streetcar.

"Anyway, the snot from my teeny cold gets stuck in the little hairs, see? You don't see. Well, no matter. But it bothers me a lot, pal. You can understand that."

The mustachioed gent was trying to understand why they ever invented public streetcars.

"So I grab a hair, grab on tight, give it a good yank. Ai! There, see, I pull out the little hair and what a relief. Ah, that's better."

Then Curro's first sneeze exploded. Above the streetcar noise, it reverberated. In aftershock, Curro's upper lip pulled his small nose up and down in silent rabbit wiggles. Big fat sneezes came resounding, one after the other. Salty curls danced to the sound of each, answered by the violent silent ride of the nose up and down his face. Like a row of dominoes, the whole back seat turned facing the rueful gent and the Gypsy.

A lady with packages and a loud voice observed, "How congenial. What a simpático fellow."

At his audacity, at the screaming irreverence of my man, I laughed, stifling my laughter into a handkerchief. The row of dominoes now faced me, as tears ran down my face. At the other end of the seat Curro laughed too.

Laughing, we jump off the streetcar. Laughing together, his arm around my waist, mine around his shoulders, we sauntered up the Ramblas toward Columbus. As we approached the benches, a small child with wisps for hair, wandered in front of us. Skirting the child, Curro placed a gentle hand on its head, like a blessing.

"Hey, pal, where are you headed? Where're ya going, baldy?" He laughed a loving laugh. "Come on?" He offered an ignored hand. The child stared after us, motionless.

The intrepid photographer asked again to take a picture of the "lovely couple."

"What'll you charge me?" Curro asked.

"Twenty duros," answered his "cousin" with the trained camera.

"Ten," declared Curro, plunking down on a bench and crossing a leg. "Come here, girl." I sat next to him, crossed my ankles self-consciously, and watched the photographer shrug and adjust the shutter.

In the photo, his short nose unnoticeable, Curro's grin was cocky, his head dipped towards mine, one arm proprietorily draped on the bench behind me. I had a wide smile and large sculpted eyes, the whites a gleaming echo of my white sweater, luminous against my tanning complexion. I was not as dark as he. But I was learning.

Twelve

Red checkered cloth napkins, crumpled amidst bread crumbs and greasy wine glasses, Sunday dinner was nearly over by four o'clock in the afternoon.

Our table was loaded: a full liter of red wine, a soda bottle, a small platter of sliced green tomatoes with onions and peppers snug between plates of steaks, panfried in garlic, and fried potatoes.

"Listen, Lita. I've got to get another suit made, you know. Lita?"

As I dunked bread into the salad, I wondered at his nickname for me, "Lita." He never remembered names, avoided them by calling everyone "Lito" or "Lita," friend and stranger alike. Including me. I wondered why I was beginning to like it. It was tinged with impudence, maybe that was why.

"Lita?"

"What."

"I have to get another suit made."

"Sure, Curro."

"Winter's coming and I need a winter suit for work. A mohair suit."

"Fine. This meat is good, isn't it."

"I'm going to arrange it with the 'daily' today."

My chewing stopped. "The 'daily'? But why him, Curro?"

"Cuz I don't have any money."

"Look, Curro," I swallowed and wiped my mouth. The silent missionary, bred into my freckled race, was raising its righteous head. "If you get your suit through the 'daily,' you have to pay him his percentage, right?" I remembered the smiling Gypsy with the sharp eye, the tact, and the little notebook, making the rounds of the nightclubs and bars around Escudilliers Street, greeting the working Flamencos sporting their gold rings and new suits. He collected a coin a day from each.

"Of course, the man has to get his little gift out of the deal," Curro justified as he speared a slice of tomato.

"But, Curro, if you put your money in a bank, you go paying little by little, too, but **before** you get the suit. And when you have it all saved up, you take out your money and get the suit made wherever you want."

"I'm not giving any money of mine to any Gachó," he interrupted.

"But Curro, it's safe there, and you can ask for it any day you want it. And you know what, Curro? You know what happens?"

"What?" Curro asked through a load of fried potatoes.

"The man at the bank gives YOU the little gift!"

"You're kidding!"

"Sure, he gives you the little gift."

"Imagine!" The bottle in his hand was nearly empty. "More wine?"

"No, I've had too much already. Let's get some flan."

"Lito!"

The waiter, tall, heavy-legged and bored, brought our flan. Then the check. As we were leaving, I watched astounded as Curro paused at the table, folded a cloth napkin and pocketed it.

"This one I'm taking with me," he informed the waiter. "And the salt shaker, too," he added, reaching over the table.

"Oh no, not the salt shaker, we only have two," protested the waiter.

"Sure, man," smiled Curro, content with the napkin.

The waiter saluted an amused goodbye as we left.

❧❧❧ ❧❧❧

Eager to shower off the grit, and sleep off the meal, we returned along Union Street. My hand rested easy on his shoulder. My hips rocked lustily. Wine set my eagerness aflow. Soon I would be alone with my Curro. He paused to covet the gold at the pawn shop. Swaybacked and tousled, he stood as absorbed as a kid with a spider, while I ogled the marbled tables of the closed milk-shop where we often gorged on milked coffee and thickly buttered bread, or a fresh cinnamoned eggnog, or rice pudding poured out on dishes as flat as full moons. Having just eaten, my stomach stuffed, I lusted anyway. I craved sugared yogurt cream, Flamenco cante, and Curro -- all at once. Like the caged monkeys on the Ramblas who did nothing but munch, crap, and jerk-off, often simultaneously.

The siesta lull along our drab street was broken by muffled screams and snarled obscenities as a drunken slut beat one of her children. As we trudged on, I shuddered, dismayed by the imbedded memory of another mother raging, back in the country of balanced meals and flannel nighties, beating my darker little sister.

My tired eyes focused on a doorway marked simply "Pensión." I froze. It was here, late one night after a fight with Curro. He had returned late, I was jealous, we argued; and I fled our room, his nearness, my frustration. Alone on the dark street, I had entered the first pensión I found. Sent to the top floor, up many dingy staircases, the night clerk for some reason at my heels ... Door with no lock, bulb with no shade, bed with no sheets.

I had removed my coat to lie down and turned to find the desk clerk still there, door closing behind him and on his unshaven face, unmistakably, the leer.

I had seen it before, on an uncle in Grandma's back bedroom, at the window of a gas station restroom, on a palace flasher, on the whispering Italian sidewalk finks, in a lawyer's Citroën on the autobahn, on a cabby near a fallen column at the Parthenon. Infrequent enough so I would forget to expect it, the leer always jarred me, invaded me. It startled me while admiring a garden of azaleas, or anticipating de-shoeing my tired feet, or basking in the jewel-light of a stained glass window, or savoring a fresh pastry. When I needed a friendly hello, it was the threat to my natural freedom, the acid to my self-respect, denial of my human dignity. The leer ravaged.

That wretch on Union Street knew I was no prostitute. I did not do it to support my household. I did it for fun, for free. I was cheaper than a whore, easier than a whore, more despicable, more fuckable - I was an American.

Panicked. I grabbed my coat, purse-whacked, kicked at his balls and missed, rushed down the stairs and out, with nowhere to go but to Curro. With him I was ugly, but safe...

"Lita!" he urged me along the bright quiet afternoon. Sighing as I admired his arrogant curly head and his tight butt under the salt-stained cotton pants, I hastened to join him.

ళళళ ళళళ

Showers in this part of the world, when available, were skimpy. I had long ago relinquished the blanketing steam and relaxing pelt of the affluent American power shower which soaked clean the feet and warmed the bones and washed my troubles out of my hair. In Spain, with goosebumps I stepped in; and goosebumped yet, I silenced the water. I unwound the towel turbaning my hair, dried my sun-splotched body and redonned the clothes stacked carefully on my shoes. Then I balanced and pliéd through the last movements of my 'shower dance': scrub a foot, dry it, shoe it; scrub the other, dry it, shoe it. My methodical water ballet avoided all freckled contact with this bathroom of strangers and its invisible maladies. My shower-dance, like my equally perfected toilet-hover, convinced me that I was untouched by the wretchedness around me.

❦❦❦   ❦❦❦

"Hi!" I greeted from between the sheets, with the smugness of the freshly bathed.

"Hello," he answered with the solemn superiority that the luxury of a bath gives a poor man. He stood at the wardrobe peacefully combing his wet hair. From the bed, my big-hopeful eyes, accustomed to the half-light, studied his naked baked back and raised arms. His relaxed face was scrubbed to a high gleam. He cleared his throat, examined the comb and continued combing with care. With the pride of a city Gypsy, he admired the blackness of his hair. Not the windburned reddish frizz of a nomadic river Gypsy, nor the sunstreaked brown of the hardworking peasant Gachó; Curro's hair was the wavy oil-black of Gypsy class.

"Hell, now it's about to start." Curro glowered as he lowered himself soap-clean and shower-cool into the bed. As we lay quiet, conversation in the street below mounted. As always, the city awakened just as we lay down to sleep.

"Can't sleep in the afternoon, and the gabby women in the kitchen don't let me sleep all morning!" His irritation built with the street noises, "I'm tired! I've got to work tonight." With fingers splayed, his short hands beseech the ceiling. "How can I sleep with all that noise?" Then he turned his back to me, stashing his head under the pillow.

I lay still on the dying wake of the jiggled springs. My feet were icy. My shoulders shivered with sunburn. The fatigue, temporarily showered out, drifted back through me, too. His smile could penetrate me, his anger exhausted me. Unhappy, I closed my eyes.

How do you expect to sleep, cranky man? Lazy, lovely man, how? How else? Make love. Works wonderfully. Make love and doze. ... Floyd would ... Floyd did all the time ... we'd both doze off. Him still inside. His head, propped on a pillow, level with mine. I'd waken first. Drink in his sweet sleeping breath. Flickering blue shadows of the gas heater ... Awake, a college orgy of milked coffee and jelly donuts, crosslegged in bed ... Books opened to study, we rubbed and tasted and flipped pages and sipped lips, then dipped into love. Deep into love, breathing in unison, ecstasy as one, in union asleep. Yes, slept interlocked again. Walked in step, hip to hip, through Berkeley drizzle. More donuts, more classes missed -- sexed through ... . Danced naked in the blue-flamed room. A slow motion hug in the center of the dim rug. Cluttered desk forgotten in the dusk. My shoulders just fit his pits, my cheek at his neck; we melted into one another, a perfect fit, a pair of burning candles set too close together. In the silence, our mouths a mutual feast. He was proud of his woman, of brand new me ... "Baby" he called me wit' his New York accent and lips I could suck all I wanted. He was mine ... Our dusky room with parchment shades ... a love box, full of sex smell, unread books, and matched white lean lovers, dozing the sweet sleep of satisfaction ...

"Well, hell!" Curro flailed. Outside, feet pounded the stairs and voices bit through the locked door. To this I had come, to this bed of grumbling indifference. Indifference everywhere. Alejandro's to his woman, his woman's to everyone. Spaniards' indifference to Flamenco, the Flamencos' indifference to tourists. Curro's impertinent indifference. Curro, tantalizing Curro, the golden toasted inedible feast. Once a day too much. Spanish standards? Or is that the way the whole world is? Were Alejandro and his woman bedded now? She was probably working ... where? Not an office, it's Sunday, and she probably did not read or write either. Maybe housecleaning or in a factory. Yes, a factory. The women back in Alcalá work in packing plants - olives, oranges ... Must ask her how she made those garlicky meatballs so crispy.

A horn below blew a long persistent drill ... as if a guy were stabbed in technicolor, lying across the wheel of his car ... Curro responded with a violent spin.

"Some orchestra out there!" Facing me, he suddenly broke into his lightning Gypsy grin, laughing at his own anger.

"Curro," encouraged to chat by his sudden warmth, I asked, "where does Alejandro's woman work?"

"Where do you think." He adjusted the sheet over him.

"I don't know, that's why I'm asking. What does she do?"

"What else is she going to do?" he answered, impatient

at conversation of any kind and finding this subject annoying. "What else's she gonna do -- fuck."

"What?"

"She fucks."

My head spun on the spongy pillow. "You mean she's a *PUTA*?"

"What else?"

"You mean it?" I propped up on one tense elbow.

"Yes."

"Then Alejandro? Your pal Alejandro is her *chulo*?" My fingers combed my hair back off my face and held it there, earnest elbow poised high.

"Of course."

"But what about their little girl in Alcalá? How do they know she is his?"

"How should I know!" His patience ended, he covered his eyes with his forearm, shielding himself from my intensity.

The squishy bed squeaked as I swung my feet to the floor. I sat, arms cocked, ready to jump up and flee. Anywhere. On my mark, I was set, but of course, nowhere to go. I sat as though bludgeoned. Bruised, mindless, I sat. Then I began to cry.

First a moan. Then a slow tear. Then a long low howl. And I sobbed. Tears ran alongside my nose, were swallowed, recycled, and cried out again. Salt itched my cheeks.

I mourned the dead life of the empty whore down the hall, of all whore-women, desperately curled, painted, and padded - despised, sought, used and dismissed. I wept for the whorebrats in their terror, I whimpered terrified for my own sister bruising under mommie's coat hanger, and for my own guilt-ridden self, watching frightened and torn. I unlocked the stored tears of my childself, ever before stifled into sneezes behind an eager compliant grin; grieved for the tiny girl of me who begged for love and was thrown crusts of approval; sobbed for the drunken woman beating her child, for my own infuriated mother, drunk with frustration; mourned my descent through a chain of bitter mothers courageously carrying their whole thankless household, and despised for it. I bellowed with the mothers shackled to their kitchens, grieved their loss, their resentment; and I wished I had a kitchen.

I wept for the love I had tasted then thrown away. Floyd was warm bread and rose petals in one precious T-shirt, and I left him. Weeping perplexed tears, I bemoaned the self-inflicted wound of severing myself from my Floyd, lamented over the jagged mismatch with this grumpy little brown man who sat watching me now, puzzled by my torrent. I regretted I would not turn back.

My face contorted into a tragic mask, water streaming from the grimaced mouth, the nose, the eyes. Orphan in the wind, I cried because I was lost.

Then I stopped. A sniffle. A swallow. A shuddered sigh. Silence. Drenched, I blew my nose, rinsed my salty face, and lay down.

Something green and hopeful had let go and washed away. Something perky within me had snapped.

Thirteen

We crossed the Ramblas at dusk, the best time of day. Lilac light settled through black lace trees, mellowed the air, hushed traffic, softened faces. Dusk was when the Flamencos came out, like night-blooming flowers: sideburns lush, eyes restless, mod suits flapping, bits of gold glinting last rays of the sun. Dusk on the Ramblas was a whole new beginning. Dusk dissolved freckles, smoothed squints, browned sunburn, whitened collars, slowed the pace, and ignited smiles. Dusk rekindled hope.

The city lamps blinked on. Curro was packed proud in his impeccable black suit, frond of chaste handkerchief at his breast, his face relaxed, his eyes widened and clean as the sheen on his cheeks, his hair a mass of oil-black ringlets behind his head. It was his custom to leave early for work, and to measure his worth by the value of his suit. His fingers were laced under his suit-coat belly and he leaned back into his stroll like a gentleman with nowhere to go.

Used to a long energetic stride, I cut my step to a mince to stay at his side. My free hand swung a small black purse alongside. In storefront windows, my mouth had the hint of a pucker and the tip of a smirk at one corner. Not a beauty in those reflections, but when I moved, my long back, supple, with the carriage of nobility, projected something vital. I felt like a winner.

We entered Escudilliers Street -- intimate carnival of nighttime amusements. Curro studied me as I stepped out ahead of him.

"Who ever taught you to walk like that?" he beamed as he caught up. I grinned over my shoulder, and continued on ahead along the crowded sidewalk. He spoke to acquaintances we passed; while I nodded and waited, pulling down my sweater, smoothing my hair. Together we melted into the crowd in Bar Escoba.

Like the crossroads of unmapped caravan routes, Bar Escoba was the tacit meeting place for Gypsies, for Flamencos on their way to work. They congregated at the espresso machine like pilgrims around a campfire.

"One coffee with cream and a tall coffee-milk," ordered Curro across a mesh of shoulders. Packed in amongst wall-to-wall Gypsies, I hugged Curro's arm and surveyed them. Neatly suited, ordering coffee and exchanging cigarettes, they chatted in loud voices and large gestures, solemn with early evening Gypsy-gentleman dignity.

"Do you want a cognac, too, Lita?"

"Yes, sure." I grinned, nervous as if I were on my way to work.

"And two cognacs," he called above the din. He flipped open his ostentatious red Marlboro pack, offered me a cigarette, and turned as someone behind spoke to him.

"Hey, how're you doing, man?" He was pleased to see

Juan de la Vara, a grave, robust Gypsy. Curro spoke to him with a special deference he reserved only for Gypsies of great respect. Some Flamencos performed regularly at the flamenco tourist shops and nightclubs of the neighborhood; others worked as free-lance artists, making the rounds of nightspots, seeking a moneyed party who might hire them for the evening. Among the independent artists were those too inept to get a job, those marking time between jobs, those of such consummate artistry they could not bear plugging it out routinely to unappreciative tourist crowds. Juan de la Vara was of the latter. He sang only *Fandango*, and *Rumbas* in offhand moments, being a Catalán Gypsy. No one in Spain sang Fandango as pure as Juan. Voiced like an oak, powered by simplicity, he sang truth and nothing more. His cante, as clean as a mighty prayer, had never been recorded, did not always earn enough to feed the family.

"Have some coffee?" Curro offered.

"Sure, thanks."

"This here's the relative," Curro introduced me in slang.

"Señora, how are you?" Juan was polite. I responded bashfully, grateful whenever Curro acknowledged me as his woman, grateful for Juan's respect.

"How's it going?" Curro's concern was brotherly.

"Can't complain," answered Juan with a facial shrug, a pulling down of the mouth. With their curt phrases and Gypsy grimaces, all loaded with implicit meaning, they discussed the work situation. Gravitating to the bar, we reached our coffees, plunked sugar lumps and stirred; all part of the ceremony, like poking at the campfire during the exchange of roadside news. I dumped my cognac into my tall coffee glass, blew and sipped. Curro finished his short glass of coffee in two draws. He fingered his small brandy snifter, ordered one for Juan, and winced down a slow swallow. The crowd leaked out, others seeped in: Manuel from the Patio Andaluz, a few faces from Seville, a dancer, other regulars. A guitarist propped his case under the bar.

"Who's that?" Curro asked Juan.

"Manuel Brenes. Works over at Los Tarantos. Manuel ... this fellow here ..." Juan introduced.

"Curro of Alcalá," Curro interrupted, offering his hand. "What's it like there?"

"Oh-hoo," Brenes began slowly as he stirred his coffee, "Lotta shows, lotta shows. Cuadro is O.K., mostly girls from Seville. Star is Maruja Garrido; pretty good rumbera. But you work like a beast there."

"Do you have to mix with the customers?" Curro was remembering the tedium of his wine shop job.

"No, none of that. It's strictly a tablao, pure Flamenco stage shows ... Listen Juan, about that matter, the Gachó says ..."

Someone stepped between them. Curro paid and I drifted toward the door. I turned and waited as he remembered to ask the barman to exchange a French ten-franc note.

"Can't. Don't know the rate of exchange," said the

bartender, drying his hands on his coffee-stained white apron.

"It's worth one-eighty. Don't worry about it. You just give me one-forty and keep the rest as a tip," Curro reassured him.

"O.K., thanks," nodded the busy Gachó, counting out one hundred forty pesetas, replacing his cigarette, and sticking a pitcher of milk under the steam nozzle.

As we left, I whispered, "But, Curro, I told you ten francs is only worth one hundred twenty pesetas!"

"But, of course," he declared with righteous Gypsy satisfaction.

We continued down the street to the Patio Andaluz. The sidewalk was too narrow to walk side by side.

"Curro, didn't I hear a fellow say his woman was leaving the Villa Rosa? That's another wine shop, isn't it?" I jumped on and off the curb, wending past people -- waiters and entertainers coming to work, some with costumes or guitars. Doors were just opening; it was early yet.

"Yes, I think so." He pushed straight through, refusing to relinquish the sidewalk.

"Well? Couldn't I work there?" I tucked my hair behind eager ears.

"I don't know, woman."

"Curro, I know how to dance, I know how." I swooped around him like a jay after a cat. "At least enough for a wine shop, I know."

"Soon you'll dance, woman, soon you'll dance," he

appeased, distracted as the 'daily' walked by.

"Howdy, Curro."

"Hello," he saluted the 'daily,' then reminded me, "I've got to get that winter suit made."

"Curro, I can't work without a dancing dress. Please let's get a dress made." Breathless, I opened my arms entreating, "I'm ready, Curro, I can do it."

"... mohair ... perhaps navy, no, black's best," he mused.

"I know just how I want it made," I insisted. "Listen to this: black bodice with three dotted ruffles, an orange, a lilac, and a yellow. What do you think?" My voracious eyes, pursued his.

"Fine, fine. But you don't have a job." He was looking elsewhere.

"Curro, I've got to have the dress to get the job." Rubbing my nose nervously, I walked backwards in front of him. "Look, with ..."

"Calm down, woman," he grabbed my arm to avoid a collision with his friend and quitarist. Quino's dark glasses, work suit, neat hair, and balancing guitar case, were all in undertaker black. He was a serious family man, with a handsome face and a typically cynical dislike for his job. He was slightly smaller than Curro -- a most endearing quality -- also an introvert, a Gachó of few words. He was a good accompanist, and they shared a perfect rapport when loaded on grifa. Relieved to see him, Curro walked at ease with him, gesturing while Quino nodded and smiled. I walked behind them to the door of the Patio, tingled as castanet chatter beckoned through the open doorway. We greeted Manuel, rocking on his heels in the entrance.

Entering, my stomach knotted. I glanced self-consciously at the owner sitting at the cash register of the bar, along one brightly tiled wall. My feet icy, I passed between the empty tables, surrounding the stage of raw wood sunk in the center of the gleaming tiled floor, and I entered the darkened back room. Thankful for the dark where my feelings could not be read, I found a chair from which to watch the show and see the Flamencos intermingle with the tourists between shows – imagining all the while how I could work there.

Nightly I sat in dark limbo, no longer a tourist, not yet a Flamenca, feeling the exhilaration of each. The tourist-me got excited by swirling dresses, mesmerized by the clocked precision of hand-clapped, foot-stamped rhythms, perplexed by the weird wail called cante, fascinated by the guitarist's busy fingers, kneading the guitar, raking holes in its grubby face, awed by the self-assurance of these people called Gypsies.

The to-be-Flamenca-me, saw myself being cynically friendly with the customers, demonstrating castanets, singing and clapping at tables, ordering more wine, sweet-talking for tips, "for the guitarist's family." Giddy, sitting in the dark, I imagined my orange and lilac ruffles flying, my feet "ticketing" to the music, dancing through the routine I learned in the little academy in Seville. I would soon be tan, and I could fake a Spanish accent. The other performers

would be grateful that I could patronize the foreign slum-
mers in English. The irony of tourists being gypped by a
tourist tickled me - their coming all the way from
Schenectedy or Liverpool to see a Californian dance
Flamenco. All I needed was that dress. And to convince
Curro.

"How eager I am to work here!" I breathed as he came
back to comb his hair. Quino entered, deposited his case,
returned to the light to prop a foot and tune his guitar. Trini
walked in, a sullen blond Gypsy with Slavic eyes, refreshed
her lipstick, stashed her purse, and left without a word.

"Curro! Good evening!" A quick laugh and the swish of
red petticoats announced the dusky, husky-fleshed Amelia.
Blanched-almond eyes glimmered in chocolate plump. A
dash of irony lacing the outer lashes of her smile, she gazed
at Curro, while he combed steadily.

"Let me use your comb, man. I forgot mine."

"Sure, here." He wiped it and slowly handed it to her,
and with her quick laugh, she combed. He watched her rich
arms under busy ruffle. "Listen, you shouldn't go around
telling people that you are in love with me."

Her eyes widened, her mouth dropped, then her laugh
tinkled. "Listen to Charles Boyer, here."

"You can't dance for shit," he concluded with the quiet
conviction of a full erection. "You don't know anything.
Why, you probably don't even have any hairs on your
'chocho,' yet."

"Hush up! You've a lot of gall." Stung by his impertinence, she added, "Here's your comb." He took it deliberately, moving in, belly to belly, staying close, grinning down at her. Her eyes glittered, their sparks bounced off his knowing, grinning cool.

"Listen," he said, "none of this gall business, eh? I am a very prudent and reasonable man." She glared, then tipped her head back in a quick, trilled giggle, and left with a flash of teeth on brown, a whirl of polka-dots on red. Curro followed her out to the stage.

Whipped by shame, I sat hypnotized, as if having witnessed a child de-wing a moth, or a dog lick at his privates. Listlessness lingered. I felt a foreigner, an inert shadow. As the show began out there, I sat ruminating in the dark.

"What am I doing here? They're a pair, like Floyd and I were, a sexual-sibling set. What do I want with this little brown man?! I'm a university graduate, bilingual, healthy, independent, and out of my element. I'm too smart to be a missionary, yet I'm living amongst parasitic pimps and illiterate Gypsies, and withstanding humiliation like this. Why am I here?"

I knew I would stay. I knew that these people lived in a different realm of understanding. I did not know what it was they knew, only that they had answers for which I did not even have questions. Curro knew. Curro of silky arm, the laughter, the rage, the irreverence of an anarchist, and the cante of my agony. As if impaled by my own blind quest, I sat in the back room. The guitar began to slap and twang, palms started clapping.

Flamencos scattered amongst the tables, smiling and toasting the customers, then collected, periodically in the center for a boisterous half-hour show. Eventually they gathered at the most fruitful table, and spent most of the evening there. They surrounded a dazzling array of empty bottles of Tío Pepé, the best dry fino of Jerez. The big spender, a pompous Spaniard with grand gestures and big claims of intimate knowledge of Flamenco, named famous singers, even attempted to sing a Fandango himself, to the overwhelming pleasure and encouragement of the house employees. There was, of course, nothing worse than an amateur Gachó singing Fandango. And no one spent money better.

Actually reigning at the table was his companion, a vivacious and well-cleavaged lady. She was a warm, wise, witty hostess; a successful professional woman, judging by her perfectly polished nails, the gold gleaming at the back of her laugh, and her poise. Noble and fun, she had soul. No two-bit pimp ate off of her, no leer would come near. Playfully, she urged her gentleman to pass out peseta bills after each round of song. Each pair of Tío Pepe bottles was brought at her gracious request. Little wonder the Flamencos welcomed her.

With the flutter of a hand, she interrupted her conversation with Paco, the dancer of ruffled shirt and high-heeled boots, to attend to the music. Quino, cigarette hanging from his mouth, sat bent over his guitar. Trini, head thrown back and hands pressed palm to palm, was singing a somber, lilting Tientos. Amelia, sitting at a virtuous distance from the Gachó, laughed as she leaned to help the man don castanets. Manual brought another pair of bottles and a platter of cheese morsels and Spanish mountain ham. Curro, at ease a moment, filled an extra glass and brought it to the back room.

"Lita, how's it going back here?" He wagged his head to pick me out in the dark.

"Oh, fine. Getting tired?" I stretched in my chair, undulating my backbone and winging my elbows.

"Not bad. Here," he handed me the drink.

"Thank you, sir." I sipped, happy he remembered me. I sipped again. "Boy, that is some lady out there! Is she a puta?"

"Of course. She's a good person, a really good person." Praise from Curro is unusual.

His benevolent mood comforted me.

"This sure is good!" I rolled the keggy wine back on my tongue. I never swallowed sherry, its nutty flavor dissolved into the back of the mouth. I sipped again.

"Shall I bring you another?"

"It looks like there's plenty."

He brought two full glasslets, we clinked them. "Cheers," he said in English.

"Cheers, Currete," I sat basking in his care, in the same benign smile I received yesterday. I had been cooking on the roof and he awoke to find me chopping carrots in the sunshine. And he smiled.

I sipped and slipped an arm around his waist. He did want me. Not as a dancer flirting here at work like Amelia and the others, but home, safely his. Not as a tourist either, to bring money and keep him like a chulo. As a wife. Perhaps I really was his woman. Flushed with wine and relief, I put my head on his side and ran my hand up under his warm jacket to the deep dip in his back. His hand paused on the top of my head. My eyes closed.

Abruptly, he returned to the customer's table.

"Put it on three for me, Quino, I'm going to sing a Bulerías here for the gentleman."

Quino adjusted the capo to the third fret of the guitar. Curro removed his jacket; swallowed another glassful; wiped his mouth by gathering his puckered lips in one hand; then grasped the back of the guitarist's chair and stared at the ceiling a moment to gather lyrics. He was feeling good; he would be singing for himself. It would be righteous. I moved to the doorway to hear better. I leaned in the tiled archway, glass forgotten, immersed in my Curro, this priest of Flamenco.

The opening warm-up, "Ti-ki-ri-ki-tiiiaaaooouuu," started with a shout, fell into a whine, filled out to a wail, then cut clean with the music.

"Ole," the others answered in unison. They had all turned towards him. Here it came. This was what they lived for. They began to clap neat, muted palmas. He sang Bulerías like it was meant to be sung. He sang short verses as they occurred to him, mostly concerning the impishness of fate. Sometimes he bent his knees as he chopped out a sound, made a fist as he gutted out the tumbling syllables. He sang in moody modes; yet hot, staccato rhythms. Palmas snapped like snares; their steady intricacy framed his coarse nasal voice. He called: burbling, howling, building tension, chuckling, through variations of stops, runs, cascades, smooth-outs, countertimes, and counter-counters. Bulerías: the most exhilarating of all Flamenco; the Gypsies' party-time Flamenco, a celebration, a sorrowful smile, a grimace, wry laughter. Bulerías: a slap in the face and a pat on the head, spiced constantly with the unexpected, then just in time, the unexpected return of the expected. The affirmation of life and laughter, heady Bulerías. Higher than wine or weed, snappier, sappier than a young tree, wittier than an ageless sage, Bulerías. The sugar of Gypsy art, gathered from many lands and boiled down in Spain through generations of suffering, laughing Gypsies.

ॐॐॐ   ॐॐॐ

"Look, Curro! Come here!" I leaned over the balcony, laughing quietly. "This you have got to see," I added in my after-work whisper. It was 4:00 a.m. and the rest of the world was asleep. He continued stirring the pot on the butane burner, so I stepped back into the room.

"A woman and a deaf-mute are down there, arguing prices, discussing business out loud with hand gestures." He smiled and inhaled the aroma of bouillon cubes. He was stripped to his T-shirt, his suitcoat carefully hung in the wardrobe. His tired singer's throat craved hot soothe. The spoon chirped inside the aluminum pot. I returned to the balcony's morose pre-dawn air. I giggled as I studied the alley directly beneath me.

"Curro, can you believe it? Red lights coming from the open doorway, red lights - and this, 1965. How quaint. A tourist's find. Hey, look at that red light there and the white globe next to it. Can you believe it? What nerve, a police precinct right next door to a screwery."

"Ole, ole, 'screwery,'" he echoed, tickled at the word I had invented. He nodded his appreciation. Mellow after a night of wine and cante, his eyes draped lazy over the rim of his smile.

"I guess a whore has to get her price before they bed because that's when the man is hot to settle for anything," I mused aloud. "But a chulo moves in afterwards, if he's lucky. She must be fed up with men, before coming home to him. So, which is the riskier business?" I plopped on the bed.

"Curro, would you mind if I ask you something I can't figure out?" I took a mug of broth from him, watching his face.

"No, daughter, what is it?" He poured his and put the hot pot on the floor. I blew, sipped, burning my lips, blew again, then asked slowly, "Why does a whore pay her pimp?"

He picked up his mug and sat facing me in his chair at the table.

"Because she loves him." he slurped and pondered, then offered, "But pimps don't love."

"But after all that fucking hasn't she had enough of men? Why does she want one more?"

"Because her profession is to fuck, but she doesn't come except with the chulo she loves."

"Oh." I sipped my soup gratefully. My questions were spent, and somehow, so were my doubts.

"How's the broth?" His singer's voice cracked with a bedroom huskiness, smoldered when he spoke, inflamed.

"Curro, it's delicious. And I'm loving you so."

We blew and slurped together. He vacuumed out the last drops, cleared his throat, took my empty cup. "Get undressed, I'm going to tell you a little joke."

"Oh, Curro, be serious; it's five in the morning -- it's nearly dawn." Ruffled, I reminded him, "You've got to get some sleep."

"Oh, just a short joke, a little quick one, won't hurt or anything." He grinned the grin of the little man with something big in his pocket. He peeled off his T-shirt, draped his pants over his chair. He looked down, and his grin widened to its limit, his eyes languorous squints. He swatted the nose-cone in his underwear.

"Hold still! You, impertinent ...! Hey, behave yourself." Clowning resignation, he dove into bed. Folding his arms under his head with confidence, he watched the peak in the sheet rise and fall.

"Come here, girl. I am going to tell you a very funny

story. You'll like it. You'll die laughing."

I eyed the taut chest flesh under his insipid tattoo, stared at the generous brown arms folded back in submission. It was an offer I could not resist. I grinned my greedy, lopsided grin, turned out the light, crawled into bed, and found myself immediately entangled in all four of his warm limbs and rudely poked in the thigh. No sweet surrender here.

"Hold on, Curro, where are you going?"

"Nothing, nothing, woman," he placated. "*Nada nada.* Didn't mean a thing by it." He relaxed his grip, nestled by my side so that he could thump my hip.

Fwump, fwump, "Now, let me see ..." Fwump, "Have you ever heard of el Solilla? Well, I'm going to tell you who Solilla is ... Solilla is this most unfortunate country bumpkin, a real hick. And one day it happened that el Solilla ..."

He did not rush me. I began to giggle at his childish cheek. I giggled, tickled by his shamelessness; giggled again, tickled because he had slipped it in while I was laughing; giggled because, helpless with laughter, I could not push him away. Laughing at the absurdity of his story -- punchline immaterial -- I laughed as he talked quietly, speaking in a thoughtful manner, pumping at me. I laughed at him, then he laughed; I laughed at us both, we laughed at each other, and, laughing, it snuck up on me and I climaxed with a gasp and a cackle. And he came chuckling at me. And laughing, we rocked to a slow-down and a stop.

"Oh-hoo," he approved and rolled over on his back,

hands beneath his head. Smiling, I wiped a tear, drank at his sweaty shoulder, licked my lips, and bounced my head back on the relentless sponge pillow. I sniffled and lay quietly. But then,

"Currete, are you asleep yet?"

"What do you want?" He did not move or open his eyes.

"Curro, look. I can dance. I know how to dance well enough to work in a wine shop. You know, it's a year now since I came to Spain. A year that I have been practicing - every day practicing in basements and rented studios. Curro, I have been watching you work and studying all the dancers you work with. I don't know much about Flamenco, but I know enough to work there in the Patio with you." I propped my chest upon his and pleaded, "You have never ever seen me dance. You don't realize - I'm ready for you to see me now. I wish you'd come see how I dance."

"Which dances do you have?" He had opened his eyes. He was looking at me intently. Hearing me.

"Well, the Sevillanas, with castanets. And the Fandangos de Huelva. And I have an Alegrías and a Soleá."

"You do? Well, all right then ... Okay, look. Tomorrow I will tell the dancer there at the Patio. Paco plays the guitar a bit, too, you know. Tomorrow I will ask him, and see if he'd mind coming with his guitar, and we'll go to where you rehearse. We'll see if we can shape you up for working."

"You mean it, Curro?"

"Yes, woman, yes."

"Oh, Currete, how gorgeous you've become!" I pounced

114

on him, bathed him with kisses.

"Okay, woman. That's enough, woman." Patting me, he turned and fell asleep.

I lay an arm across his sleeping warmth, and stared at the promising dark. I chewed at my lips. Visions of auditions kept me wide-eyed. I slipped out of bed, pulled a coat from the wardrobe and stepped out onto the balcony. I leaned against the iron bannister, shivering with excitement, one naked foot propped warming the other. I hugged my green coat around me.

It was the magic hour between the closing of the screwery and the opening of the precinct. Only a cat scouted. Somewhere a watertruck sizzled, washing down the streets. Further, produce trucks hacked and hummed to market. A late couple scurried under the rising sky. The street lights blinked out.

Fourteen

Curro's nostrils flared with distaste at the sour pungence of that wine cellar. Kegs and crates lined the wall. Daylight eked through a fogged window. One bulb illumined the dust webs, a stained cement floor, and me.

"What first?" he asked.

"Alegrías." Quivering, I stood in the middle of the dusky room nervously picking skin off my lips. I felt suddenly very American, in street skirt and a tie around my lengthening hair. I wore thick, cracked, dance shoes.

"*Vale.*" Curro wiped his mouth and said to the guitarist, in his husky morning voice, "Put it on three, and play me a bit of Alegrías."

The guitarist, actually a dancer where Curro worked, propped his leg on a broken chair and strummed the basic skeletal music for the commonest of Flamenco, the Alegrías. I had been practicing it alone in silence, in murky rented places for one year. No one had ever seen me dance.

Softly Curro sang. I could barely hear his beat above my own pulse pounding in my ears. I counted under my breath. Counting I launched, and counting I danced out my little routine.

"*Uno dos TRES, cuatro cinco SEIS, siete OCHO, nueve*

DIEZ. Uno does TRES ..." I had never danced with a guitar before, nor a singer, but I had heard hundreds of Alegrías by then. Curro's quiet noonday singing somehow eased me and made it fun. How my blood stirred to be dancing to that man's voice, even in a rotting basement. How he could sing, when he wasn't even trying.

When I finished, Curro was squinting and beaming like a Buddha. "But woman, you can dance!"

My eyes grew round. "I told you I could dance."

"But you need a dress! There's a job open at the Villa Rosa, across the street from where we work, right, Lito?" The guitarist nodded.

"You'll be working in a week!" Curro predicted.

"I told you I needed a dress!" Triumphant, I threw my sweaty arms around him.

He grew businesslike. "Now, let's see your Fandango and the Sevillanas."

Fifteen

"Ole, Susana!" Music to my ears was my name shouted in Spanish. "Susana, *bien!*" Shouts, clapping, and rousing rasping guitar, backed my dance. They called out many encouragements, but I was too busy counting to decipher them,

"Uno dos TRES, cuatro cinco SEIS, siete OCHO, nueve DIEZ. Un' DOS."

I danced scared, bolting around a stage as small and precarious as a table top, intimidated by the men in black suits behind me, the musicians who knew what they were doing, and knew I did not. I danced nervous about the audience scattered around the room. I smiled at them when I could remember, as I stomped and swooped. And counted.

"Uno dos TRES, cuatro cinco SEIS, siete OCHO, nueve DIEZ. Un' DOS ..." So much to remember. My routine (what comes next?!). The edge of the stage (in three steps I was out of bounds). The compás (stay in step with the music's irregular accents). Move my arms at the same time I was counting out my steps (how to do everything at once?) Hold my head up...

"One two THREE, four five SIX ... EIGHT ... TEN ... TWELVE. One two THREE ..... SIX ..."

Looking down was easier. Glimpses of my polka-dotted ruffles -- an orange, a lilac, a yellow -- rimmed with black lace, made me feel safe, encouraged me that I was indeed a dancer being paid to struggle here.

I had never attended a rehearsal. In Spain, it seemed, Flamenco rehearsals did not exist. Like a Forties' Hollywood musical, one day I was in the audience, hankering, next day on stage tapping my way to stardom. Without any rehearsal, I just got out there and danced.

It was not easy.

"*Ele, Susanita.*"

"*Chiquilla, baila bien.* Dance good, girl." The waiting dancers were paid to shout and clap out the beat for each other. This *jaleo* and *palmas* was part of the show.

Sweating, hair a mess, I accelerated my footwork, hanging on to my new skirts. My feet became two pistons clicking faster than the music behind me, speeding out of control. I had lost count entirely.

"*Asa Susana. Asa toma!*" The cheering voices quelled my panic. I was in trouble, but the enthusiastic group did not show it. They pounded feet and hands, signaled the end to the music so forcefully that I managed to spin and stop with it. Almost. I put out one last foot to steady my wavering final pose.

The audience, a tableful of English tourists, one of French tourists, and a few Catalan Spaniards at the bar, applauded the sudden silence. They did not know Flamenco enough to judge me.

Panting, I smiled shyly at the guitarist, avoided the eyes of the others, and took my seat among them. Grateful for their backup, I intended to return the favor. I twisted my hair up off my wet neck and clapped loud and fast for the next dances.

Yolanda circled the arena, a stumpy thing with dyed black horse-tail nearly as long as her short ruffles. A left-over from Spanish classical dance, she danced her number with castanets, sequins, and the chronic smile of an old circus performer. Her smug performance looked silly to me, but I clapped as though for a master.

Then the *maricón* danced. Pepito wore eyeliner, pointed his pretty toes, and constantly fingered his vest with long nails. His dance was a series of cute poses. I sat with my shoulders bunched at my ears, concentrating on my clapping.

While I clapped, I mused that this Barcelona wine shop cuadro was a tacky crew. Unlike the exciting flamenco tablaos, the performers here were older, uglier, and possessed more cheek than ability. As a beginner, I fit right in. Comforted, I could plug along, hoping with practice to achieve the polish of a real tablao dancer. Just a few streets away, "Los Tarantos," flamenco tablao, my grand prize, glimmered. Soon I would dance there, I was determined. Curro was already working at Los Tarantos.

"Strong palmas!" noted Ramon with a diplomatic smile, as he parked his guitar and left the stage. "Really loud."

I grinned at him, pleased, until I noticed him exchange

a glance with the dancer Mercedes. Tough as an old wait-ress, Mercedes intimidated me. Although Mercedes' angle-armed, hollow-chested, mundane dancing was genuinely forgettable, this wary woman anchored the cuadro with her commanding palmas, seemed an old friend of the guitarist, and was high on that intangible pecking order found in every workplace.

These dauntless old pros would rehearse me on the job. Dancing these three precious nightly shows at the wine shops in Barcelona was my Flamenco graduate school. The price I paid for that school was the mandatory mixing between shows with the customers. "*Alternando*" they called it. I had to guzzle lovely sherry wine until I hated it.

"Where are you from?" I approached the most promis-ing table of tourists with my own gypsy guile.

"Liverpool. That's in England."

"England!" I fumbled for words. "Mmm, do chew lie Flamenco?"

"Lovelih, simply lovelih." The guests nodded vehement-ly. They sat in "quaint" wicker chairs, beaming with tourist expectancy, their red English faces sipping wine and turning redder.

"May we join you?" It was my job to charm them into buying many rounds of drinks. Grabbing a chair from an empty table, I offered my castanets to a bashful girl, sat and helped her put them on. Ramón ordered wine, the other dancers found places to sit.

"Good, good," I encouraged the girl's attempts with the

castanets, while I drank my wine thirstily and held out my glass for more.

"How do you clap so loud?" asked the man across from me, as if on cue.

I grasped his wrist, straightened his fingers, then aimed my fingers at his bared palm, to produce the explosive pop of Flamenco palmas. Delighted, everyone tried it. A most chummy lesson ensued, amidst much pouring of wine.

"How well you speak English," praised one enchanted lady.

"Thank you," blushed I artfully, feigning pleasure at the compliment.

"How did you learn?"

"My mother she kwus from Sevilla. A Cheepsee. The American, mmm, airbase ... mmm ... es by Sevilla. My father he kwus Americano ..." I shrugged and grinned to let them fill in the rest of my story. They were charmed. I gloated.

"Maybe," I whispered to my new confidante, just as the other dancers had taught me, "you could give nice tip to guitarrista. He has big family, too many mouths ..."
Smiling and nodding, the 'Flamencos' took leave of their English pals. They regrouped at the square of wooden flooring to carry on again for another show.

"Look, Susana. I need to tell you something ..." Mercedes discreetly drew me to one side, while the guitarist tuned up. "I don't want you to get mad at me," she whispered, "but I am going to ask you a favor."

"What's the matter?" I was apprehensive.

"You've got to clap more quietly. Play *palmas sorditas*."

"Why?" I began. "I clap well." At least, I had assumed, I could do palmas well. What is in clapping? Just hit your two hands together. Infants do it. The criticism hit hard, shamed me.

"You do clap well," Mercedes lied. "But too loud. *Tienes que tocar las palmas sorditas.* Clap softly, mujer," she said with the same Andalucían charm used a moment ago at the table on the other foreigners. I glanced at the dancers taking their seats. They pretended not to notice.

"But you clap loudly." I was stunned, I could not let it go. "I clap like you do."

"There are times to clap *fuertes*, times to clap *sordas*."

That humiliation would teach me stage etiquette. I would learn to distinguish between just clapping and the impeccably exact Flamenco *palmas*, the percussion of Flamenco music. One day I would modulate my *palmas* too, and blend with the other musicians.

Meanwhile, I would not mention my embarrassment to Curro.

"Listen," Mercedes said, "don't forget to ask for the little tip for the guitarist and his family."

"I did, I did. I always do."

"You forgot last night." Glaring at me, Mercedes made it clear. They would cover my mistakes on stage only if I, with my English, would pay my dues at the tables.

"*Vamos a Sevilla, chiquillos. Vámonos.*"

"*Ole, Susana. Asa Pepito.*"

My arms circled, my castanets clacked around my head. The cuadro was ending the evening with Sevillanas, a couples dance and a crowd pleaser.

Pepito was feinting and ducking around me.

"*Asa Pepito,*" Mercedes and Yolanda laughed behind us. In a spin, Pepito did not see my arm coming and he received a glancing blow on the back of his head. A castanet in a flailing hand can hurt like a brass knuckle. As I jerked past him, I did not notice I had hit him. I was always dizzied by my own frantic turns.

Doors were closed, money was on the table. While Ramon counted it out, Pepito bickered quietly with Mercedes, as usual.

"Next time it's your turn," he growled.

"*No señor,*" she snickered, "not me."

"I mean it," he pouted, "I won't put up with her any more."

I was oblivious. I never knew it was a hazard to dance Sevillanas with me, until years later when it ceased to be so. The simplest is often the last to be mastered. Meanwhile, my redemption was my endless awe and respect for Flamenco. Real Flamenco. And my awareness that this wine shop dancing was pretty bad, all of it.

Sixteen

Curro was my only friend and I was his. I was his only drinking buddy, his own-ly woman, the only one who loved him. We lived alone together, two helpmates, consoling each other, too lonely otherwise. I earned for room rent. I danced. He earned for food. He sang. I moved my body in space to pay for the space of our room. He sang his soul out from his belly to pay for the food we ate. We lived well, bedded and fed, in a pensión where whores lived with their pimps, with one kitchen down the hall, one communal bathroom. Amidst the misery of the street and the pensión, inside our one small door, the narrow room was ours. It was our clean home. We kept it scrubbed, from dusky brick floor to gleaming wash basin and tiny oil-clothed table. The narrow bed at the table's edge was ours. The sheets had the smell of clean. We bedded with the smell of clean and satisfaction. Every night we would burrow together in our narrow bed and sigh deep sighs and Curro would recite his gratitude:

"*Que camita ma' buena.* What a good li'l bed."

"*Sí, Currete, que camita ma' buena,*" I would chant. And we sighed together in luxury.

After breakfast of toasted bread and café-con-leche, we

would shop for our daily food. We bought it fresh each day at the market place.

Entering the market was always a shock. Lanes and lanes crossed rows and rows of awninged stalls, with piles of fruits, bins of vegetables, swinging carcasses of dripping meats, iced marble counters of fresh fish, coffee aroma from the tiny outdoor bars. Curro chose the fish, I chose the meat. We met at the tomatoes, haggled over the peppers, offended the garlic lady, joshed at the olives. Passing again the sour-faced garlic lady, we paused at a flaming pyramid and worshipped and chose oranges with joy. Orange, olive, garlic, pepper, tomato, sausage, fish -- the market was a celebration. Marketing with Curro was always a celebration, an homage to abundance and to being alive.

Bread was separate. Bread came from the bakeries away from the scramble and flies of the market; from warm flour-dusty, quiet, clean bakeries. Curro bought bread in individual buns and carried it with deference, always set it right-side-up on the table. Every time he broke open a new bread, he first marked a cross on it with his pointed finger, like his mother alwys did. He ate a sandwich on the bread-bun with the heaven side upwards. He was not a religious man, but he fervently revered bread. He was irreverent of everything and everybody; he was anarchy and desecration and irreverence incarnate, that crazy Gypsy. But he was gentleness to me, and he revered bread. He was always telling me to eat bread. *"Come pan,"* he always, always told me. Never "have more meat," not "eat your vegetables," always simply, "eat bread."

Curro de Alcalá was proud of his little hometown. Alcalá de Guadaira was known over all of Andalucía as "Alcalá of the Bakers" because Alcalá's bread was so famous. Up in Barcelona, bourgeois affluent Barcelona, they had nothing because their bread was not that of Alcalá. Curro had tried most of the bakeries in the Ramblas area to find good Alcalá bread. He tried to find the heavy white bollos with the tough crust and the fragrance of virtue. Nothing put Curro in a nasty mood faster than bad drinking water or bad bread.

The day was cold, rainy. The Ramblas trees were pruned, naked fists gesturing obscenely at the thick gray sky. The market was dripping and chilly. Curro and I spent more time and more money than necessary. Two voluptuaries with steaming breaths, gleefully collecting vittles. We chose fresh eggs, tender pork, bacon. From a mountain of pea pods, we bought a paper cornucopia of peas. Tomatoes, some green, some red, some red-green. And blue-backed, sharp-nosed, silver-streaked, water-new sardines.

We trudged our loaded net bags home in triumph. Under Curro's direction, I cooked on our one butane burner in our one Gypsy pot, in the communal kitchen down the hall. As I cooked, Curro went out again, as usual, for bread and wine, and that day he found some artichokes to season the pot. He carefully placed the breads on the little table in our room, then joined me in the group kitchen. We shelled peas together drinking wine and laughing. Curro talked to the other women in the kitchen and made them all laugh.

Curro and I sat down to eat. We sat facing each other in our narrow clean room next to our neat narrow bed with our two bowls and two spoons and two wine glasses and two breads. The stew of peas and pork and artichoke steamed of heaven.

"We are eating like rich folks," Curro was proud.

I answered with thick gray words. Perhaps I was offended by his rapport with the others in the kitchen, by jokes pitched too quickly for my foreign ears to catch. I was cranky. Then I said it. Tossing my broken hunk of bread on the table with contempt, as it rolled to a stop upside down and rejected, I said, "This bread is shitty."

His eyes jumped from his dish, to my bread, to me. His spoon halted halfway up, jaw stopped in mid-chew. As if I had hit him, his face of celebration turned to pain. He would speak no more, nor eat. He could not swallow, he would not eat. His bread lay heavenward at his place.

I knelt by the side of his chair, barely fitting between the chair and the bed, and asked what I had said that hurt him so. I begged him to tell me what I had done.

After a long moment, he put his arms around me. Without a word he pulled me up off my feet, and in silence put me back in my chair, at my plate and my wine and my broken bread. He returned to his chair.

Curro sat and studied me. Then quietly he spoke. Watching me, Curro told me the story of bread.

"Suesee, bread is sacred. There is nothing more pure

than bread. There is nothing more clean than bread. There is nothing more honest than bread. There is nothing more pure, more good, more clean. There is nothing more noble, more simple, more honest, than bread.

"Suesee, in North Africa I saw the Moors, when the wheat had grown high, kneel down and pray to that wheat. I saw the Moors show their gratitude because God brought them that wheat out of the nothing. Out of the nothing, Suesee. God brought that wheat out of the nothing and they were on their knees to that wheat."

Curro was calling me by name, pronouncing it in the soft Spanish way.

"Suesee, I have been so hungry that I have eaten old bread out of the gutter. I had to eat banana peels, I had to eat potato peelings, and I picked up old hard dirty bread from the gutter to eat. And I ate that gutter bread. I'm not ashamed to say that to you, Suesee, to say that I ate bread people threw away, that I ate bread out of the street ..."

My name became a caress.

"Suesee, all bread is sacred. Some bread is badly made. But that is not the fault of the bread. That is the fault of the bakers who throw in other stuff to make more money. That's not the fault of the bread. Bread is good, Suesee.

"After the war - the war of brother against brother, the war that killed my father before I was born, the war when they shaved my mother's head -- after that war, the only bread in all of Andalucía was made in Alcalá. There was no other bread but the bread of the bakeries of Alcalá. There was hunger everywhere and people stood in lines that wound around the little streets of Alcalá, stood in lines for the bakeries of Alcalá. Suesee, I knew a baker in Alcalá. The man had many children. Every morning, after baking bread all night, every morning he would tuck breads into his socks to smuggle them out of the bakery for his children to eat. Every morning he would leave the bakery with burning hot bread from the oven, inside his socks next to his shins. Every morning he would burn his legs again with the hot bread so his children could eat. Every morning during those war years his children ate bread. And his legs still carry scars from the bread ..."

While he spoke, I wept. In remorse, I wept. In wonder, I wept. He came around the table to me and drank my tears. He held me and kissed my teary eyes.

"I love you very much, Suesee. Much more than anyone would have believed I could love you. We are two, a pair. My life is yours and yours must be mine."

Then he told me to eat and he sat, and we ate.

Seventeen

"Currete, I got it! My card!"

"All right woman! I knew you would." He sat down next to me at the back of the empty Flamenco club.

"Those Catalán Gaché don't know Flamenco from nothin'! There were four of them on the panel. While I danced my Alegrías, I just smiled as if I thought I was hot stuff, and I was careful not to count out loud. So I guess I looked like an 'entertainer' to them. Poor things."

"Ole." Curro grinned.

"I go back next week to pick up my syndicate card. Woo! The American Gachí is a bona fide Spanish Flamenco dancer named Susana. Whatta joke. They said with this card I can work anywhere in Spain. Yea!"

"Hush, woman," Curro looked about him, but no one else had arrived. The chairs around us were all empty. It was nearly opening time at Los Tarantos. Curro brought a cognac for each from the bar, and in the dark club, we toasted my career.

"Cheers, Chochete," he said in English.

"Cheers, Currete." It was our little ritual.

He swigged, I sipped. Then with a pat on my head, he left me to go backstage, and I settled in my seat for another evening of good Flamenco. Another evening of serious "advanced study."

Red velvet curtains lined the raised tiny stage which swelled out into the audience. The yellow haze of the empty stage inflamed me. Dancing here amongst the best was the ardent goal of my young life. But I had much to learn first.

"*Señora,* aren't you working tonight?" Maruja's mother, stately gypsy matron with knotted hair, saluted me politely. Dancers' mothers were allowed to loiter on the edge of an audience in Spain and keep watch over their daughters. As a singer's wife, I enjoyed that privilege as well. I was considered Curro's wife by Flamencos who seldom bothered with legal marriage.

"No, I quit at the Villa Rosa." I fingered my hair self-consciously. "I'll start at the Mimosa next month. Contract is signed." The Mimosa was the highest paying wineshop in town, a step up for the American, but small potatoes to the mother of the lead artist at Los Tarantos.

"*Bien, bien,*" she nodded as she crossed the hall straightening chairs like a mother-in-law. Cognac seared my throat and I watched with glee as the club filled.

That peculiar lush tinkling of two guitars exploded into my veins as the show started. Curro stood at the guitarist's elbow, clearing his throat with that "Hee!" he used to test his voice before an evening of singing. The cuadro girls, in spectacular colors and prim shoes, drifted on, squinting at first in the bright light. They settled in their seats as though bored, adjusting their ruffles about their feet, donning castanets. They were mostly from Seville; I knew by their blasé look and the length of their dresses. Flamenco styles changed first in Seville, and were now long, flared skirts with one ruffle hanging at the ankles. The Catalans dwelt in the fashion of twenty years ago, with one-piece dresses, full crinolines, short ruffled shirts, and bare legs. The short dresses seemed more provocative, but the longer, limper, heavier ones could reveal greater surprises - and had an action of their own which was causing a whole new style of dance. But I did not understand this yet. My two dancing dresses were short. And the ladylike, antique appearance of the Seville girls still puzzled me.

I envied those pretty cuadro girls who danced to Curro's cante. There were other singers too, but none with the raunch and poignance of Curro's deep song. I watched how the group clapped and shouted for each girl as she took her turn to dance; how the tension and excitement of each dance was built by the hands and voices of the backup behind the dancer, by the acceleration and sheer musical stops of the cuadro crew.

I picked and chose. The way a girl paused and looked over her shoulder became mine. How one tossed her hair and it landed at the beat of the music, now mine. One dancer in yellow was quick and cute, a Gypsy, I recognized by her perfect footwork, but her elbows were ugly angles, her fingers dead twigs -- not for me. One in long shimmering fringes and with combs above her temples had a queenly demeanor and smooth I wanted. One with pouting lips and gobs of curly hair was as wild as my fluttering heart. How to show that wildness? One stomped a counter-beat while her blue skirt, like a cheerleader's flag, caped swirls to the downbeat. I could do that. I chose the stretch of a certain arm, its twist of wrist, and ripple of fingers. A magical turn. The different ways to gather hair, to place a rose. Which colors in the stage light stole your eyes. Oh, the costumes I designed while sitting in the dark.

After a closing group number and an explosion of flashing colors, spinning skirts, thundering palmas, the stage was cleared for the soloists. Curro and a guitarist remained alone. Curro unbuttoned his suitcoat and studied the floor for lyrics.

The guitar began a melodic interlude in the dampened amber light. Then in brown, fitted, high pants and vest, appeared CaraEstaca, solemn and intense. He shone with the dark facial beauty of a prince of India, bovine round eyes and puffed lips.

Curro sang the tragic *Sequidillas,*

Se han cambiado los tiempos, y me he cambiado yo.
Times have changed, and so have I,

CaraEstaca marked time. A small man with the steel shanks and rock buttocks of an Olympic runner, when CaraEstaca began his footwork, he transformed from human into dive-bomber. He jack-hammered around the stage, hands in fists at his chest, berserk with speed and countertime. His guitarist sweated to keep up with him, and Curro did not even bother to clap. CaraEstaca's feet were a zipper opening the stage.

Flamenco genius, CaraEstaca usually insisted that Curro sing for him -- partly because he could hear the pitch of Curro's voice. CaraEstaca was deaf, yet he was rhythm incarnate, an expert's expert. He would bank on the compás that was his essence, ignore others, and dominate the stage like an autocrat.

Backstage, his eyes were quick as birds to catch all that his ears missed. I never saw him smile, yet he always spoke with tongue in cheek, in his palate whisper. He always made Curro laugh with his inside Gypsy jokes.

After he sang for CaraEstaca, Curro came out to sit with me and watch Maruja work. It was time for the star of Los Tarantos to overcome the night -- with only two guitars and her sister as vocal back-up -- to vanquish every spectator in that dark house.

The Catalan Gypsies gave Flamenco its Rumba. They borrowed it from the Latin American four-beat rhythm. The rumbera was a specialist who both danced and sang her Rumba. And among rumberas, Maruja Garrido was Catalan cream.

Her guitars first played a lovely melodic duet. Then a tornado swept onto the stage, a one-woman skirmish of hair, skirts, and footwork. Suddenly she stopped outside of the lights, in the gloom with the audience, arm outstretched, pointing accusingly at them, hair a horse's mane, head thrown back as if trying to get away from what her heaving chest craved. No one breathed. The place was so quiet one could hear her blood pounding. Her hand turned over and fingers beckoned, yet not a hair moved. With eyes closed, she made the sign of the cross on herself, as her earthy voice whispered:

> *Voy a mojarme los labios, con aqua bendita*
> *Para borrarme los besos, una vez me diera tu boca maldita.*
> I'm going to wet my lips with holy water
> To erase the kisses from your damned mouth.

Then she was a raving maniac again, storming about the stage. And suddenly still, to shred the people with another passionate verse. Whenever Maruja left the stage, the world reverted to a dreary bog. Her dresses were awful -- short and outdated Catalan things. But her Rumba altered you for life.

After the show I sat absorbed, wondering at Maruja's passion, at her matchless timing. While people ordered drinks and began to move and talk, I noticed Maruja's mother wending her way amongst the tables. Maruja had made records, had bought her father a car, in a country where only the richest classes owned vehicles. Yet her parents came to her show every night, and now, between cuadros, it looked like her mother was hawking socks to people in the audience.

"Curro, look at her!"

Curro was fetching two fresh cognacs. I pointed out Maruja's mother bending over a table down near the stage.

"Watch her," I whispered. "Currete, is Maruja's mother actually selling socks to people?"

"Sure is," he chuckled.

"But Curro! Maruja is a star, known throughout Spain. She has money. Why is her mother selling socks like she had nothing to eat tomorrow?"

"Because," laughed Curro, with that candor which made me fall in love with him every time he sprang it on me.

"Because we Gypsies can't BE without cheating somebody."

కళ కళ కళ   ఌ ఌ ఌ

After work, Curro and I walked home. Every night we mellowed in the deserted streets of Barcelona. We strolled the wide lamp-lit Ramblas by ourselves.

"... Two new girls from Sevilla on the show. Oh hoo! One called me to sing three times in her Seguidillas." He shook his head. "Man you really sweat at Los Tarantos," he grumbled, glancing at me for sympathy.

I envisioned his black alpaca suit under hot stage lights, grunting out his deep song. But instead of commiserating, I entreated, "Curro, please ask them where they get their shoes made." How I craved to be in their shoes, those Sevillanas, to look like they did, to have Curro sing for me.

"All right. I said I would find you a shoemaker." He followed me around sidewalk café tables with chairs upside down on them. The brick avenue was freshly washed and puddled.

"They let me try my Soleá tonight," I began. "Half of it went OK ..." I shot him a look, "... until my heel fell off. Lucky it was the last show." I had managed to finish without hobbling.

"We'll get that shoemaker, *Chochete*," he promised.

Distracted, I wandered ahead of Curro. He caught up and studied me. He glanced at the naked strip in the paint on my eyelids, where I had pulled off my false eyelashes I cut daily out of black photographer's paper, feathering them fine with my tiny American fingernail scissors. He knew I was miffed. Really angry. He read me like a barometer.

"What's the matter? Woman, what's eating you?"

"A Gachó at the bar, an American," I admitted reluctantly. "He kept watching me. Know what he said to me?" I glared at Curro as if it were his fault. "He said, 'You're no Spanish dancer, lady. You've got the map of Ireland written all over your face.'"

Peals of laughter from Curro danced on the fresh night air.

"Damn house lights," I muttered. "Bring out every freckle. Just wait 'til I get up on a TABLAO stage. No one - not even Spaniards - will know I am a foreigner."

He would not stop laughing. I swung at him, missing. I pouted, then my nostrils flared. A giggle strayed, deep chuckles broke loose. And our laughter blended with the sudden swish of hose water hitting pavement. Arm in arm we laughed off tension from the night's work, happy we both had jobs.

We entered a dark side street, joined other Flamencos off work.

"*Qué hay, Manolo?*"

"Curro, how's it going?"

"Doin' ok. Not bad."

"*Señora,*" one customarily saluted me with click of heels and swift nod.

"Antonio," Curro remembered, "did you get the name of that shoemaker? Wife's dancing on one leg now."

Their jokes echoed off the stone walls and cobbled alleyways. Mostly I stayed out of their conversation, could not follow it all anyway. I was content to be accepted among them.

They wended to the marketplace. At the all-night coffee stall they huddled around an open counter under dripping awnings. The men bought hot drinks for each other. They threw dice from little black leather cups onto the counter between coffee and cognac glasses, exhaling steam and chortling together.

Heading home through blowing fog that peppered our faces, we passed a man dressed only in shirtsleeves, ogling the dark. The insane black-skinned man, the Moor, as Curro called him, was a fixture on that Ramblas street corner. He always stood on a curb as if about to cross, never crossing. He stood statue-still amidst moving people by day, solitary by night, silently gaping at the sky. I was chattering, my arm in Curro's. I did not notice the Moor until I felt Curro drawn back, his shoulders touching mine, as he twisted to look back at the lost creature.

At the bakery, Curro bought three breads, then returned to the Moor and handed him one. The Moor quickly consumed it, and resumed his job of gazing at the solid black sky. In the lamplight for a foreboding moment, I watched my troubled Curro watch the Moor watching the solid black sky.

അഅഅ ഏഏഏ

"No, no," I screamed, and threw myself on Curro to protect him. Men with clubs were about to attack him.

"Just try me, you son of a bitch," he sputtered, straining to get beyond me. Curro was picking a fight with a customer in the wine shop where I worked.

"Please, Curro, go. They're going to hurt you." With my embroidered shawl, long hair, and castanets, I shielded him from the house employees. "Wait outside. I'll be out soon. Go. Those sticks will hurt me too ..."

He left. The men melted away, adjusting their suit jackets, avoiding my eyes. I was shaking but I did not cry. People turned back to their drinks, their conversations. The Flamencos, pretending nothing had happened, managed a perfunctory last show.

Many such humiliations came along with Curro. A waiter treated us with the disrespect due a Gypsy and a foreigner, and it irked Curro. He never understood that his own behavior hurt his woman worse than the waiter's. If the coffee was bad, I drank it; Curro griped. A cabby drove in circles to run up the meter. I fell silent and helpless; Curro accused, picked a losing fight, then backed down to save messing up his costly alpaca suit. Never knowing when he would blow, and traumatized each time he did, I reverted to my childhood passivity, disassociating in the face of wrath, unaware that Curro's belligerence drew me. As an angry young woman, I shared his hostility, but I forbore mine. Maybe his behavior gave me relief. His insolence was the existential outcry that resounded in Berkeley. It wedded me to him, as long as I had no way of expressing my own rage.

Once I could really dance, I might no longer need that rabid Gypsy -- having found my own means of spewing my ire and my grief. The time might come when I would notice that instead of opening the door to Flamenco for me, Curro was obstructing me from it. Then what?

❧❧❧　❧❧❧

"Hey, Currete!" I put down the dance skirt I was peacefully lengthening. "How was the game?"

"OK," he trudged into our room and pulled off his dirty striped jersey. How proud he had been of that jersey when the owner of Los Tarantos furnished it for his employees' soccer team.

"Did you guys lose?"

"No, we won by two goals." His eyes glinted a second, then lost all luster.

Curro loved tussling, lunging, raising dust - a tough player. He had insisted that I take photos of him kicking the ball.

"So, what's wrong?"

Ignoring my concern, he left to shower. Soccer games had been great release, great therapy for Curro. Where was that euphoria now? Back from the shower, he sank onto the bed, stared at his towelled lap, listless. He was unshaven, his shoulders slumped.

"I am so sad. I don't know what's wrong with me." Brown eyes appealed to me, then gave up and dropped to the towel. "*Qué angustia!*"

That rare moment of candor made me love him so, I embraced his wet head protectively, kissed his temple. "Curro, you have so much. Your cante. No one can steal that from you." I spoke ever so tenderly. "You have me. A good woman who loves you. And you have a savings, a fat bank account to protect against the winter." At least I had taught my Gypsy to use a bank.

"I work without any desire. And those sonsabitch guitarists never give me my chords. I don't know why everyone is against me," he sighed, nearly in tears. "What anguish."

"*Ai mi Currete ...*"

However I ached for him, my words never touched him. Curro dwelt out of range of reason.

Curro had been grateful and polite when he began working at Los Tarantos. But he soured, became petulant, then suspicious and obnoxious. He worked a year there, until his paranoia overcame him. Troublemaker, he was fired from the best house in Barcelona, dashing my hopes for his career and ruining my own chances of ever working at Los Tarantos.

So we packed up and left Barcelona. Three years after I arrived in Seville as Susie, a foreigner, I returned to Seville as Susana, a Spanish dancer.

III
Seville

Eighteen

The door was ajar.

"May I?" we asked in unison, peering into the dark hole of an office.

"Come in, *queridos*." Antonio Pulpón was haloed by the glare of the desk lamp. He glanced up from the illumined clutter on his desk and smiled wanly. He did not look like power. The man who single-handedly represented all the Flamencos of Andalucía, upon whom careers and the existence of Flamenco itself greatly depended, looked pale, his blond hair graying, his blue eyes large, drooping at the outer corners.

"Sit down, Susana." I did. Curro stood near me. Power in America meant ordering people in and out of your plush office; copious lackeys, files, and phones. This man was alone.

"How are you?" asked Pulpón, buying time to finish writing something.

"Very well, thanks," Curro said.

"And you, Antonio?" I asked with concern, as he looked exhausted.

"Fine," he replied, glanced at me, then refocused on my gaze, reading in it that I really wanted to know. "I'm dead tired." He tossed away his pen and ran fingers through his thick hair.

"Antonio, you need rest. Is there no one who can do your work?"

"No one I trust." He closed his tired eyes to rest them a moment then squinted at me, "I'm going blind, you know." He retrieved his pen, "Gotta hurry and get things done. While I can ..." He shuffled and wrote. "Curro, I'm sending you out with Cristina Hoyos. You start Friday." He handed the job slip to one of his best singers, who was not always dependable, but seemed much tamed by this woman who spoke two languages and was considerate.

"*Vale*, sure, Antonio," Curro nearly saluted the man in whose hands it lay whether or not he ate.

"Antonio, why don't you have a secretary?" I admonished.

"I did, it was a disaster. I cannot trust anybody."

"Your typewriter just sits there in the waiting room." That 'waiting room' was waiting for lots of paint, a window, a new sofa, and a scrub. "I was wondering if ... I could use that typewriter."

"What for?" Pulpón studied me.

"Nothing important. I have this travel journal I'd like to type up before it disintegrates."

"Sure, go ahead. Could you do a letter or two for me?"

"Glad to."

Pulpón was the only Gachó in Spain who treated me like an equal, an experience so rare, it endeared him unequivocally to me.

"Good. How'd it go in Mairena?" He was shuffling papers.

"Bien, bien," Curro answered.

"Good cuadro, went well," I agreed. "Drive's not bad. And the Festival was great!" I considered every job a glorious gift, but I withheld enthusiasm to not sound amateur. To the "Concurso Nacional", and the "Festival del Cante Flamenco," and all provincial fairs, Pulpón would send a cuadro of artists he picked seemingly at random. The richly costumed dancing girls were accent between the serious concert performances of grand old Gypsy men and women who sang the deepest of cante. Cante Jondo. The Flamenco greats of Spain would gather with their superb guitarists, and I would be sent in Pulpón's cuadro, and paid to hear them. That way I heard Antonio Mairena, El Chocolate, Camarón de la Isla, Fernanda and Bernarda de Utrera, el Lebrijano, and the best of guitars in Spain. Even Curro was thrilled to go, if he were to admit it. But his feelings were conflicted with envy and a complicated history I knew nothing about.

"And you're going to Jerez tomorrow, right?"

"Right." I was already mentally packed.

"Be at Bar Iberia at 3:00. Car leaves from there." He started to dismiss us. "Oh, something else ... here it is." Pulpón pulled up a job slip from the mess. "A tablao in Córdoba needs a girl for three weeks." He wrote. "Start first of the month."

"And Curro?"

"No need for a singer, just a dancer. You want to go?"

Three weeks out of town without Curro. Pained, I hesitated and looked at my man, the glow from the desk lamp on his face. He looked back and raised his eyebrows, insisting I take the job.

"Sure, Antonio. Thank you." Three weeks on the same solid stage. It would turn out to be outside, and very small, too small for my little *bata de cola*, which I would wear anyway. I would dance my *Caracoles* with a fan.

Pulpón usually sent us on different gigs, separately. Partly because I belonged in ordinary cuadros, and Curro could sing for soloists. He was an artist way above my caliber. For now.

Pulpón stood up to dismiss us. Shaking our hands, he added, "Listen, Susana. You need a new dress. I want you to go have Lina dress you."

"Lina of Seville? Will she sew for me?"

"Tell her I sent you."

Arm in arm, we exited into the Plaza del Duque, near La Campana, heart of downtown Seville. The Duque was the center of sustenance for Flamencos, because Pulpón's might radiated from a tacky office there.

Triumph bubbled up in my throat. Barely able to control my voice, I squeezed Curro. *"Fíjate, Currete, Lina de Sevilla."*

"Ole," he beamed. "But calm down." He looked about us, some heads along the sidewalk were turning.

Curro understood my triumph, although I dealt in

abstracts while he measured in peseta bills or chicken in his puchero. But the triumph was the same: the scorned becoming admired, the discounted finally in the spotlight, the envious amongst the enviable, the ugly duckling growing into swan, the American tourist being fitted to dance by Lina of Seville.

༄༄༄ ༄༄༄

"Hurry! Muchacha! They called for the cuadro." Three painted girls left in a swish of ruffles, leaving me in the makeshift dressing room amidst empty open suitcases strewn on the floor.

"Coming, coming." I stuck the stem of a pink silk rose into the elastic around my long hair, grabbed my castanets, and ran to catch up. As they scurried through patios, down a driveway, I said to anyone, "Man, I'm stiff from sitting hours all squeezed in that car." Ingratiating myself, I asked, "How do you dance without warming up?"

"You'll warm up with Sevillanas," the kinder of the girls offered.

I stiffened. I was developing a Sevillanas-phobia. Sevillanas - a set of four simple folk dances, choreographed in waltz-time, always danced the same. Somehow the girls made it a game to see who could avoid dancing these Sevillanas with me. I did not blame them. They had been dancing Sevillanas in every family gathering since they could toddle. They were blasé, and bored with my inexperience.

I shivered, though the night in Jerez was balmy, dismayed as we approached our outdoor stage. It would be a trick to dance here.

The music had already started. We scampered onto the makeshift platform, lifted our skirts, picked our way over floor cracks and speaker chords.

"Ole!"

"*Vamos a Sevilla!*"

We stepped right into our dance, ruffles gaily twirling, faces smiling, castanets trilling. It took me nearly the first dance to figure out which girl was my pair. Then they alternated. Passing my partner and turning, I was never sure where to mark my terrain. I danced ill at ease, dizzied by all the turns, arms wheeling in stiff arcs. But I got through it safely. We sat down.

Ruffles jumping, feet stomping, hands clapping, we worked from our chairs, raucous and shouting taunts. The guitarist's hands fanned and plunked at the face of his beat-up guitar. The singer cried out his opening call.

I danced first. The urgent music struck stage fright in the pit of my stomach, put a chill on the back of my neck, made my armpits sweat before I even started to dance. These Seville girls, of course, never bothered to perspire. Waiting to start, I quickly scanned my audience.

A grand outdoor private party at a famous winery, socialites chatted, milling in the lantern light, grazed at tables of food and drink. The night breeze wafted fresh under the starry Andalucían sky.

Whenever wine vintners or bull ranchers in the swamp-
lands threw parties, they hired a Flamenco cuadro from
Pulpón's office. The Flamenco show provided the decor, the
background music, set a "quaint" mood for the aristocracy.
Working these one-night stands for Pulpón, I danced in
Seville, Morón, Málaga, Mairena, Utrera, Jerez, Huelva.
Not a star, I was satisfied to be just one of the girls in a
genuine Flamenco cuadro in Andalucía.

It was a disadvantage to dance first. No one had yet
tested the stage, where to drum out footwork that would
resound well and would not rattle mike stands? I would
experiment, mid-dance, while the others would watch and
benefit.

As I got to my feet, the girls snickered. My Barcelona
dress, a sheath to my knees, three layers of ruffles to my
ankles, was out of style in the Flamenco-Mecca of Seville.
It was the best I had, my longest dress, closest to the floor-
length flairs of theirs. Soon enough I would dance in a dress
by Lina.

Ignoring them, I danced with head high. No counting,
no getting lost, I kept the musicians at my chosen pace. I
could hold my own, and my figure must have been pretty
enough on the stage, long with natural grace and enough
energy to do the job. I still danced by rote the first dance I
learned in Caballo's academy. But it had become a harvest
from the best of all the girls' I worked with -- a copied arm
here, a borrowed footwork pattern there. I had planted
Caballo's bareroot academy routine and slowly grafted onto

that. And so I was flowering.

"*Asa, Susana.*"

"*Vamos a Cádiz, niña.*"

My apple-green ruffles flowed smooth and confident. My white underskirts bounced. It was a good Alegrías. The singer joined comfortably with his little interlude, where traditionally the dancer passed and turned four times across the stage, "*Cuando venga conmigo,* When you come with me ..."

Then I was sitting on the floor in a pile of green ruffles, legs extended, staring at my shoes. Astonished, I looked back to see what had happened. No one was near me. The girls, still clapping the music, sat laughing aloud at me.

I must have slipped. Once I figured it out, I was on my feet. Red-faced, but undaunted, I finished the dance smiling gaily at the audience who paid such scant attention, most of them missed my fall entirely. My final turn stopped on a dime with the music.

In my chair, on my sore bottom, I began clapping for the next dancer. I clapped a strong clean downbeat, as well as any cuadro girl, with the humility sufficient to leave fancy counter-time clapping to the Gypsies. While clapping, I pondered my fall, proud of my recovery, hurt by the girls, my innate sense of human kindness violated. They had laughed instead of helping me up. Well, I did not need their friendship. All I needed was their dancing. Off of their dancing, bit by bit, my skill was fattening. And I had Curro's loyalty. That was enough.

Perhaps cuadro girls resented that a "rich American" was taking jobs that Spanish girls needed. I was a handy scapegoat with foreign accent and different costumes. And I had not yet learned their effortless easy dancing. In my zeal to dance like a Gypsy, I did everything with a foreigner's artificial fury. I had not yet learned the different flavors of each dance. Sevillanas, a gachó dance, should be sedate. Alegrías and Caracoles light and playful. Seguidillas mournful.

Not until the Soleá became mine, much later, in my best dress, the stark black one, did I finally learn to dance from inner inspiration. To release the rage from the bowels of my own being. To use the power of the pause.

૭ૐ૭ૐ૭ૐ   ૭ૐ૭ૐ૭ૐ

We stuffed dresses back into suitcases, readying for the long ride home in the wee hours of the night. We were offered food, but were too tired to eat. No one spoke of my fall. Offended, I could have made a fuss like Curro would have, but I 'knew my place,' and never caused trouble, so Pulpón kept giving me jobs.

"Anyone seen my sweater?" the saucy one called Rocío asked.

"Here," I was embarrassed. "It got in my suitcase by mistake."

Dark-eyed impish girl who made the others laugh, Rocío started heckling the American.

"Hey Susana," she started on me. "How's Curro?"

"OK, I guess, thanks." I was on my knees, bagging

shoes, boxing flowers.

"Where is he right now?"

"Asleep probably," My watch said 4:15 a.m.

"Maybe not ..."

I glanced up at her, then back to my packing.

"Is he yours?" Rocío kept after me. The others were listening as they dressed and brushed hair.

"No one belongs to another." I closed my suitcase and stood up.

"Are you married? A church marriage?" The girl's voice was taunting. The others had stopped to watch.

"No," I eyed her steadily. "Why? Do you want to marry him?"

"Well, let's see," Rocío giggled. "What does he do in bed?"

"None of your business." All packed, I knotted my hair then started to leave.

"Tell me what he does." Rocío's face was in mine, with an insistent hand at my shoulder, prodding me. She reached to my crotch, laughing at me, and spoke an obscenity.

My American hand whacked the face of that Spanish girl.

Rocío retreated, holding her cheek, feigning pain and whining, "You slapped me!"

Astounded at myself, and at such language issuing from the mouth of a provincial virgin, I turned away from her, confused. The others were statue still.

"I'm going to tell," Rocío threatened.

Shaking, I faced her again and pronounced,

"Girl, Curro is my man. And you speak to me with respect. You speak to me with the same respect that I speak to you." I turned my back on them all, grabbed my bags and headed out for the car.

After that, cuadro girls, although seldom kind, were always civil.

ᕱᕱᕱ ᕱᕱᕱ

Lina of Seville provided wardrobes for half the dancers of Spain. Curro and I were intimidated by the wealth of her home.

"Please wait here," we were told. We nodded politely, huddling together, then turned and stared at ourselves in the giant mirror. It covered an entire wall. It reflected the rich hand-painted tile floor, velour sofa, the million-crystalled chandelier, and us. There we were, short bronze Gypsy and freckled foreigner towering half a forehead above him.

I chuckled first.

"Ole," Curro murmured with raised eyebrows. Then his velvet cheeks creased into a winning grin. Arm in arm we stood laughing aloud at the ridiculous couple in the mirror.

"Chochete, how you've grown!"

"No, it's you, Wide-Face, you must have shrunk, no wonder people smirk as they walk by us on the street. Look at us." Out of habit, I placed my hand on his shoulder and cocked my head towards him. My eyes softened and I sighed, wondering at this incongruous love between us. "Funny how you don't notice differences when in bed ..."

"At night," Curro shrugged, "all cats are gray."

❧❧❧   ❧❧❧

A week later I stood alone in that salon. Slowly turning, I watched my new blood-red dress in the mirror. Sleeveless, backless, with pinched waist and belled skirt. Faintest of freckles showed around the straps of the heart-shaped bodice. I held up my tumbling hair, imagined it slicked back in a conch bun with red roses at the nape of my neck, the petals lopping down nearly to the slope of my shoulder. My head, with shadowed cheekbones, swiveled gracefully towards the mirror whichever way my body turned. At that moment I discovered that I might yet be beautiful.

This dress would begin to change the way I danced, would eventually put some style and dignity into my moves. I would wear it first in the Spring Fair of Seville - four years after I had tailed Curro and hankered all night at that Fair.

Nineteen

September 1967, Seville. I'm getting quite fuzzy now, Jessica. Alone in bed, washing down little bitter cherries with red wine; missing Curro who has gone to the movies. I have no other friends.

Jessica, it works like this: Curro is a perfect, needy child. He can't keep a job, was starved of mother's love, is little and dark and curly-haired like my baby sister. I'm needed! Two neurotics, dependent upon each other. Happy love. Happy happily-ever-after.

Curro is the answer to my dilemma. I'll be the husband! Curro is a good cook who loves the tiresome entertainment of children. Calm at home, and gentle, he'll be a perfect mother. So I will read, and be out in the world and earn money. And he can be the ignorant housewife. How's that?

November 20, 1967. Marbella, near Málaga.
Dear Jessica,

... Then in early September, Pulpón sent me here to Marbella to a little Flamenco tablao. They already had two singers and didn't need Curro. But I managed to manipulate him in.

Business is bad. In the rainy winter the "house" is empty; so it's not a secure job.

We live outside of Marbella in a bungalow amidst pine trees on a bluff over the sea. A path of 152 of my steps leads down to the foamy surf. The tiny house is fully furnished, kitchenware and bedclothes, hot water, fireplace, clean pine air, and no sound other than the sea. Every day we say, "Esto es la gloria, *this is heaven.*" Curro studies guitar a couple of hours a day -- insurance against the day he might lose his voice. I practice dancing in the living room with the bay windows, shutters closed to act like a mirror. Curro swims and runs and exercises on the beach, gathering wood and cones. His copper muscles gleam and so do his loving eyes.

They don't do Halloween here, but we made a jack-o-lantern out of a skinny Spanish gourd and put it in front of the house to scare witches. Curro was as thrilled as a child. He gets that same delight out of the fires he builds in the hearth, out of the pots of beans he stews up, the hot shower, the fresh sheets -- from everything simple and good. He gives me life.

Curro gloats when he eats. He measures his worth by the good food he eats. He can tell himself he's not the miserable hungry wretch he used to be. He is somebody, like a priest or a mayor, somebody who eats well.

Gypsy style of eating turns a stew pot into a three course meal. First, you set aside the meat, bacon, sausage from the pot. You drink up the broth. Next you spoon up the potatoes and garbanzos, or beans and greens. Then you bringar. That is, with hunks of crusty bread you mash the meat, fat, and sausage, *together. The* bringue *from the mashing process butters the bread. Then between the bread and your thumb, you scoop up a mouthful of the mash. Gypsy thumbs are often double-jointed. The sign of a true Gypsy, and the brunt of ghetto humor, is the dexterity of that thumb* bringa-ing. *Curro mashes with his bread chunk studiously and maneuvers his thumb like a backhoe. At a recent dinner juerga the famous recording artist, Lola Flores, dropped in for a few minutes. When her husband wanted to leave, she said, "Wait a minute, I've got to watch this Gitano finish eating." She stayed, delighted, while Curro, unaware, packed in a huge* bringá. *She watched until he finished his last bite.*

Here in our perfect cottage, Curro is serene. But as we dress for work, he begins to get testy, then raving at work. Each job we've worked, our employers love me and cannot bear my husband, because I am nice but Curro is nasty. Everything infuriates him. He is compelled to shout at people, even customers, that he is not a piece of shit, and he calls them awful names, with meek Susie shushing him as best I can and making amends.

Curro is an incredible singer for accompanying a dancer. God, he's good. I can lean back into his song and it charges me; creates coraje *(passion) and compás in me. His cante dances through me. Now I know why fellow Flamencos have put up with his obnoxious attitude. Also I know why more and more they don't. The tension is aging me. Bags and wrinkles swing beneath my eyes. I'm twenty-seven, and I'm skinny and "dried up" as Curro says. He likes women plump -- flesh is beauty in Spain.*

As we walk home from work, we bicker for a while, then we laugh. And I sigh, "Well, one more day safe, five hundred more pesetas in the pocket, and our little house still ours for tomorrow." We hope we can last here 'til Christmas ...

My dancing is progressing. But not as fast as the aging process. It is a losing battle and the loser gets no children.

Curro has been begging me for his own "Corrillo" for years, for a son to be the solace of his old age. (Sons are the only "social security" Spaniards have). I have finally consented to have his child. I am no longer taking pills. I have designed a little house like this cottage. I have his respect and my health, and somewhere a glimmer of hope that life could be good for a child.

I have written a letter to my folks because I need my christening certificate so that the church here will allow a marriage. I wrote them that Curro and I have been living together for three years; that we are going to build a house; that we want to have a child; and if we do, we'll get married.

My folks might not like that letter.

December 10, 1967, Marbella.

Oh, Jessica, sometimes I am suffocated by fear. Fear of shouts at work, fear of no work. Fear of pregnancy, fear of childlessness. Fear of losing Curro, fear of jealousy. Fear that dancers will clap badly for me to throw me off when I dance. Fear they will start a fight with Curro and he will cause us to be thrown out. Fear he will be hurt by a car or by the Guardia Civiles. If I had chil-

dren, I would die of fear for them. My fear would be unbearable and I would go crazy.

So last night, when the owner's wife insulted my husband, I simply said, "Fine. We'll go." I walked out. And it was done. Anyone else in this business would have out-shouted her and continued working. But I said, "Curro, we are going." I was astonished at myself. I guess I could not stand the strain. Losing the job was more tolerable than the fear of losing the job. We'll stay a few days in this heavenly bungalow, then return to Seville. Oh, woe.

Remember that banal letter I wrote to my folks saying that I only live once and I've got to live now, so I'll marry Curro and live the life of insecure but cheerful poverty? As soon as I got it down on paper I was revolted. I think he'll be a stubborn, tyrannical father; one who resents the children who are smarter and more educated than he. He will be jealous of them.

December 30, 1967, Alcalá de Guadaira, near Seville, and jobless. Dear soulmate across the seas and far away,

Your letters open my mental jail and let in fresh air. Sometimes I don't write back because I'm frozen up inside. You want my dreary present essentials? My short waning history as a Flamenco dancer?

Age 27, healthy, childless, sharing life for three years with a small, bad-tempered man who treats me with care. Both ignorant and stupid, this man. Yet I love him. Actually I just like sharing life with him. Because if not with him, with whom? Alone here is too cruel.

Afraid to have children, afraid I won't ever.

After Marbella, winter threatened Curro's family, so we are sharing an apartment with them in Alcalá. Our banked money -- stashed for house building -- pays the rent. With the pesetas Curro and I would spend on groceries, his mother knows how to feed the whole family. From her Gypsy stewpot, we can all go to sleep with warm bellies. To eat, we depend on whatever jobs come up. Flamenco jobs are scarce. Curro and his brothers work between rains as day laborers. On some rainy days, all we eat is garlic toast and hot milked coffee, just before going to bed...

Twenty

Curro's family seemed to camp out in that apartment, to never really settle in. His mother kept chickens on the balcony; cooked stew on a butane burner atop the cold stove; poured kitchen bilge down the toilet.

Coral's tin cup clinked as she dipped out dirty sink water into a bucket. Her flattened slippers scuffled as she carted the bucket to the bathroom. Her ankles were swollen full, she was small-boned, plump, with dark dimpled elbows in her pink nylon blouse, her mahogany face matured by laughter. If pressed, Coral could not say whether she had had seven or eight children. She did not know exactly how her own name went. She could not write, and she counted her age by peseta bills, being at the time, five greens and two browns.

One son, Joaquín, sat glum as a saint. Rooted to the short sofa in the minuscule parlor, he inhaled the odor of burning coal from the brazier under the table. Joaquín was narrow, with a long gopher ugliness to his drooping passive face. His brothers taunted him, and he always looked off to the side while mumbling a response. He wore a Spanish military recruit's khaki uniform. He was repeating his three-month boot camp training because he was too dumb to succeed the first time. After every weekend leave, his old man, el Viejo, had to take him back to camp in Córdoba on the bus, or he would not go. He seemed to prefer silently moping near his mother, listless, his head to one side, eyes downcast, like a thin, silent creature of Picasso's blue period.

Coral glanced at him as she threw feed to the chickens on the balcony. The stairs barked, the door bonked. Coral's youngest son stomped in. A panting gangle of skinny four-teen-year-old energy, he was as dark as she, so they called him "CocaCola." His words were loud and droll as he yelled store news to his mom. He dumped his purchases on the table. Coffee beans and warm breads tumbled from his shopping bag, thudding onto the blue oilcloth.

The grimy chipped grinder growled as Coral hugged it to her belly and twirled the lever in jerks. She dumped her ground coffee directly into boiling water, then poured CocaCola a muddy glass of it. As sediment settled, he dunked toasted bread rubbed with garlic and fried olive oil.

"Here's six bits. After your breakfast, get me *sisco*." With another bang, CocaCola left again to buy coal chips for the brazier. Coral set down Joaquín's coffee and returned to the kitchen. Hesitantly, he gravitated toward his breakfast.

Miguel breezed out of the bathroom, grabbed two breads and Coral swatted at him. Dressed neat and clean, Miguel was surly and brutish. *"Bestia"* they called him, because his perfect matt-brown muscles worked like a "beast" with pick and shovel. Miguel recently brought home a salary from a few weeks of heavy labor, looked around the house, remembered that no one else was working, and quit his job again. His big seventeen-year-old head bore the heavy-lidded eyes of his father and cinnamon jaws and a flashing white smile. In the rusted bathroom mirror, Miguel combed his reddish, sun-bleached hair with much care and with the Gachí's lacquer, then left in beauty, strutting and elegant. The girls in town would not know he had only five pieces of clothing wadded up in the family wardrobe. They would see him and be swooning for him with those hot inner deaths.

Coral leaned out the window to test the clothes drying there, and she checked the overcast sky for the thickening of rain. The rutted dirt road was puddled. She gazed across the lumpy green pasture, speckled with clods and distant reddish sheep. Beyond, coming over the crest of the bare hill, was the overcoated figure of her husband. Carrying a package, Antonio Román, *el Viejo*, dragged heavy feet over the red footpath, tired from a day of walking, from a lifetime of walking, selling yardage in the ancient Gypsy way. His package probably contained unsold material, a tablecloth, some suit-cuts.

Coral returned to the kitchen to add potatoes to the pot already steaming with chicken and garbanzos. She burned her fingers on the pot lid, dropped it, grabbed a rag - someone's shirt - to gingerly lift it again. She heard her son Rubio weeping.

Three young men slept in his bed under sour blankets,

head to feet. During the day Rubio was alone in it. He faced the wall and wept. At sixteen years old, rheumatoid arthritis made his legs twitch and jump with pain. There was no circulation in his hands; they kept going to sleep. And he ate nothing but aspirin. Perhaps he would die. It was no good going to the county hospital, the Macarena in Seville, where interns experimented on poor folks, where he would lie in dreary terrifying wards with people dying on either side of him. No, he would stay home with his mother and weep. Perhaps Rubio would get better. Some days, on his fallen arches, he walked around the apartment as if hobbled, pushing one foot ahead of the other.

Rubio was an infant when Antonio Román left Coral, when he went off to Madrid to marry Fernanda de Utrera, a great Flamenco singer. The ban had been said. Coral took her nursing Rubio off her breast and left him with a bottle at the neighbor's. She took Miguel in her arms and hid Joaquin beneath her seat, so she only had to buy one ticket on the train to Madrid. She went to a city she had never seen, whose street signs she could not read, to find her man. She found him and she brought him home. They had one more son, and then a church wedding, a ceremony doubling with the baptism of their last baby, CocaCola.

But Rubio was weaned too soon, and Coral always said he would be sickly, having been deprived of his mother's milk. She was resigned to his pain. There was no money for the rich folks' doctors and private clinics. Maybe Curro would manage something one day ... She stood at Rubio's bed and stroked the forehead of her tallest and fairest son. She took a blanket from her bed and bunched it around him. Then she straightened her bed while she listened to him cry.

In this small bedroom the six of them, the Viejo and Coral and their four youngest sons, slept in these two beds. Curro and his woman had a twin bed in the other room -- a room so small that even the wicker trunk that housed their belongings would not fit.

Today the old man came home to the aroma of stewing chicken. He removed his coat and hat, exposing big paunch and big bald head. He sat down at the warming table and pulled the table-skirts over his legs.

"Oh-hoo," he groaned, and glanced heavenward, seeking patience for his hard life. He would die soon, in the Canary Islands, while selling cloth goods and sending money home. His huge eyes, wide-set under heavy, lowered lids, wore deathly grey circles. Big mouth and buck teeth hung under his eagle-hooked nose. Antonio Román had been a good man, a civilized Gypsy, always bringing home a day's household expenses. He had been handsome like Rubio, a rounder like Miguel, with passion for his own people's Flamenco. Coral was the last of three women. His women were cousins of each other and he sired mostly sons by each of them. Some sons were shameless bums, some good salesmen like him; some fine Flamencos, some barely able to clap compás. Coral's youngest children were his last, and not very promising.

CocaCola affectionately prodded his father's bald head.

"What's new, Billiard Ball?" he teased, landing in a chair next to him.

"I walked all morning. Not one sale. Going to have to try the Canaries. They say business is better there." El Viejo leaned heavily on the table. "And Curro?"

"He went to Seville to ask about work."

"Rubio?"

CocaCola nodded toward the bedroom.

"Rubio, come eat," the old man called out hopefully.

"Not hungry," came the muffled response.

"Oh-hoo," the old man shook his head, eyes returning skyward. Coral scuffed in with plates of steaming puchero, and they broke their breads and spooned and chewed in silence.

ॐॐॐ ॐॐॐ

"Do people live up there, Curro?" I wondered as we walked into Alcalá.

"Up where?" His mind was already in Pulpón's busy office.

"In the castle." I pointed up to the ancient Moorish ruins, the crumbling vine-covered parapets and dark window holes. Deserted as a wasp's nest, the hilltop castle was collared by the old town of Alcalá de Guadaira. Rings of white houses mounted the hillside.

"Joaquin de la Paula never left el Castillo.

"No, not the caves underneath." I knew 'el Castillo' was a Gypsy neighborhood somewhere behind the castle, where

Manolito de Maria lived, where cave homes were approached by narrow footpaths and no one paid rent. "No, I mean the castle itself..."

"How should I know, woman?" Curro rarely gave a straight answer, even if he had one. But he was mellow today, and I kissed his cheek as we walked, and he began to reminisce.

"Joaquin de la Paula was a Gypsy who lived in el Castillo. Manolito de Maria was his nephew, and learned his cante from Joaquin. Joaquin was an ironmonger. But the rich folks of the towns would go to his house and take him with them on juergas. He got a group together with his sons and his nephew, Barcelona, and they sang in the towns around here, singing his songs, which he made up out of old Moorish lyrics."

I stayed quiet. Rarely would Curro tell me things...

"Joaquin always wore an overcoat. He put it on in October, and in August he took it off. He was a Gypsy who loved to sit in the sunshine more than anybody." Curro smiled fondly, and closed with a shrug, "And that was the life of Joaquin, who never left el Castillo."

And that was all I got. With no further sound than our footsteps on stone streets and a donkey braying, I reflected. Manolito de Maria. Joaquin de la Paula. Gypsies named themselves after their mothers. I wondered if that was the cause or effect of Gache's disrespect. The English used fathers' names – Johnson, Paulson... Allison in my family. Decent dwellings in town were not allowed to Curro's family. The flimsy apartments where we were renting, under my name, were scattered over empty lands outside town. The farthest dwellings were the *"casitas bajas,"* government housing without plumbing. There dwelt Curro's married sister Regla, and there his mother Coral would live out her old age.

Heading for the bus depot, Curro turned down a tightly packed, cobbled street. The castle disappeared beyond peeling white walls with mud-stained bases and firmly closed doors. I never knew this town well. The city of Seville was my home, more mine than any place I had ever lived. But in Alcalá I was under Curro's auspices, and I only went where he did. He grew up in Alcalá. It was his turf and his struggle.

"Currete," I said as I walked proudly beside him, thinking of all the singers named after their home town, "what do you think of this? Your stage name is 'Curro de Alcalá,' right?"

"Of course, mujer."

"And I'm your wife."

"Well, yes, mujer."

"So, could my stage name be 'Susana de Alcalá?'"

He merely raised brows and curled down mouth, in the gypsy shrug of non-committal.

"Curro, look," I pressed, "'Susana de Pasadena' just won't do."

He snickered.

"Worse than being 'from Cuenca,'" I admitted, skirting a donkey pile.

"Really?" He was delighted that I might be teased. He grinned sidelong at me. I gave up discussion and relished his good mood, ever thrilled that I was a part of his life here. After all, I was "from Alcalá" right now. I was living here, sharing roof and food with Curro's family to wait out the hard wet winter. And because of my partnership, Curro was able to provide for his stepfather for the first time. Old family rifts were healing.

Jiggling and squeaking, the bus whined the nine miles to Seville. I peered back at the highway as it curled around the Moorish castle and followed a curve of the Guadaira River.

"Chochete, did you know that Manolito de María died?"

"No!" My head spun around. "He died? When?"

"When we were in Barcelona. In a glass coffin, they carried him on their shoulders from Alcalá to Seville, and buried him there with honors."

"Too late!" My eyes brimmed righteous tears.

"Yes, woman, too late."

I wondered if that would happen to Flamenco. Honored too late. I looked back at the highway and imagined the throng of people inching along, coffin aloft and glinting in the sun, surrounded by bowed heads.

"Do you remember when we slept in that hayfield with Manolito?" Curro reminisced.

"Not much ...," I responded coolly, and he stole a merry glance. I could be as huffy about Rose as I was about Curro's tattoo.

"Manolito was sweet; he called me 'daughter.'"

"He was a good man, a very good man," Curro added huskily. Manolito de María had always been unfashionably kind to Curro. And he had taught Curro to sing the Soleá of Alcalá.

Many bored Flamencos lingered in Pulpón's drab little waiting room, sitting on chair arms, pacing. Finally our agent appeared, saggy-eyed and somber. He did not usher Curro and me into his office; he merely stood at his door.

"Sorry, sweethearts, I haven't got a thing for you right now. Come back next week." His familiar refrain.

Twenty-one

Coral and Miguel were still eating when Curro and his Gachí seated themselves at the warming-table for puchero. CocaCola pretended to help his father into his coat, teasing him with it, preventing him from finding the arm hole.

"There, you got it, Pa. There it is ... no, here."

The Viejo grunted stoically and left for Bar España to play cards with his cronies. Gambling and juergas seemed the few recreations available to a bright but illiterate mind in southern Spain.

I sipped thick chicken broth, my legs warming under the table. I tried to steal potatoes from Curro's plate whenever he glanced away - my little sport. I never succeeded but it was fun trying, he glowered so. The table had a lot of traffic, which brought in cold draughts across my knees, but I loved eating with men coming and going. Raised without brothers, I was exhilarated dwelling with that masculine family.

Glamorous Miguel packed away his stew and second bread, then jumped up to wash and dress for town. Coral followed him to the back room. There he did something to anger his mother, which was unwise. Called *"La Negra"* as a girl, after her dark skin and her black temper, Coral could be fierce.

"No, Mom, now wait a minute." His shirt half buttoned, arms raised and velvet belly bared, Miguel shielded himself, backing around the dining table. Coral attacked him with a broom. Scolding, with broom aloft, suddenly, mid-swing, she broke into laughter. She laughed at herself and her broom. I sat amazed. Such tinkling kaleidoscopic people, these. The American who had been raised by unrelenting household hostility found Coral quite novel. With merry gypsy eyes she stood, hands on hips, and griped.

"Ole-ole-ole." Curro was grinning. He resembled his mother the most, and they shared the same blend of rage and mirth.

Coral doled out pieces of chicken breast, sausage, and sidepork, and she and her "artists" mashed their bringá together.

࿔࿔࿔ ࿔࿔࿔

"I'd catch my death of pneumonia," Coral fretted, "if I washed my hair that much." She was on her knees cleaning the hall floor with bucket and rag.

"Try it, woman," I insisted, bending over, towel-drying my hair. "I do it all the time and I'm not dead yet." My hair hung to the floor, my head level with Coral's.

"Well, before you leave, bind your hair. Don't go out looking like a crazy woman."

"But if I slept with a wet head, I would die of pneumonia." I swung upright and my hair flew over my head. "I need to dry it in the sunshine."

"I guess neither's going to change," Coral shrugged, rattling her bucket. Water pattered as she dipped and wrung her rag.

"Probably not." I admired Coral's wavy, peppered, black hair, which she kept in a loose twist on top of her head all day long, with only one hair pin. "You remain Gitana, I remain crazy foreigner Gachí turkey egg."

"Turkey egg?" Coral's mopping rag halted.

"That's what the girls call me in the dressing room. What does it mean?"

"Turkey eggs have spots on them. Freckles."

"Freckles? The bitches." I ranted and swore, imitating Curro. Coral's laugh, like my own grandmother's, was a lopsided cradle exposing crowded teeth. I was so fond of this limited country woman who was so much wiser than I. Coral's dark face with mischievous glint, her graceful Gypsy nose; her lack of vanity and her sense of the ridiculous; her unconditional love of her sons, whose names she could never remember; her resemblance to Curro and her acceptance of his Gachí amongst her own; endeared her to me.

"Coral, listen." I had pulled on an old pair of Curro's tailored suit slacks and two English sweaters. Combing out my long wet strands, I followed Coral to the parlor. "By Spring, Pulpón will have work for us. Would you like to come watch me work sometime? See the show? You could play mother-of-the-artist and sit in the dressing room with the other mothers!" I chuckled at the irony of it. "You'd be my authentical and veridical Flamenco mother. You could sit and be mending my costumes ..."

"Me mend? I can't see to thread a needle."

"Then who mends your boys' clothes?"

Silence. Then both burst out laughing. No one in that family mended. If something was torn, it was tossed.

"Well, I'll mend for you." I stood up and grabbed the packed lunch bag on the table. "And you come to my dressing room and keep those women in place. You can tell me what they are saying behind my back ... and to my face." I opened the front door. "It would be fun. Will you?"

"I'd like that ... just once to see what it's like in those places where Curro works ..." Pondering Curro, Coral balanced her twist of rag on the rim of the bucket and sat back on her heels.

"Susana," an intimacy in Coral's voice caught me.

"What?" I turned back in the doorway.

"Susana, how do you put up with Curro, *como lo aguantas?*"

I searched her eyes, found her earnest -- his own mother asking how I could stand to live with that man. I smiled at her, grateful for the woman's awareness. His brothers called him *Majara*, "Crazy" in Caló, but in the original Sanskrit, Majara meant "Saint." Both fit. Curro was the Goldilocks of Alcalá. When he was good, he was very, very good, but when he was bad, he was horrid.

"Coral, he thinks the world out there is against him. But with me he is so gentle."

Her eyes twinkled a mother's gratitude, then slipped

away with concern. Coral shoved open the glass balcony door. "Buk-buk-buk," she clucked as she went out to clean the chicken coop.

ॐॐॐ ॐॐॐ

Fragrant with Spanish perfumed soaps, wet hair loose behind me, I set out to bring lunch to Curro and CocaCola. I wore my husband's pants in a land where women wore skirts. Walking warmed me. I walked beyond Alcalá, along the vía, the wide yellow path left by the railroad. There were no people, only an occasional olive tree on the deep blue horizon. I remembered Coral's ignored request and swung my hair like a crazy woman, and I dreamed of dance costumes. Imagining my new dress by Lina, its stark red under stage lights, I strode.

Just as I entered the railroad tunnel, my crotch hairs itched, and distractedly I scratched, unselfconscious on the deserted path. Then I glanced up at the lone highway and saw a man in the distance. He had seen my gesture and thought it was an invitation. He cut down onto the railway, running to overtake me in the tunnel. Thunder-hearted, I grabbed a huge menacing rock and continued striding resolutely. He got the idea, and fell back. But I kept the rock in my hand long after I left the dusk of the tunnel.

Curro and his kid brother were working pick and shovel for masons. He had told me where to meet them, away from the worksite so that the workmen wouldn't see his woman, nor watch them eat. This modesty of poverty, I had never known. I sat on a wall at the Venta del Junco and waited with their food.

Dusty and sloppy, they rounded the corner, jabbering with the joy a simple job in the fresh air and promise of a meal gives. Happy grins flashed from Curro and CocaCola when they caught sight of me. Belongingness flooded me for an instant.

"*Caco en diez, el tío no sabe callar. Habla mas que un barbero,*" Curro raved at his droll best. "Damn it all, that guy doesn't know how to shut up. He yaks more than a barber."

"Relax, Majara," CocaCola teased as he plopped down beside his sister-in-law. He was a shy, ugly kid with no skills, but outside of that, CocaCola was splendid; he had the nerve to call his handsome oldest brother "crazy" and make him laugh.

"No, no. He won't tire out, mind you." Curro paced, gesturing his ire comically to the sky with cement-powdered arms. "He's going to talk straight through until that house is roofed."

"Shoot! We're only pouring the foundations."

"*No te lo digo yo?*" What did I tell you," Curro insisted, "it's going to be a long damn winter!"

"Stuff your *bollo* in his face," CocaCola said with typical gypsy humor. His words were loud, but his laugh was silent. His huge buck teeth in dazzling moistened array, his head back in short quick nods, were his laughter.

They perched on the wall at either side of me. I unwrapped cloth and brown shop paper. My ever-gnawing anticipation of Curro's explosive anger was momentarily at bay. This humble lunch was a respite -- one of life's little treats. Squinting in the sunlight, and jolly, we ate bread and Spanish omelette, savory with golden onions and potatoes. Still chewing, the brothers rushed off to work again. A happy woman watched them go.

ॐॐॐ ॐॐॐ

I sat leaning against a wall in the afternoon Alcalá sun and read two years of Jessica's letters -- my nourishment, my source of balance and sanity. Sun-warmed, I took off my green coat, rolled it to cushion me from the cold pebbly ground. Then I wrote:

December 30, 1967, Alcalá de Guadaira.
Dear Soulmate across the seas and far away,
    ... Flamenco jobs are scarce. Curro and his brothers work between rains as day laborers.
    Christmas? Spaniards don't do Christmas trees, nor Sanny Clause. But I made such a fuss, that Curro and his brother stole a tree, gypsy fashion. They foraged out and found a pine-ish looking thing on some government land, and dragged it home after dark. For decorations we hung oranges and sausages and wrapped candies on the fool thing, with two bottles of Christmas spirits beneath it. I had to stand guard or the brothers would swipe sausages from it on their way out the door. But it got a few laughs, and it cheered us all a bit.
    On Christmas ...

I stopped writing. I stretched out my legs on the chill ground, squinted at the cold sky to check the sun's position, swept the empty landscape, with its scattered trees standing like random tombstones in an abandoned graveyard. I was hungry. From the apartments, I heard tomatoes sizzling in oil, the wail of an infant. Somewhere a lonesome cock occasionally crowed. I wondered why he didn't wait until dawn. The crow of a cock on a cold day would always remind me of austere winter in Andalucía.

I stared off, gathering words about my Christmas in Alcalá. I envisioned the gloomy days before Christmas with no money coming in. Days of cold feet and short tempers. No one complained, but bellies growled. Luckily I had Curro to warm my bed.

Then, on Christmas Day, the Viejo came home jubilant. After a morning of fruitless walking, he finally sold one bedspread. He gloated as he took off his coat, "The minute I saw him, I knew he was my man. The fellow bought it for an enormous price -- for Christmas. Enough money for a good Christmas dinner!"

The boys applauded and hooted. And he took his place triumphantly at the warming table. CocaCola rushed out for groceries, and Coral prepared a sumptuous stew. The house filled with the comforting pungency of frying garlic.

"Here, Pa." Miguel swooped a liquor bottle from under the tree up onto the table. "Here KeeCola, catch." And he ripped a sausage off the tree and tossed it. He tossed another to Joaquin. Sausages flew around the room. Rubio

got out of bed and made his way out, like a man on crutch-
es, pushing from wall to wall. And a sausage came flying his
way. He gathered the skirts over his legs at the warming
table. Curro opened the anise and they toasted one another.

"*Salud,* Pa!" "*Salud!*"

"Cheers," Curro said in English.

"Cheers, Currete."

The clear licorice syrup burned throats on its silky way
down. We wolfed the formerly forbidden sausages with
crusts of bread, waiting for our stew. Curro was sitting with
his stepfather when the front door burst open. Someone I
had never seen before, a stepbrother, an older son of the
Viejo, came in out of the cold. He was unshaven and in
shirt-sleeves. An alcoholic, he had sold his last jacket for
wine.

"Hey, hey," he greeted them. He was wired, would not
sit at the table, paced the room. In fact, he knew he was
unwelcome and did not care. He was a rumpled bum and
totally audacious. A Gypsy's Gypsy, he called everyone
"Manuel" with awesome cheek. He was obviously the
source of the greatest pride and greatest disappointment of
Antonio Román.

He swigged a drink, and began clapping a little
Flamenco compás.

"*Canta, Manuel,*" he commanded of Curro. A genius
with palmas, this man could clap compás with an artistry I
never heard elsewhere.

"Ole-ole-ole," was Curro's dimpled reaction to this

man's flair. And Curro cleared his throat. He sang a few opening syllables, then began a bit of raunchy down-home Bulerías.

"Oh, Ma, *Baila un poquito,* dance a bit," CocaCola called. Coral came out of the kitchen, mincing a few steps to the rhythm in her flattened slippers, her fingers snapping before her twinkling eyes, her brown face puckered with whimsy, her gold Cordoban earrings shimmying. She pinched her skirt with one hand, scat-singing the rhythm through her crooked grin. To Curro's song, Coral gestured a little Bulerías pass, a little old woman's gypsy dance.

"*Quilla... Asa mujer*"

"*Asa toma,* Attababy"

"Go for it" "That's it," murmured Miguel and Rubio in rhythm.

"*Allí, asaaa,*" called her stepson while he clapped out his perfection. "There ya'go! Right on!"

CocaCola's head bobbed with his silent bucktoothed laughter. Even Joaquin managed a wan smile as his eyes followed his mother. I sat enchanted, curled in the armchair, reveling in their mirth, lost in Curro's voice.

අංඅංඅං අංඅංඅ

Bleating sheep, tinkling bell, thumping stick -- the symphony of a passing flock -- brought me back to my sunlit writing tablet. I flexed my back muscles, grown stiff against the cold wall. I resumed writing about Christmas, when a shadow fell on me. I looked up. Rubio stood grinning down at me.

My heart jump-started. I masked it with cheer.

"Hey, man! Rubio! Time to go shopping?" I folded my papers.

On his best days, Rubio would come out and seek me. The two of us would walk to the corner kiosk to buy lottery tickets, and dream together over how we would spend the winnings.

"Time to go shopping," he nodded, grinning. Rubio most resembled the Viejo: a large-headed, big-boned Gypsy with heavy-lidded eyes, high cheekbones, overlapping teeth, shapely mouth. Skinny from his illness, he was nevertheless an attractive kid. And, ripened by pain, he was compassionate and knowing beyond his years.

"This is our winning day," he announced. "We've got six bits, enough for only a quarter-million win. But that's enough for one day." His eyes swam in mine. Our grins were automatic reflexes whenever we looked at each other. We grinned so hard, it hurt.

"What'll we buy?"

"You start."

Together we headed for the street. After hours in bed, Rubio's thick hair was badly combed, and he plodded as if his feet were strapped to big wooden blocks. He kept repeating hip slang, like any teenager anywhere in the world who had watched American films. He also seemed to rise above all differences and just be human with me. He actually sought my opinion.

"Let's see. A house for Curro," I began fantasizing.

"Shower and hot water so abundant that it fills the whole tiled bathroom with steam. I had already designed our house on paper. The first thing I drew in was the lemon tree in the back yard ..."

I stopped. "Look at those children! They can fly!"

Red dust swirled around urchins playing soccer in an empty field. Scrambling and kicking, crowding and scattering, utterly intense. Even the tiniest grubby child was masterful at diving to the ground unharmed, clouting the ball with his head mid-flight.

"So brave." I stared, enthralled. Then I glanced at my sick brother-in-law, caught him wincing as he moved laboriously along. "With today's lottery, I'll fly you to America to the best doctors. Then I'll buy the castle of Alcalá for Coral," I continued, "with a room for each son."

"*Ole, lo propio*," Rubio approved with a chuckle.

"For me ..." I kicked pebbles. "Let's see ..."

"Susana," Rubio said quietly, "what you seek, money can't buy."

"What do I seek?"

"I don't know," he stopped and turned to study me. "It's not money. You left money to come here." I peered back at him, my head cocked. Then I flushed and looked away.

Somehow he knew me. He saw me and he heard me. Few did. The difference about Rubio was subtle, a light.

"What do you really want?" I challenged him and resumed walking, inhaling the crisp air pungent with coal smoke.

"Shoot, I can't think beyond the pain. I just want to be well."

Rubio greeted the vender at the little corner stall, imprisoned behind tobacco, candy jars, and strips of lottery tickets which beckoned in the breeze.

"Hey Rubio, you're back."

"Yeah, well, they just let me out."

"How are you feeling?"

"Alive. You can't kill a bad bug." He handed over his three tin coins and pocketed the row of flimsy tickets. "Is this the winning number?"

"Guaranteed. We didn't win yesterday, so it must be our turn today ... ."

With difficulty, Rubio sat on a wall near the kiosk, and I squatted near him.

"Today we're going to win. Gachó told me so. I'll get the latest clothes for Miguel. Style, man. He knows how to dress. Curro, I'll get to a head doctor. Ma says the Majara was hit by a car when he was a kid, and his head's never been right since." Rubio paused as a noisy truck cranked by. "CocaCola. I'll send him to school, then get him a job as a stand-up comic ..."

"*Hombre, lo propio!*" I imitated him, and we guffawed.

"And me ...?"

"A car," I offered. "A red-hot roadster."

"Yeah. And cool shades."

We sat and laughed in the thin winter sun. Basking in each other. I could have loved Rubio. I wished he were older and that I had met him first. No one knew my thoughts, for I was a decent woman, and he was very young, and I belonged to his brother.

Twenty-two

"You lied!" I bellowed at the kid. "CocaCola, you lied to me!" Scowling murderously, I socked him in the back as he cowered at the warming table. I pounded on his narrow shoulders. His brothers quietly disappeared. Coral stayed in the kitchen.

"You lied to me," I wailed and plopped like a teenager over the chair arm in the claustrophobic parlor. I shook with rage of the wronged. I cried and sniffled and pounded the chair.

CocaCola ran out the door without looking back.

Like the Ugly Duckling, I had forgotten that I was different. CocaCola owed me no special allegiance. He was Curro's favorite brother and often we were a hilarious threesome. But he was not my little brother to send out on errands.

I had inadvertently left my American coat in town. He had said he talked to the Gachó at the post office, and he would get it later. That night no coat appeared and I interrogated the kid. He admitted that he never did anything about the coat, that it was gone. He had lied to me. The betrayal, the exclusion, the enormous financial loss, blinded me with rage.

Curro found me in bed facing the wall when he came

home, and nothing was said.

The next morning a smoldering daughter-in-law was the last to dress and leave the house. Coral, who had avoided me until the others left, barred me from leaving as I was crossing the parlor.

"Look, Susana, you're a good woman," she began. Her lips were pursed, her dark eyes overcast. "I love you. I can't help it because you love my Curro. And I'm grateful to you both for this roof this winter," she added. "But it's not right that you hit my boy. CocaCola is my son and I can do what I want because I'm his mother. But you have no right to touch him. Don't you hit him again."

I looked away, studied the ugly blue oilcloth, greasy and crumb-specked, on Coral's table, and disapproved. This woman had so many children she could not feed. Curro ruined every job. I had nowhere to dance. We were all helpless.

Head down, I turned back to my room. I sat on the edge of my little bed, in the thin box of a cold bedroom, listening to the clink of the tin cup as Coral dredged out the sink while I muttered and sulked.

სოსო   ის

Her dark hair was pulled smooth, her eyes flashed. She wore Spanish pearls in her ears, behind the curved high-boned cheeks of an elegant Spanish woman. In her Spanish fitted coat, the woman in the antique mirror behind the bar glanced back at me. She didn't look much like an American, except that she was standing in a small town bar amongst men.

Lulled by Spain's national anthem -- the hiss and cough of the espresso machine and male banter -- I sipped satiny anise and licked my lips. I was standing by Curro's side at Bar España in the plazuela of Alcalá de Guadaira. I did not speak. In jobless January in Andalucía, five words covered everything anyone had to say, anyway.

"*Como va?* How's it going?" a neighbor asked.

"*Hombre, la cosa está muy mala.* Things are bad all over," another answered. And heads would shake. Yet there I stood, looking like money, like a successful artist home on leave. I took another sip and caught my man gazing at me.

"*Y qué?* So what?" I asked with a tiny toss of brow and head -- the Gypsy's challenge -- my confidant green eyes in his.

"Ole," was his grinning praise, his cheeks in deep folds, his eyes lazy.

It was Three Kings' Day, the day Spanish children received Christmas gifts, brought by the Wise Men to the Christ Child. In Alcalá, the Three Kings swept through the center of town that night, each in his own carriage. Curro had brought me to see the evening parade.

After waiting awhile in the warmth and haze of the tavern, shouts and a strange splattering noise drew us out into the sharp air. The Kings, in flowing robes and false beards, were raining little candies on the crowd. The sweets fell on the street like hail.

"Look, Chochete. There's CocaCola. Is he scoring!"

Curro laughed, remembering his own boyhood in this very street. These were the only Christmas gifts his family ever knew. Through the crowd I glimpsed the kid, his long arms raking up candies and warding off people. Hovering close to the wheels of the Black King's carriage, CocaCola was part of the parade. Assigned to keep tiny kids from under the wheels, he was loping the whole route at the source of the treats.

After the festivities, Curro and I walked home, my arm warm in his. The moon swathed us in white light, reflected off the whitewashed houses of Alcalá. It tagged us along the highway. It shadowed Curro's ruthless beauty in that cold moonlight while he softly crooned a pretty Spanish song to me.

Salí de mi campo un día, Llorona, cuando al pasar yo te ví.
Qué rico pelo llevaba, Llorona, que la Virgen te creí.
Leaving my land I saw you, Llorona, I'd never seen you
    before
I thought you were the Virgin, Llorona, for the rich hair
    that you bore.

Viva el vino y viva el ron, Llorona, viva el ron y la baraja
Viva la mujer bonita, Llorona, y viva el hombre que no
    trabaja.
Long live wine, long live rum, *Llorona*, long live the
    cards where luck is lurking
Long live a pretty woman, *Llorona*, long live the man
    who's never working."

I knew that "*Llorona*" meant "weeping woman." "*Llorona*" was what Curro called me when I moaned making love. Endless verses were sung to this "*Llorona*" in Spain. I always wondered who she was.

Everyone was asleep in the dark apartment when we tiptoed in. Fumbling and jostling, we shut the door of our tiny room and turned on the light. Lo, we stood transfixed staring at the bed. It was strewn with the Kings' caramelos, all one hundred fifty-three bagged by CocaCola. Every inch of our bed was covered with the confetti of sugar candies wrapped in clear cellophane which caught the light. "In gay profusion lying there ..." I thought, remembering a song from my childhood.

"*Mira Currete, parece seña,*" I whispered.

"*Sí, Chochete ...*" concurred my velvet-voiced Gypsy. And we gazed at the candies in silent wonder.

"Look, Currete, it looks like a sign," I said.

And that night my baby was conceived in that bed.

Twenty-three

No longer alone. My belly with me. A baby's in here, and I'm in love with my belly. First time ever to revere a part of me. Loving my belly and my baby inside nearly loving me. Hand pat-patting this belly. Proud of my body for doing a beautiful job, creating a baby with ease. No fear like Spanish women have. Childbirth for them is the shadow of the valley of death. Me, eager for the life of it all. Wondering at this creation, one pea fitted neatly in the pod of me. Shape of watermelon on end, packed high in my core. Amazing belly to belong to this hand, until tonight together on the stage. Flying skirts, twenty clapping hands, shouts of jaleo, raucous guitars, bright lights, and me. Sitting serenely, my belly and me. Sitting in a row of dancers. Clapping. Singing. Beaming. Baby stirring within, camouflaged by fringe of a long Spanish shawl, secret kept quiet in my pocket, tickling me in loving conspiracy, come to be just in time to dance with me in London.

෴ ෴ ෴   ෴ ෴ ෴

Blessed by the gift of the parading Three Kings and two bodies, naked because of our own close heat, with no erotic intentions, no modern love-making of mouth-play, tease and tickle, touch and titillation, no fantasy arousal of the jaded, no he-said-that-she-said-that-she-came-when- he-came game. 'Twas the old world modesty of a crowded Gypsy family. One body receiving another in the dark and hardly a movement of the bed.

❦❦❦ ❧❧❧

Hand-in-hand at the desk of Pulpón. To confess and receive his blessing. Great white father. Blue-eyed ruler of the dark Flamenco empire. He looked up at us and didn't see. "Papers arrived. Your name on them, Susana. You leave in three weeks." Looking at each other. Hand-in-hand our secret kept. To London without my Curro! Bawling like a baby with contorted child's face, swallowed hard, sighed, and went anyway.

❦❦❦ ❧❧❧

Piccadilly Circus parade of Flamenco dancers. Newspaper pictures. Five-month belly behind fringe and silly grin. Flipping the bone at my race. Exotic imported Flamenco is secretly an Anglo defected. Triumph of a Wasp from Pasadena with her secret Gypsy belly. Glare of the lime-light all dimmed in the great glory of my secret belly. Walking in light in Piccadilly Circus. All traffic stopped for me. Hoping for two, maybe three, weeks' work. Finished two-month contract, renewed option, staying another week, yet another, and another. My dance the last of the show, like the last bull of the afternoon. Careen around carefully. Head proud and head-dressed tall. No turns to expose the belly under red skirts, no heel-work to jar its repose. Cuadro of good Flamencos not doing their best, restrained by the picky English. Funky is rude. Clapping must be muted. Thus, my matronly gait overlooked. A bovine belly couldn't pass in a real *corrida*. Companions help with silence, their Spaniards' compassion for the mother. Spanish waiters whisper, but English don't notice such things. Not nice. Time I learned a new art for me. "A Gypsy without a lie is a bird without a wing." Learning to lie in London.

❧❧❧ ❧❧❧

What good fortune. I saved the money for our land, proud I needed no help, sad I got none, but God's. This belly took care of me as if there were God within.

❧❧❧ ❧❧❧

Ooze of milk! Tiny droplet of amber dew on plump pink satin nipple. Great wondrous body, milk in my breasts. Breasts not for the dirty fifties' smirkers to ogle, breasts for the flowered sixties for an infant to suckle. Revelation. *Como Diós manda!* "Just as it should be!" A cry of discovery of the droplet. Rush to Ana, another dancer, below. Held as though by a mother. Bewildered weeping, and triumph shared with a stranger. Grieving for my mother, needing her so but never letting her enter my mind.

Le canto a mi madre que dió vida a mi ser
Le canto a la tierra que me ha visto crecer
I sing to my mother who gave life to my being
I sing to the earth which has seen me grow up.

Mothering my belly.   Receiving food of my own hand.
Fresh ground beef, green watercress, oranges, and milk each
day. Feeding my belly with love. Five flights up to my quiet
attic room. Not even out of breath. Ana and the others lazy
and listless beneath. Sitting alone in the peace of my room,
patting my belly, watching the moon shift night after night,
swell and subside and swell again like me. Sitting, rocking,
reading love from my Curro. Seventy-two letters he wrote.
The illiterate Gypsy to his Tourist love. Seventy-two letters
in fifteen weeks. *"Dale con la manito a mi Corrillo.* Pat my
Corrillo for me." Rocking, my hand on my loving belly.
Moonlight on my shoulders like my shawl.   Alone in
London. Never less alone.
   Ai a la La, la la La, la la Lai.
   Lai la la La, la lo Lai.

Twenty-four

Near the silent center of Seville, under the shadow of the towering Giralda, clustered irregular solid-packed city blocks. Old houses heaped wall to wall, eroded by centuries of thick winter rains and congealed together by the unrelenting summer sun. Their uneven rooftops, at odd angles from one another, displayed random collections of laundry drying in the September air.

One roof was mine, where I stood washing clothes. My long brown hair piled off my bare neck out of my way. My summer smock of sunbright print exposed long freckled arms which moved insistently over the corrugated concrete of the laundry pila. I pressed a most swollen belly against the sink's edge as I reached over it into the suds. I sang a simple song as I scrubbed, a sorrowful sunshine song I sang.

"Ai a la La, la la la la lo La? ..."

Suddenly I needed to stop mid-song and mid-scrub. Leaning on my soapy knuckles, I inhaled a few slow deep breaths. Then I resumed sloshing and squeezing and humming. It was my very first laundry here, and this sink pleased me. It had a generous faucet, a low sink for filling buckets, plenty of clotheslines and sunshine, and all just a few steps from my front door. I rubbed the chalky disk of soap across a shirt collar, slapped up water and kneaded the collar between my fists. I whistled my melancholy tune, rinsed and wrung. Again I had to pause a moment, breathing deeply with my head thrown back. Then I hung the dripping shirt, squinting at its whiteness in the late afternoon sunlight.

This was my second day in this house. Curro found it just in time for my return from London. I and my beautiful belly had been due back within days and he could find nowhere in Seville for us to settle. After years of using the crowded kitchens and foul bathrooms in unkempt pensiónes in unfamiliar towns, we sought a home where we had begun together, in Seville.

His triumphant letter to me in London told how, in desperation, he had climbed the Giralda, panting like a tourist. From the top of the Giralda he had spotted this house. With a determined angel perched on his shoulder he had walked through the maze of the city directly to it. Miraculously, it had a roof apartment waiting for us. Alone in my London attic room, I hungrily consumed his misspelled concern, his awkwardly phrased eagerness, his barely legible love. After my last portly Alegrías in the London Flamenco show, the next day I was on a flight to Spain, my riches in my purse, my baby in my pocket.

"Damn." I dropped my snowy sweater onto the dusty roof floor. As I re-washed it, I felt the panic of a woman soon to become a mother, of a human about to relinquish her human rights. London days had been peaceful without

Curro. The peace of solitude would soon be ripped from me. Wail would replace silence. I craved a warm downy baby from my belly into my arms, suckling my milk, but did I want a child to hound me for years of motherhood? This child was Curro's - his child, his life's desire, his son, the sun of his life. I was sharing this child with him, like our meals. But I often cooked alone, and too often I mothered Curro. Now I would have two. Two was too many. Would I reject the surrogate once I got a real son? Would I regret them both? Why must men be children? Why couldn't they be fathers? Love would shift. Would he and I revert to strangers, foreigners again? Would his son pacify him and heal his rage? Would I, in exchange, become an entrapped woman, recreating the hostility I had come so far to flee? Then I remembered the meals, the bread we had celebrated together. I remembered Curro's smile, his anguish, and his cante. I remembered his soft urgent pleas for a son. As I held my belly with both hands, the jagged doubts slowly melted into nectared tenderness and sweet yearning.

I stooped to gather the colored clothes piled near my feet. As I dumped them into the pila to soak, I paused again, gripping the edge of the sink, breathing heavily. The child heaved. Reaching down reminded me of the sudden cramp on the airplane when I reached under my seat to pull out my heavy overnight case, weighted with forks, knives, and spoons, each engraved with "Lyon's Corner House" -- a Gypsy gift collected by the other dancers of the show.

Wondering if that strain disturbed my belly, I drew a wet garment up from the soapy water onto the scrub ridges, Curro's green knit shirt. My hands pause as I inhaled the cool thrill of green: green tree, grass green, apple green, dappled above a stream green, shimmering field green, evergreen, emerald green, lucky green, London money green, patio fern green, babyleaf uncurling green. Curro wore this green when he welcomed my green eyes home green, incandescent at dusk green ...

After those months apart, the flight and the airport bus through balmy evening air, sweet Seville air, tender with orange blossom and jasmine, fresh with fountain spray, and down down the aisle of Seville to the muted fanfare of provincial traffic -- outside the Bar Iberia, polished clean, at dusk a burnished copper in the emerald green shirt, grinning at me, stood Curro. My heart expanded to wheels of burning jewel petals.

"Touch it, Curro." His hand was timid on my sacred swell.

"Oooh, how big it is!" No prayer so lovely as his throaty awe. No blessing greater than his hand upon his belly of mine. Patterns of soft amber and diluted violet glided across ageless columns of my mind, the worn floors, hidden chapels of the ecstasies.

"*Qué bonito,*" he chanted through his old sensual grin. In my lovely new belly I bore his life. Our seeds wed at the altar of mysteries, gentle Seville breeze blessed us with flowers and holy water as we embraced, a holy bulge between us. I paused again at my laundry, breathing long deep draughts.

"Keep still a while," I admonished my churning belly. When it subsided, I sighed and resumed kneading the green jersey, whistling my sad sunny melody. We had come home to this house I had never seen. To the nest feathered by my male, I came. Impatient with the cabdriver, Curro directed him through the snarl of short one-lane streets to Gandesa -- not really a street, rather an open-ended courtyard encircled by a continuous mass of houses. We entered a bare inner patio, climbed to the second floor, passed through its dingy, garbage-strewn kitchen and up a narrow brick staircase to the fresh air of the moon-bright rooftop. Instead of turning out onto the uncovered roof, we continued along a covered corridor to our door, a crude wooden door painted blue. Over the threshold he carried my suitcases. I stepped across with my belly and my joy, through our own private door, into our own home. I saw only a narrow high-ceilinged living room with its table, two chairs, and wardrobe; a kitchen nook with our butane burner, two stew bowls and pot; a tiny bedroom with a bed for two, neat with our own clean sheets. The walls were newly whitewashed; the floor of worn deep-grooved bricks scrubbed clean and cool by my proud man. Quiet as a monastery. Humble, immaculate, secluded. Secure.

Kneeling, I dipped a navy blue dress in the rinse tub, and as I reached for the clothesline I paused, my handful dripping, while I measured out slow breaths and the child prodded and flailed within me. I wondered if I harmed my belly yesterday, scrubbing the kitchen floor.

Gasping, with hands on my belly, I leaned against the flaking wall outside the rooftop toilet. I murmured to my belly between breaths. When the commotion settled, I remained a moment admiring the sweet mound under my wet hands. I wondered how much rounder it would grow. I contemplated my bright smock. I had only been wearing it a few days. For a few luxurious days I had allowed my belly to bud forth under its flowered print.

My belly tormented me again, and I circled the rooftop, seeking relief in movement. Remembering my English paperback about deep-breathing for painless labor, I practiced breathing in readiness for next month's labor. Breathing calmly against the commotion of my belly, I held onto the iron railing at the roof's edge and peered across the drop to the peeling green sunshade rolled down over my window. Inside I knew it was clean and soon to be cooled by the evening air, my clean bed quietly mine in there. I smiled as I remembered last night. Late at night, I could not sleep. Compulsively, I turned on the light and, out of my little English book, I, the ignorant American college graduate, lectured my sleepy Curro on childbirth. My wise, illiterate, Spanish Gypsy humored me. Side by side, the two of us sat in bed studying birth. I held an endless elated discourse. My energy lit the room, and he listened, wondering at me in our tiny bedroom, brilliant in the clean light of anticipation.

Fishing in the murky water for his black socks, I caught one, soaped it, and waited as the child's turbulence barreled through me again. I paced slowly into the house, moaning each breath out, until my belly relented. Then I returned to the sock. Squeezing soap and water through it, I pondered my growing discomfort. Would it be like this the whole last month? I tossed the sock into the plastic rinse tub, reached for another and halted again, pumping air in deliberate gulps.

"Hold still a while, baby!" I pleaded. After our midday meal, Curro had left from Bar Iberia with a carload of Flamencos, to sing a show in Málaga. The round trip, a long uncomfortable drive, would not bring him home until nearly dawn.

"Oh, this baby just won't stay quiet," I moaned, remembering to breathe against the scrambling whirling dervish within. When it stopped, I remembered Curro's words of concern as he left. If I felt bad, I was to go to the neighbor women living beneath us. They had had many children and would know how to help me. As he left, something made him hesitate. At the top of the stairs he looked at me intently for a moment with a dark Gypsy eye. I was cheerfully filling buckets, and he left.

I dropped a soaped sock on the scrub-board, a few were afloat in the rinse tub. The unrelenting inner churning impelled me into the house and onto my bed. Perhaps this belly would rest if I did. In the late afternoon light trickling through the sunshade's cracks, I lay in fetal position, my

hand on the struggling fetus within. I gasped through a
spell of great tumultuous discomfort, then, when relieved,
quietly murmured,

"Baby, what are you doing to me?" I rubbed my belly
affectionately. I patted it and gasped again, rolling my head
on the pillow. After hour-long minutes, I sprang from the
bed. Unable to endure lying down, I returned to the wet
smell of the laundry. For each sock I washed, I paced a
harrowed circle around the roof. I rinsed the black socks,
paced again, and hung them in a row. I emptied my buckets
out on the roof floor and watched the water wash across the
red bricks.

By late evening my hectic belly was in torment. Nothing
relieved me. I walked the length of the living room. Perhaps
this baby was in trouble. I paused at the wardrobe mirror.
My hair had loosened around my grimacing face. I stalked
the corridor to the roof faucets and back again. Perhaps I
should find a doctor. I lowered myself onto the rumpled
bed. I could wait here for Curro's return. His words of
concern echoed. Groaning on the edge of my bed, hands on
my knees, I tried to imagine those women beneath, whom I
had never met. I peered over my iron bannister into the
depths of the courtyard. Perhaps they would know what was
wrong. I remembered their dank seamy kitchen, shuddered,
and determined to wait until Curro came back. I paced
from my unlit kitchen, the length of my shadowed house,
around to the dusk-cooled roof, and circled the laundry,
avoiding the cold touch of the wet clothes on the line. As

alone as a tourist, I panted and I paced.

At midnight I bolted from my house. Leaving my blue door ajar, I strode down the corridor, hesitating in the waning moonlight, then slowly sank down the dark stairwell. I left the laundry stirring in Seville's September night air, on the deserted rooftop under the Giralda.

Twenty-five

The small kitchen in the midnight light of one weak bulb was smutty. Wall gunk was vapor-coated from frying Spanish oils. The one round window, cross-barred like a berry pie, opened into the same airshaft that ventilated the toilets of each floor. The sink, a shallow brick-red half-globe, was encrusted with grime. The floor was slippery with forgotten bits of garbage.

One woman was slowly scraping something; another entered, returning her husband's empty plate from his late supper. They paused when I appeared. I began to speak, and was interrupted by the terrible agitation of my big belly. I gasped. They watched me. Then shook their heads. I could see in their somber faces they believed I was giving birth.

"No, but it's not time yet, it's only eight months. Do you suppose the baby is just turning a lot? Does this happen in the last month?"

"I don't know," the young mother said, "You don't really know until the blood comes."

"Oh, oh, oh, the poor thing," the deaf grandmother chorused. "Look at her, she's nearly there, nearly there, oh, the poor thing. Look, there she goes again."

I held the wall until the pain subsided. Confused, I

climbed the stairs back to my room, lay down and soon found myself surrounded by the four women. I vaguely resented the intrusion of strangers yet, no longer caring about the world outside my body, I lay on my bed without protest.

The youngest -- a small, curly-headed girl -- stood away from me, watching me with the curiosity of a child, occasionally frightened by the turmoil on the bed, then turning and looking out the balcony window to the dark street below.

The smug young unmarried woman feared nothing. Worldly and indomitable, dark-skinned with mischievous black eyes, she was in the habit of going out at odd hours leaving a wake of perfume in the house, and she had no intention of this ever happening to her.

The young mother watched with the black eyes of a captured rabbit. She had lain under her husband, had been close to death each time she bore a child. She knew little else of life than delousing her infant's head in the sun on her balcony. This caged woman watched the struggling stranger on the bed, knowing it would be her own turn again soon. Afraid, she kept leaving the room to serve her husband, then reappearing.

The old woman was beyond fear. Usually she was relegated to frying in her filthy kitchen, to laundering gray sheets and leaving them on the line grayer still, reeking of sweat. Like a domestic pig that eats where it excretes, she peed in her kitchen garbage bucket. This old woman with her little black bun, her stupid black eyes, placed a chair by my bed and sat with her hands folded. At each contraction of mine, she would sigh in unison and murmur,

"Oh, the poor thing," shaking her head. The old cracked hands resting in her lap had scraped greasy pots, disposed of garbage, pulled entrails from fish, plucked and hacked chickens, cleaned excrement from animal cages, wiped up brats' puke and infants' runny shit, mopped up a drunken man's vomit, washed the cloths from her own bloody cunt, aborted sisters, bathed smelling belching cadavers. These woman's hands were now willing to attend to yet one more messy childbirth.

The night labored on, and the age-old sisterhood of women in mutual gore, grew between us. The intruders became welcome, my freckles and their dirty fingernails forgotten. We women had become one, like the women at a Greek wake, sighing together, waiting together, sharing pain. It was a place where men did not belong, where men would pale and faint away. This was the women's battlefront and we fought as one. No training required, no regimentation. Our instincts united us.

They offered to bring me a midwife and I refused, between grimaces. I was determined to do nothing until my Curro returned. Finally the wild one, familiar with the street at night anyway, went out to find a midwife.

Then I sprang from my bed, left the room and squatted over a chamber pot in the dark. The rush of liquid that poured from me, convinced me that I was indeed giving birth now. No waiting. I turned on the light ... and saw bloody water.

The midwife, a glum young man, cranky at having been awakened at 3:00 a.m., felt my belly, said he couldn't handle this birth, would give no reason, said I must go to the hospital, and five hundred pesetas please.

In the cab with the three sympathetic women, I sat quietly, half lying on towels, unaware of anything but the abundant fresh air from the window and the absence of pain. Then I was standing outside the high wrought iron gates of the Macarena Hospital. The night watchman ambled out.

"What is it?"

I was doubled over in pain.

"Let me in, please."

"Do you have papers?"

"No, I have no papers. I have money. I'll pay money. Just let me in."

The echoing hospital corridors had no sounds to repeat except the squeak of the wheeled bed and the footsteps of the silent orderly and the three women following. The stillness of the hospital echoed the stillness within me. Tiled walls tilted past me.

My bed paused and the crazies came - the delirium, the headiness, the speckled lightness. I knew it was "The Shift" that my little book had explained. Now my gate was open. Now my wise womb was fully dilated, and ready to reject.

At the door of the maternity ward, the orderly, who said his name was César, told the women to go.

"Tell Curro I'm here," I begged with desperation of someone being thrown in a dungeon. There was no phone to Curro. I was abandoned in the Macarena. In the hands of strangers. And my baby was coming out.

తతత ⁊⁊⁊

"How many children have you had?"

"None."

Green frock coats flapped in and out of the maternity room. Medical students, a dozen of them, each had his own officious clipboard.

"What is your last name?"

"Shoemaker."

"Chew-may-kuh?"

"Shoemaker. s.h.o.e.m.a.k.e.r."

"How many children have you had?"

"None."

I had been offered a folding metal chair to sit on. But I felt my baby coming out, and didn't want to sit down. I just wanted someone to do something.

"How many children have you had?" asked yet another supercilious frock.

"What?"

"How many children have you had up to now?"

"I've never had a child before."

Any minute now, one of these busy milling people would stop and help me. Would just look from his clipboard and notice me. I was giving birth.

If someone would just look me in the eye. Coral could see my baby in my eye at four months -- couldn't these medical men see in my eye that he was coming out now?

"How many children have you had?"

"NONE!" I bellowed in exasperation.

"Speak politely!" commanded the gestapo voice. The frocked man glared at me with contempt, adding, "And SIT DOWN."

That chilled me, as I saw I was not safe here but powerless at the mercy of strangers seeking their own interests.

"Yes, sir." I sank to the chair, hanging on to the back, sitting on the side of my thigh. Tears fell and I began to whimper. "My baby's coming out."

Someone called in a nurse, a woman, who looked me in the eye, smiled and spoke kindly. They told the nurse to prepare me for the examination chair, a raised throne with stirrups at one side of the room, with a pool of blood on the floor in front of it.

Without waiting another moment, I pulled up my skirt and mounted the chair and its stirrups, exposing my crotch to the roomful of people. Revulsed by my immodesty, they reviled the nurse for not controlling me. She took one close look, announced my exact condition, and they ordered me down and immediately into the delivery room.

"I have to go to the toilet first," I protested, standing in the middle of the delivery room.

"No," the smiling nurse explained, "That's your baby coming out."

"Oh." NOW they were talking MY language.

"Can you climb up on this table?"

"SURE!"

They surrounded me, all the cold-eyed green frocks. When someone tried to put an I.V. needle in my arm, I protested,

"What for?"

"We must put you out, sedate you."

"But I want to stay awake for this!"

"No. It's our policy to use the drip." Scent of danger ...

"Ok, but you're all my witnesses," I drew my pointing finger around their circle of faces. I had remembered Ana's story of a baby retarded because delivered by the "suction cup".

"No 'suction cup.' You must NOT use the '*chupón*.'"

Their disinterested faces fogged and faded away.

I awoke alone in the same room, and morgue cold. I called out,

"Hey, where is everyone? I'm cold!"

The kind nurse came in, covered me.

"What happened?"

"You had a baby boy."

"Where is he? I want to see him."

"Can you see?"

"Yes, yes."

I squinted and blinked to focus my eyes on the shriveled gray monkey in a cloth in the nurse's hands. Then he was gone.

César, the orderly who wheeled me in, wheeled me out cheerfully.

"My *chocho* hurts," I complained.

"Hey, watch your language," he chided with a grin.

"Listen, they didn't use the '*chupón*', did they?"

"Yes."

"Oh, no," I bawled. "I told them not to!"

"Hey. They had to use it," César tried to calm me. "The baby was struggling. Otherwise, he would have died."

"Better DEAD than STUPID," I wailed, sobbing uncontrollably. So they gave me an injection.

સ્ર્સ્ર્સ્ર   ৯৯৯

I awakened in morning light in a room full of women with their babies in baskets attached to their beds. I had no basket. Someone told me my baby had a little trouble breathing so they were giving him extra oxygen. I dozed again and Curro awakened me. Together we went down the hall to the "showcase", the "*escaparate*" as I nicknamed it, to see our baby. So many incubators, it was hard to pick out which baby was ours. His tiny hands trembled strangely. Curro took me home in a cab, both of us empty-handed.

સ્ર્સ્ર્સ્ર   ৯৯৯

With a gait as wide as a sailor's, from a telephone at the bank, I put through a call to my sister, awakening her in the middle of the California night.

"Hey Nantz, guess what!"

214

My sister's groggy voice traveled around the edge of the earth. "What?"

"I have a baby!"

"Oh yeah? Where'd you get it?"

"It's mine. I made it. I gave birth. But guess what, Nantz. He looks just like Daddy."

"That's all right, Sooz. He'll get better."

☙☙☙   ☙☙☙

I wept. The little glass trumpet slowly filled with yellow milk. It stung my nipple as it stole my milk from me. I emptied it into a cup and milked the other breast. Tears flowed as abundantly as milk. No one told me what to do with this milk. No fridge to put it in, not even a jar. Ashamed somehow to expose it to the light of day. It should be slipping unseen down an infant's throat. Sick with grief, I walked the corridor to our laundry roof, and poured that precious milk down the smelly toilet. For five babyless days, I sat on our bed and milked my breasts and cried. How I hated that little glass trumpet.

Had I been pregnant? I had worn a maternity smock only a few days. Had a baby actually been born of me - while I was out cold, while his father was out of town? Something must have happened, because I couldn't stop crying. Something must have happened, because I hurt between my legs, and an ugly rash ran down my inner thighs. My belly was gone. Perhaps there had been a crime.

Superstitious, Curro and I bought no baby clothes for

our non-baby. "Grave" condition might just lead to grave. But we stood our daily watch at the display window of the hospital.

❧❧❧ ❧❧❧

The "escaparate" was smudged with fingerprint and face-smooch of frustrated mothers. Beyond lay a museum of infants in individual glass cages, some wailing silently like de-barked dogs. I watched the one they said was mine. He lay still. There! Arms flailed and hands jerked. Then still, again. I compared with other babies -- none moved so strangely. He needed to be held close. Tucked so close within me before, now so far away was my shriveled infant, out of reach in his glass box. He was not done yet. Why did he eject? Reject me? Glass coffin on his way in from immortality ...

Intent, I inched closer as the crowd thinned. A stuffy smell of too many people, and my instincts violated to a shambles, I clung to Curro. Before us at the display window, a small woman in flowered kerchief wept and muttered,

"Oh, the poor thing."

Curro and I squeezed in beside her to better peer at our baby.

"*Mi po'recito*, my poor lil' guy," she repeated so sorrowful-ly, I glanced at her.

"Coral!"

Unrecognized, under a head scarf she had donned "to protect the newborns," was Curro's mother. She had bussed from Alcalá to see her first grandson.

"What's the matter?" Curro asked her.

"Well, just look." She had picked out as hers the darkest baby in the room, a baby with club-feet. "*El po'recito ...*"

"No, dummy, ours is that one over there, the whitest one," Curro chided his mom.

"Oh, for heaven's sake!" Her tears still spurting, she laughed aloud at herself, as only Curro's mother could.

❧❧❧ ❧❧❧

After a day of house cleaning, Curro and I came rushing late for our visit. The nurse poked her head out with, "Good. You're just in time to feed him." Dismayed because I was unbathed, I washed my breast with their boiled water. Suddenly in my hands was a screaming miniature gargoyle who grabbed onto the nipple as if unfed for his first five days. The tiny creature was drinking! He growled and drank. Smaller than the milk-swollen breast, he drew upon it like a landlord. He drank so thirstily they said I could take him home.

"Now?" I was horrified. He didn't weigh five pounds. Suddenly I wasn't ready. And, they instructed, he was to be left in bed until he got bigger. I was not to hold my baby.

An ecstatic Gypsy father took us home in a cab then rushed out to buy supplies. All we had for the baby was his father's name, which had been given him two years before he was conceived.

I was alone when I unwrapped my infant for the first

time, like a belated gift. The party was over, everyone had gone home, there was this one gift left. Gingerly, I peeled back his wrappings, then gazed dismayed. Blue "X" marked the scalp where delivery damage had been done. Wrinkles hung from miniature curved bones. The tiny survivor was a speck on the sea of my bed. I stared at him with the panic of a female American displaced in a land of no running water, no Kleenex, no Gerbers. A straw shade in our bedroom was keeping out hot sun, filtering in fresh breeze. The monastic simplicity of this room became dangerous.

"One big germ could just knock you over," I whined like the motherless child I was. Curro found me crying again, when he returned with a stack of new diapers and a crib. Sniffling, I unveiled his infant for him. All four pounds. Most of this baby was genitals which he would have to grow into like a puppy grows into its paws. Precisely then, the baby peed with such force, the urine hit the wall over his head behind the bed.

"Ole-ole Currito," his father laughed. "*Ole su' cojones allí!* That's my man."

Twenty-six

"No, Curro, you don't wear a wedding ring out of the store."

"*Eso no me lo quito yo*, I ain't takin' this off," Curro declared with the conviction of a man who'd never before worn gold.

"Currete, no."

"Well, why not!?"

"Not until you're married." I giggled helplessly, like someone being tickled. "You put it on at the wedding."

"Why?"

"*Yo que sé - es la postura*. How should I know - it's the way it's done." I appealed to the fat jeweler, who nodded solemnly. The jeweler held out the envelope that already contained my band. Curro plunked his in, snatched up the envelope and stashed it in his pocket. On the bus to Alcalá, he kept checking it, to see if it still contained his first very own gold.

I waited in the doorway as Curro entered the bar to get Miguel. They stood talking and laughing as if Curro had just told a joke. They had grown up together. Miguel was saucer-eyed Alejandro's brother, and Ana's husband. He was better looking than his brother and made a decent living as a singer. He started to order drinks and Curro stopped him, pointed to me in the doorway, and showed him the little envelope with the two gold rings.

"Why, you're serious!" Miguel was astounded. He looked out at me and back at the rings. Then they doubled in gales of laughter again. It was, indeed, the biggest joke in town. Even I started chuckling in the doorway.

"Yes, and we're getting married right now. You are best man."

"I am?" Miguel glanced down at his rolled up white cuffs and tennis shoes.

"Doesn't matter. Pope's not marrying us. You're fine." With big grins they came out together into the sunlight.

At the church, Curro called some men down off the roof they were repairing. They became the witnesses. Inside, the little plain chapel smelled of incense and candle smoke. The pews were empty, except for a record player in the second row, scratching out some wedding music for the deluxe fifteen-dollar wedding. During the quick ceremony, I kept wondering if this round-eyed, satin-tongued priest actually did molest all his acolytes, like Curro had said.

We struggled with the rings in the envelope. They wouldn't tap out; then fell on the floor; were nearly identical and we argued over which was whose. Finally, Curro put on his own, and I put on mine, and Miguel's nostrils flared so I thought he would burst with laughter.

"Now you may kiss your wife," the priest allowed. Curro's cheeks creased to their most benevolent, their most sensual. I tucked my favorite kiss in at the corner of his grin, so that his mouth paused in the edge of my smile. It was our standard twin-cheek-kiss. A sweet familiarity we had. Sort of an ironic tenderness.

"...Now place thirteen coins in Curro's hand," the priest instructed Miguel, who dug in his pockets, counted out the coins into Curro's upturned hands. Curro gave them to his bride as promise of provision, and I passed them into the acolyte's hands. The kid in a white bib pocketed the coins as a tip, we found out later.

"Son of a bitch," Miguel complained as we left the dusky wax smell and returned to Alcalá's September sunlight. The witnesses climbed back onto the roof.

"Filthy priest robbed me." Miguel was not prepared and did not have little tinny coins, only peseta pieces. The wedding cost him more than it did Curro -- who laughed with a Gypsy's delight, waving him off with a gold-banded hand.

๛๛๛ ๛๛๛

We let Currito lie in his crib at the head of our bed. But when he would cry, I would cup him over my heart. With my lips on top of his warm head, I would anxiously chant a teeny march to him. "*Chiquitín,* lil'guy," I would say. "*Chiquitín, Chiquitín, Chiquitiquitiquitín* ..." It soothed me, but my bony self never seemed much comfort to him. His head would clunk on my clavicle.

"*Cuando te pone' grande, tu papá te va a comprar un borrico.*

221

Your daddy's gonna buy you a lil' donkey," Curro promised. Murmuring his country-Gypsy's endearments to his infant son, he dried him and pulled on his doll shirt. The fatherly short brown hands were huge and safe around his miniature baby, in our clean home. Pinning a diaper, Curro gingerly scooped him up, cooing, "*Ya vamos a la vaquita.*" "The little cow", I waited on my bed, having just washed my powder pink nipples with boiled water. I cupped my tiny baby's head, smaller than my rutted palm, and directed a plump nipple into his mouth. He growled like a cub as he glommed on and drank. The other breast spurted on him, awaiting its turn. The pleasure of the drawing milk drew a new love from me, a sunrise within me. It was just as things should be, easy, never a doubt. Years and years I had awaited this. I was more important than I had ever been in my life. This was MY baby.

Then one day I had a thought. I would give my baby a bottle to accustom him in case Pulpón should call me to dance. That did it. I guess the bottle was easier. The baby stopped wanting the breast. The breasts stopped spurting. Rejected by the one sure thing - my own child - after only two months, in despair I handed the baby to my man and said, "Here, you feed him. He doesn't want my milk." And I went out and got a daytime job. An office job. Heartbroken and relieved, I became father. Curro mothered my son.

As the baby fattened, he spent hours in the big double bed with Papá, lying on his father's chest, tiny head to loving heart. Packed solid as a sofa, Curro was his son's best cushion, his best pal. Floors were cold and drafty in Spain, the milky baby wiggled on the clean soft bed, in the protective curve of his Papá's nurturing copper warmth.

"The Gypsy with the baby on his head," people labeled Curro. To market, out for coffee, to Pulpón's office, his son went everywhere with him. While I worked. Curro carried him on his neck, even before the baby could sit up. Curro was a short man and his son gave him stature.

"Ole-ole-ole," the swarthy father bathed his son in his blue plastic tub in the rooftop sunshine, delighted at the baby's two-toothed grin and wicker-colored curls.

"*Ole, su' cojones,*" Curro rooted in time with the baby's tiny hand as it slapped the water, splashing his own blinking little face, and his father's creased cheeks. Curro's lips, often hidden behind the hard line of his mouth, were turned out, yielding and full. He was happy. Droplets sat on the father's lashes as he spoke guttural fondness and shampooed his son.

Bell pepper and onion savored the Seville afternoon while Curro's stew simmered. His husky mammy voice lullabied as he sat at the playpen, plunking the guitar for his diapered yearling. Strumming and slapping, babalooing and crooning, Curro charmed the child. Currito of baggy diapers hung resolutely onto the playpen bars, gumming the railing, drooling, and bobbing to the music. Tousled Curro was at peace with him there. While I worked.

His Papá dressed him, his Papá entertained him, his Papá fed him. To induce him to eat, Curro did tricks, told stories, imitated little animals; to fatten his skinny son, to compensate for lack of mother. A meal became a full circus. Curro labored for each bite the baby swallowed. While I worked.

Currito drove his first wheels on his first birthday. His walker. Two aluminum rods, bent into moonlanding legs, ran on little caster wheels and suspended a cloth seat. With a drooling grin like a torn pocket, Currito's feet churned vehemently, wheels stalling, then he shot across the floor, eyes bulging with thrill. The rutted brick floor thrummed like a washboard while he banged into doors, drawers, zoomed from one noisemaker to the next with a drummer's frenzy.

"Ole-ole-ole," laughed Curro of mellow eyes. The baby's delight was his father's balm. And my satisfaction. No American man I ever knew wanted a baby like that Gypsy had. Not one of my countrymen would ever have treasured my child as much.

But I never forgave Curro the baptism of our son.

Twenty-seven

"Now now, Francisco ..." The flustered priest extricated his wet gold cross from the mouth of our baby. In the priest's arms during baptism, a plump and cheerful nine-month-old Currito preyed upon the gold hanging on the man's frock -- reaching for it, as fascinated as he was with his grandmother's medallion every time he sat in her lap.

Grinning, and wearing all her gold, Coral watched him, and so did Rubio and CocaCola, dressed in their best, standing around the baptismal font with the new little family. It was one of the rare times those Gypsies entered a church. After the baby was blessed, the real party would begin.

The Gypsies' highest celebration was a baptism and the ancient Gypsy custom of a baptismal party. The parents of the child spend all they have on food and drink for a splendorous party that lasts all night, even for days. In Spain, the greatest of Flamenco was created at the juergas of Gypsy baptismal parties. All the trials and joys that the child could experience in a lifetime were vented in cante, at that high night of his baptism. I had never been to a Gypsy baptism, and here was my chance, at the baptism of my own son.

Our party was to be in Regla's two-room house. Curro's only half sister, Regla, was a pretty, dimpled woman with a

wide mouth and thick ankles. She was barren and sometimes had convulsions. She lived with her young husband, a
first cousin from Utrera, in the *"casitas bajas,"* Gypsy ghetto
outside Alcalá. For the celebration, she whitewashed the
walls, scrubbed the cement floor. The curtains over the
doorway flapped a welcome.

Curro had planned a joint baptism, to save money, with
Casquele, his next brother who had just produced the
second grandchild of the family. Casquele was crippled and
sold lottery tickets in downtown Alcalá, and knew everyone
in town. So he invited everyone in town to "his" baptism --
a big brag at Curro's expense. Curro's resentment, as he
bought all the supplies for the party, brewed for days ahead.
The two brothers spent all day stewing a pot of beans at
Regla's house. Together they mixed a tub of sangría with
liters of red wine, cognac, sugar, oranges, cointreau, and a lot
of sampling.

By the time the people started arriving, Curro was pretty
well drunk and hating the brother he had already spent a
lifetime resenting. When I arrived with the baby, our nine-
month son, the house was filled with anger. I put our son
with Casquele's tiny baby girl, on Regla's big bed in
the other room. I was frightened already at the violence
radiating from Curro.

Men who stood around drinking and talking, as they do
until the juerga warms up and begins to roll, were becoming
wary too, as tension built and Curro fussed and swore while
serving beans onto American paper plates I had bought on

the air base. The plates were soft and shallow, and beans were running over the sides. Pity burned in my gut as I stood frozen, helpless, watching him struggle with the beans.

The first man to gamely take a plate was smaller than Curro, a good-natured regular at juergas. His smiling good-willed gesture would have ordinarily broken the tension, but a lifetime of sibling rivalry roared through Curro like a loco-motive.

Hoping to shock Curro and break the tension, I said, "Calm down. What do you want to do at your kid's baptism, damn him instead of bless him?"

He blew. He threw a plate of beans at the little man. Like a planet it spattered bean meteors in an arc around the room. Yelling, snarling men scrambled, and Curro was the wild center of the holocaust. The ball of men rushed outside and Curro threw something and shattered the window. Glass showered all over the bed the babies were on.

"The babies, the babies!" people screamed. Ignoring the glass, I grabbed our son and held him, terrified. The gob of shouting men came back in, to the doorway of the bedroom. Many men held the maniacal Curro at bay. Sobbing and pleading, I held the baby up to Curro like a cross in the face of a demon. I shoved my silent infant into that knot of men, into Curro's arms. He calmed and held his son. Then he allowed them to stuff the three of us into a taxi, before a Gypsy war between cousins could begin. Curro and I skulked away like culprits from our own son's baptism. It had lasted less than an hour.

The father's storm subsided. He forgot the baptism. But what had it done to the son? Was that the memory locked away behind the child's speechless confusion?

The next day, with a broken heart, I went out to Regla's to help scrub beans off her walls.

Twenty-eight

We built our own home on the edge of Seville. A tiny house. A simple, poor man's house. A full-grown olive tree enveloped the backyard. The walls, as thick as a castle's, allowed windows east and west, to let in the light of Andalusía. I designed the house and Curro hired the workmen. His brothers dug the foundations. The Viejo had died, and Coral wore black, the twinkle gone from her eye, the day the concrete was poured. For good luck, she tossed a turd from the baby's diaper into the foundation -- a Gypsy's blessing for a Gachí's home. CocaCola leaned on his shovel and grinned. Miguel kept on shoveling.

Coral wanted her first grandson, begged to take her "little cream puff" white baby home to Alcalá and fatten him on her garlic soup. His parents refused. We would raise him ourselves, thank you. In our little rooftop nest, while we built our house, Currito was never near another child. Restrained the long damp winter in his blue high chair, my baby was cocooned in the colored afghan of mismatched squares I had begun knitting in London and had laced together hastily after he was born. His hazel eyes sad, mouth hanging, sometimes banging his head against the back of his high chair, Currito would sit quietly, cooperating, for hours. He never crawled. He would sit and wait for us to finish our insanity and come to him.

Our insanity was our house, built of hopes and needs. It cost us. It cost us his babyhood. We worked more than beasts, beyond exhaustion. Curro sang by night, supervised building by day, shopping and cooking daily. I worked by day and scrubbed diapers on the roof by candlelight. Worn to bickering frayed nerves, we were often too tired to bathe. It was too much to drag the filled laundry tub into our apartment, add stew pots of boiling water, bathe, then drag it out again to dump onto the laundry roof. Some days I could smell myself in my little cashier's cage at work.

The two months of sacrifice had dragged into two torturous years. But it was finally done.

In September, 1970, on Currito's second birthday, we moved in. Our new house shone like dawn after a snowstorm. And it was ours. Our very own.

What roaring joy. Neighbors kept their distance, streets were still unpaved and water was not yet piped to our plumbing. But what splendor we perceived in our gleaming white-tiled bathroom with telephone shower, well-windowed living room, solid table and chairs, big cushy platform rocker, immaculate white-tiled kitchen with built-in sink and food shelves, silvery faucets, double laundry sink out back, and secluded bedrooms. Humble luxury for us. Now we would be happy.

But we were not.

We fought in our tiny backyard, while we planted the lemon tree of my dreams.

"It's too deep, take it out!"

"No, the roots can spread here. Just turn it this way, dammit!" We tugged on it, spitting wine-breath at each other as we swore and wrangled. When we planted that lemon tree, we buried our sense of humor. We buried the detachment which had been keeping us together.

"Woman, come here! Look!" Curro shuddered, one morning. A black hearse was parked in front of our pristine white home. Superstitious Gypsy, Curro always avoided a funeral procession, but he could not avoid this hearse. It chilled us both. The baker's donkey with his fragrant baskets delivering daily sacred bread could not quite wipe away our sense of doom.

We were out of work. It was wintertime. Neither had a job.

Our dusty street, houses flush with the curb and wall-to-wall, felt like a prison compound. Curro left me alone in the house for hours at a time while he desperately sought ways to earn food. He gambled away what cash we had, and came home sour and mean. Our bedroom sequestered all our unused stage wardrobe in a sumptuous alcove but scanty love-making on our new double bed. The baby had his own bedroom but no toys nor playmates in it. I did not know how to mother my son, and Curro could not support his family.

One day, he brought home a whole crate of fresh

mackerel. He claimed it had fallen off a delivery truck; I suspected he had stolen it. We boiled, fried, marinated mackerel, and ate it to disgust. We gave mackerel to neighbors and even bussed a bucketful of mackerel to Coral in Alcalá. But nothing improved.

Bored, I kneaded clothes on one new pila, rinsed them in the other. Like my neighbors, I hung out my clean wet sheets on the roof, blinded by their whiteness in the winter sun of Seville. My chickens bickered at me from their rooftop coop. A neighbor voiced astonishment that my sheets could be so clean. As if a Gypsy's American wife was expected to be trashy. Was I to be toiling for the approval of a handful of neighbors, instead of dancing for the applause of crowds?

ॐॐॐ ॐॐॐ

"No! No, that's a big branch. Not that one!"

Another branch fell. Silvery foliage was mounting at the base of our olive tree. It was a huge lush old tree and balding by the minute. Parcels of sky were growing larger while I peered through my olive from my bedroom window.

"No more. Please don't cut any more."

"Look Señora, your husband hired me to prune. This is how I prune. I know pruning."

Curro was gone. A crew of pruners, cutters over shoulders, had finished a neighboring orchard and passed down our street. Curro, newly landed gentry, hired one on the spot, then left for town. That pruner was amputating all our summer shade. Would this tree ever recover?

"Please stop. Please," I begged, fighting tears.

"Trust me. You'll have double the olives in two years."

"We don't need more olives, we need shade." Wringing hands, I paced around my living room and back out to the yard. As each branch fell, something was cut away from my heart. But I was only a woman, a city person, a foreigner, so he pruned away. All but the trunk fell.

I stayed inside after that. It was Curro's job to get water for the lemon and the olive.

❧❧❧   ☙☙☙

"Our living room is so big! Look. We can put a counter here, inside the front window. Wall off a tiny store," Curro paced off the space, to show me. "You can sell thread and buttons from your house. And we'll get by nicely," was the Gypsy's ancient solution.

"Maybe later, when we retire." No way would I sit here hour after hour, selling sewing supplies to disdainful local ladies while he gallivanted and squandered and stirred up trouble everywhere. To a defected American woman who thought she had escaped the shackles of housewifery, my husband was offering solitary confinement.

"For now, I can dance. Spring is coming." I sniffed.

"*Mujer*, we'll starve before summer work opens."

"Just speak nicely to people and things will improve. Try it!" I was shelling peas at my big table, my heart an anvil in my chest.

"I spoke nicely to Pulpón." Flamenco jobs were always scarce in winter, and Pulpón had lost the habit of giving us work.

"And?" I twisted open a pod, raked out its plump peas with my thumb.

"Same old story. 'Nothing *querido*, I haven't got a thing for you.' Susie, we have no other choice." He sat down facing me. "We have to go to the coast. I hear there is lots of work in Palma, Mallorca."

"I'm not leaving this house." My hands clutched the peas.

"Just for a season. Money's good there."

"But we just moved in here. This is our home."

"My mother needs money for groceries." Curro chewed on a raw pea. "She said we live in such a beautiful house, we need to think of my brothers. I said, 'Ma, there's no money. We have a house, but you can't eat bricks.' She doesn't believe me." He glimpsed something in the street, swore, and stormed to the window.

"Look, they did it again! Took off my hose and hooked up theirs."

"Currete, let them have water too. Our two tanks are nearly full, and they have only one tank each." I tried once more to placate him. "Don't hoard water. We're okay."

He ignored me, rumbled out to the main water hydrant and switched hoses. It was becoming a major war. A neighbor approached, then another. I sat helplessly shucking peas. Curro returned to rave and sputter around his sunbright home. Then he left for town, leaving me with my chronic uneasiness.

"Mamá ..." my son was awakened from his nap, sweaty with one cheek pink.

"Chiquetin, Chiquetin, Chiquetin-tin-tin ..." I chanted. I kissed him, diapered and dressed him and absently set him down with his tricycle. Too little to ride it yet, he liked to push it around the house.

I watched. Curro had bought that tricycle. Currito had never played with another child, his Papá his only companion. Now his tricycle was the child's only friend. He steered it from room to room, barely reaching both handlebars at once, purring through his pacifier.

I dusted the white tiles of my empty kitchen shelves. On my knees with my bucket, I admired my gleaming granite floor. Like butterscotch and cream, it ran throughout my house. On it lay my little boy. He had turned the tricycle on its side, and lay down beside it like a buddy, tapping toe and sucking his chupe.

"Ai, mi Currito," I scooted over to stroke his hair. "Go play with the kids." I heard their laughter in the street. "Eh?" I perked at him with an inviting grin. "Go." He was only two and so little. But they were small too. The street was safe. No cars since that hearse. My son needed other children. "They're having fun!"

His head lifted with their laughter. He brightened, left his tricycle and stood in the doorway a moment, then disappeared. My long arms dipped in the bucket, reached and swabbed. While my luscious floor was drying, I would check on him.

As I cleaned my house, I washed out denial from my mind. Finally entrapped in my own home, there was no way to avoid the reality of Curro's chronic belligerence. No one in Seville would give him a job because of it. Waxing and waning over the years, Curro's behavior customarily offended all the tablao owners in one area, then he would move on. Pulpón would periodically blacklist him, forcing him to seek work for himself on the coasts in tourist resorts.

"That's why we went to Barcelona when I started dancing. That's why we left Barcelona," I confessed to myself, reaching in swoops over my treasured floor. "That's why we went to Marbella. That's why we left Marbella." I finished both bedrooms before I finally admitted, "And that's why Mallorca is next."

My heart as wrung out as the rag I was wringing, I finished scrubbing around my oaken table, under the fringed hanging lamp in the center of the house. I wiped hands on my old flowered smock, went to check the chicken simmering in the kitchen.

It was our rooster. I had raised him from a chick. We had gradually sold off a zillion baby chicks as our coop on the roof grew too small. We had kept this rooster, and the best hen, named Hope. Now with nothing to feed even chickens, Curro had gamely killed and plucked the rooster. I did not watch. But I was stewing the fellow who had scratched overhead, whose majestic crow awakened us in our new bedroom, the fellow who was our future in full plume. Dead now.

"Mamá ...?" Only two and tiny for two, my little boy stood in the front doorway, perplexed.

"Did they play with you?" I asked hopefully, spoon in hand.

He nodded, frowned.

"What are their names, did they say their names?"

Silently he worked his fingers. Something sticky on them. He looked up at me as I approached, his eyes deep and lost.

"Dogshit?" I recoiled. My little boy stank. Smeared with excrement, his cheeks, his arms, his hair.

"Did you play with dogshit?"

He shook his head, soundlessly, tears gathering and spilling.

"Did those children do this?"

He nodded big nods. He began to grimace, still silent.

His angelic innocence was what struck my heart most. He was not alarmed until he saw his mother's alarm. He was baffled by the kids' giggles, baffled by the stink, baffled by his mother's anger, baffled about what he must have done wrong.

I stripped him, and carried him at arm's length to my new bathroom. In the basin, a half-globe white as a hole in the snow, I scrubbed my son until he bawled.

I could not get the smell of shit off his skin, nor the stench of prejudice out of my nostrils, nor the oppression of insanity off my shoulders. Defeated, my house-joy had soured to dread. My safety had become imprisonment. My marriage was punishment.

I wrapped my child in a clean towel and held him and rocked him, lonely woman, too thunderstruck to weep.

☙☙☙   ❧❧❧

"Look," Coral moaned on the last day I ever saw her. My mother-in-law was cleaning our last chicken, Hope the Hen, for a farewell stew. The smell of singed feathers hung on our fresh air.

"Coming," muttered a bitter daughter-in-law. I upended my iron. I was packing and closing up my house. In the morning, with husband and baby, I would leave for Palma, Mallorca. Coral and the boys came from Alcalá for dinner and instructions on house-watching.

"Look at these," Coral's small brown hand cupped a string of mustard seeds. Not mustard, each was bigger than the last, yellow as yolks ...

"What is that?" I studied it.

"Eggs. In Hope." With pity in her eyes, Coral held out the other hand, "Her first egg. She would have laid it tomorrow."

My mouth hung open. I touched the hard shell then backed out the kitchen door. "Ooooh noooo," I uttered low and slow. "An egg. Hope had an egg ..." My head wagged. "No no ... Hopeless ..." I stood shaking my head, "Hopeless, hopeless."

Rubio, seated in my rocker, was rolling an orange to Currito. The orange wobbled away, forgotten, as the baby and his uncle watched me.

"Two years to build this house," I reminded hapless Rubio. "How can I leave my beautiful house after only six months here?" I ranted and paced. "There were eggs in that hen. Eggs. EGGS," I bellowed. "Hope was going to lay an EGG tomorrow, the very day we leave this house."

My shouts brought in Curro and CocaCola from the back yard where Curro was showing his brother how to water. They stood at the door, wary.

"This is your home. Yours, Curro. You are supposed to be HAPPY here for godsakes." I pointed out my broad windows, "It has an olive and a lemon and two pilas and the most beautiful bathroom in Spain. And we have to leave it," I roared, "and kill Hope!" Spouting tears and mucous, I stomped from room to room like a mad broker on a selling tour.

"Damned suitcase. I don't need it," I yowled, kicking the open suitcases on the bedroom floor, full of all our clothes. "I don't need a suitcase, I've got my own closet."

The brothers looked at each other and wondered why all the fuss over a chicken. But they knew Curro was impossible to live with, and these Gypsies, accustomed to deep enduring loss, knew enough to keep quiet. Even Curro understood my disappointment. They all stayed out of my way.

"Never again!" I swore through clenched teeth. "Never

again. Never raise chickens, never be a homemaker." The
depth of my vow was unspoken. For the rest of my life, I
would keep my silent vow: Never own another home.
Never marry again. Never bear another child.

I threw myself belly down on my new bed, where the
working singer and dancer could have slept in peace all
morning, where my other children could have been engendered. I stayed on that bed and wept until dark. Ignored,
my son pushed his tricycle to the foot of my bed and
watched me cry. Then he allowed Coral, his beloved
Abuelita, to rock him and hum a little gypsy lullaby.

After Herculean effort to be unlike my mother, I had
inherited her lie: Make the house beautiful enough and it
will generate marital contentment. That frantic mother had
lived a life compulsively redecorating her home, even formed
a club of housewives who mutually redecorated their homes,
hoping to find they had redecorated their marriages and
their roles as women. That great lie of the 50's was carried in
me like an infectious disease, and this disbelieving American
daughter, in spite of herself, had built her own house on that
lie. My house had failed me. And those tiny eggs exposed
it all.

Coral scrambled the unborn eggs and fed them to her
wide-eyed grandson, while he played with her gold medallion. She smiled at him with each bite. Between smiles her
eyes were as bereft as her black dress, lifeless as the clefts in
her pursed lips. Her eyes were full of goodbyes.

Curro and his brothers and mother, somber as undertakers, sat for that last meal at the table in the center of my new house. I stayed in fetal position on my bed. In silence the Gypsies ate my hen.

IV
Soleá

Twenty-nine

Ocean air cleared my head and revived me. With wicker trunk, suitcases, tricycle, our seasick toddler, and the new hope that sea breeze brings, Curro and I sailed to Mallorca.

Together we were hired at Los Rombos, a renowned Flamenco tablao on the beach outside Palma. Overjoyed, I forgot all past disappointments. I was finally a dancer working nightly on the same stage with Curro.

We worked seven nights a week plus matinees on Sunday. And by day, I was allowed to practice alone on the dark stage. Empty chairs in the gloom witnessed my drumming feet, strengthening thighs, building speed. Tightening, weeding, cultivating my dance material, I rehearsed my Alegrías, my Fandango, my Bulerías, my Sequidillas, my Rumba, my Sevillanas, my Caracoles, my Soleá; purifying, sweetening them all, thrilled to finally be getting enough dance, and enough of Curro's cante. His peerless cante.

The three of us were a family with just a staircase and a few paces between home and work and beach. Curro and Currito played together every day. By night Curro de Alcalá, swarthy Gypsy versed in all the Flamenco styles of

Andalucía, and I, of fluid moves, long-haired, well-painted, eager as a new filly, were respected professionals, on top of our careers. And our bright apartment was on top of a narrow building with sea view out both sides and clean sea air blowing through. We were finally okay.

My golden little boy had cheeks like mine, cheeks glossy as his knees, my apricot kid, my very own tiny Gitano. Fawn hair parted and slicked back every afternoon, he circled the village quad on his beloved tricycle with his Papá. Meanwhile, a bathtub full of soaking diapers and sheets attacked my tired dancer's back, punished me as I rinsed my laundry on my knees until one merciful day when the first laundromat in Spain opened next to the restaurant beneath us.

Curro's two younger brothers joined us in Mallorca. Camped in the little living room, bored and listless without jobs, whimsical Cocacola and affectionate Rubio cared for Currito while his parents worked. They even potty-trained him.

Then CocaCola became a painter for a construction company. His cola skin paint-flecked, he came home telling scary tales of walking beams seven stories high; and he soon left us to return to the safety of his mother's one-story house in Alcalá.

Rubio could sing. When a singer left Los Rombos, Curro got him his first job there. We had sent him to a doctor who freed him of pain. He still could barely walk, but singers mostly stand, and his big hands and generous nature were good for cuadro clapping. Then Rubio found a home. His first girlfriend was a dancer in the show, a Gachí with milky thighs and motherly manner, who looked as much like Curro's wife as Rubio could find. Rubio and I never did look at each other, even in the cuadro, without grinning.

After his uncles moved out, Currito slept in his mom's wicker trunk in the dressing room, beneath my swinging costumes. One night, I returned from the cuadro with my shawls and my castanets and my charm, to find him crying hysterically and covered with vomit. Swooning with pity and guilt, I cleaned him up, but I did not miss a show, not a beat. So his first baby-sitter was hired.

Our little boy had been sleeping for hours in his rumpled bed, when Curro and I finished work at four a.m. We inhaled his sleeping fragrance, kissed his hot cheeks. Hungry and animated, gabbing in whispers, we wolfed toast and bringá at the kitchen table. Then we slipped into bed. The black photographer's paper, carefully taped over the child's windows, failed to keep him asleep past dawn. Drowsy mother played quietly with bright-eyed boy, until Papá could sleep off any potential ire, just like I had done twenty-five years earlier with Baby Nancy, when Mommy had migraines, codeine, and similar rage.

My little Currito and I breakfasted together high above the bay, in our little apartment kitchen, watching boats out the window. Salt air filled my bar room lungs, smell of the sea composed me.

247

"*Es mío. Es mío.* It's mine," my tiny boy chanted through a mouthful of egg, as he pointed to a black and white checkered cement mixer unloading way out on a jetty.

இ~இ~இ ~இ~இ~இ

Two dancers from Seville shared the crowded dressing room with me and my wicker trunk. The mirror on one wall reflected skirts, mounds of ruffles dipped in candy colors, with matching blouses and long-fringed shawls. Costumes reeked stale of tobacco and sweat. Starched velvet roses hung over a mirror. Tins of bright plastic earrings - hoops and dangles -- strewed the dressing table. Castanets sprawled amongst them, cast off hurriedly during a quick costume change. Cluttering the floor underneath, tired shoes yawned for tireder feet.

"Good evening, ladies." Breathless, my excitement sparked the tiny room. I came fully made-up from my own bathroom mirror, just two stairways away. My hair was gathered high behind my smooth head.

One dancer, puckering lips at the mirror, responded with her typical haughty silence. But Amparo, whose breasts and wit and grace I emulated, turned to greet me. Amparo was also a Gachí, as tall as I, with many Gypsy relatives of her own. She had sufficient confidence and imagination to be kind to a foreigner.

"*Qué hay, 'quilla?* How's it going, girl?" Amparo spoke the Andalusían Spanish of Flamencos, which I no longer noticed, for I spoke it too.

"Oh, Amparo, you're wearing that dress. I love your black dress!"

"I'll give you the name of the dressmaker."

"Could I have it copied? How wonderful." I lifted my trunk lid to deposit clean blouses, knocking someone's slippery shawls to the floor. "Sorry. Guess I'm nervous. Was that CaraEstaca I saw downstairs?"

"Probably. I heard he was coming to work here." Amparo replaced the shawls, choosing one to wear.

I stepped into my green bodice, hopping in place when the elastic harness hung up on my heel. Fleetingly, that old stage fright iced my gut. CaraEstaca was dancing here. Last time I saw him, I was an awful beginner in Barcelona.

I never knew whom I would be dancing with. In Flamenco cuadros, artists were hired and fired like waiters. They honed themselves alone, then jammed together on stage. Each knew the compás, and the protocol. The dancer called the changes with foot signals but had the courtesy not to do so during the singer's verse or the guitarist's solo. I knew to call for a song after my footwork, knew when to speed up, knew to drum out a signal to stop the music entirely. And in a good cuadro such as this one, whenever anyone faltered, the clapping carried them. Singers like Chato, the leader of the cuadro, and Rubio, were valued for their strong palmas as much as their cante.

I was an accomplished professional dancer. But for a moment I was awestruck that I was paid to dance on the same stage with CaraEstaca.

I watched my mirrored self pin a white rose to the side of my chignon. I checked my eyes. Perfect. They loomed eager, painted larger than life on my moon-shadowed face. I smiled at Amparo in the mirror.

"Don't you miss your home?" Amparo asked when our eyes met. "I am so homesick."

"*Po'recita*," I commiserated. "Seville is the most beautiful city in the world. It is my home too, Amparo ..."

Ah, my abandoned house. My shining white tiles, gathering dust. Was the olive filling out? Did the lemon get enough water? Was the street paved yet? Foundations thick enough to support a second story ... rooms for children, for Coral. Would those rooms ever be built? It was there awaiting us... My mind shut it away.

"But what keeps you in Spain all these years?" Amparo insisted as she brushed her long hair.

"Cante." I was pulling a mass of green ruffles off a hanger. "Cante keeps me. There are jobs for dancers in America, and good guitar. But no cante." Crowds might flock to the dancing, but cante was the soul of Flamenco. Dancing was just the lace around the edges. I knew that. I would stay in Spain as long as they would let me dance here. I pulled my skirt into place, shimmying to zip but catching the zipper anyway. Amparo picked at it, while I explained over my shoulder,

"Flamencos don't sing a song you can hum along with. A Flamenco never sings the same way twice. It's not written down. So what foreigner can learn cante?"

I stopped. Amparo was not listening. The chasm was always there. These girls danced here so they could make a living. I made a living here so I could dance. They could not fathom my fascination with Flamenco. I could not participate in their boredom.

I savored the soft husky way the Flamenco fit his few pungent words and scat-syllables into the compás rhythm. A Gypsy drank that compás with his mother's milk. Manolito de María ... and the other rumpled old geniuses ... and my Curro singing with them since a kid ... I remembered the naked babes in the dust of Alcalá; Coral teaching her first grandbaby, my own Gypsy son, to lisp "oday, oday," laughing as he clapped his tiny white hands. I could hear the cock crow on a stark winter day; felt that old allure of Andalucía.

With a sigh, I tossed a shawl around my neck, grabbed my castanets. They dangled and clinked like wooden wind chimes. I pulled their cords around my thumbs and tightened them with my teeth. Then they caught at the shawl fringes. Twenty inches long, the silk fringes tangled easily. I picked at them as I headed out.

In the tiny green-room, the men were waiting, all in tailored black. One tuned his guitar, twanging a string to loosen it. A cleaning cloth squeaked over frets. Curro nodded and twinkled at some droll word of CaraEstaca's, whose eyes darted and fingers tugged at his vest. We women slipped in amongst them. A girl rubbed lipstick off her front teeth. Rubio's girlfriend brushed off his shoulders.

Castanets, tightened and tested, chirped and hushed.

I pressed in the hairpins loosening at the back of my neck and shivered. Shyly I kept my eyes averted, peering beyond the men to the stage, to the row of chairs awaiting us. Chato snapped his arms forward to free his cufflinks from his jacket sleeve, then reached behind someone to hit the light switches.

Costumed, groomed, and tuned, we all sauntered into the daylight of the stage and took our places. The Flamenco Cuadro at Los Rombos, an hour show, was beginning. The guitars raked out a familiar jaunty song. Castanets chirruped gaily. Girls in bobbing colors shouted encouragement to the rhythm -- audacious banter that roused and excited.

"*Ole, Brujo.*"

"*Vamo' a Sevilla.*"

"*Vámono', 'quillo.*"

"*Asa, Pedrito.*"

In pairs we danced Sevillanas. I danced happily in the cool green with a sheen to it. The white silk shawl shimmered around my neck, hung down in long fringe, like icicles over green lawn. The shawl and the rose low on my high head, I knew, underscored the whites of my eyes.

I felt hospitable, as if the stage were my own living room, and the audience were friends who had dropped by. I glided with rakish confidence, my raised curling arms framed an irrepressible grin. Castanets whirred like an ensemble of ratchets. I preferred to snap fingers and clap like Gypsies did, but even Gypsies on stage danced Sevillanas with castanets. I tolerated it fondly, this regional folk dance of my beloved Seville, which I had danced in the Spring Fair there. Dipping and turning I danced, flowing past each partner with the easy draw and pause of a matador. Languid and smiling, I moved as though suspended between delight and tranquility.

Thirty

At the water's lapping edge, in the glare of beach-light, my black-lashed stage eyes were reduced to pink-lidded squint. My Anglo face scrubbed pale, my hair knotted like a Spanish matron's, I was dressed for town. I paused a moment, watching my child, with that old uneasiness. I remembered how Currito first played with another child on the sand, eagerly offering bucket and shovel. But after a week, that child left. Then another, who left also. And others. The beach was peopled with European tourists, and all his friends left him. After a year of it, my child stopped making friends. He would fill his bucket listlessly, wade in the surf holding his father's hand, then just stand watching the water while Curro swam 'way out to sea.

Today Currito squealed and chased his ball. I watched them play soccer, molasses Papá and honey son. They kicked more sand than ball, Curro's springing curls powdered, giggling child taking dives. Satisfied, I waved, then headed to the village for groceries.

At the meat shop I greeted Amparo, with her own washed face and shopping basket. With no explanation, Amparo suddenly said, "There is a Gypsy family I want you to see. Do you have time? Come with me and meet Chato's family."

Chato, the lead singer in our cuadro at Los Rombos, I knew, was a Catalan Gypsy, native to Palma, Mallorca. Chato had glass blue eyes and an abundance of princely nose hanging down over his mouth, way beyond what was necessary for smelling. His great dignity outweighed both name and nose. He was a strong Gypsy of discretion and personal power, who led the men of our cuadro. His presence at work comforted like each reappearance of the hero on the movie screen. My own husband, darker and an Andalucían Gypsy, sang with much greater depth and soul-out intensity. But, Curro's nose was very small, his presence seldom soothed, and he commanded no one.

Half an hour later, as I entered Chato's home, it seemed a silent gallery of faces. All Gypsy faces -- young ones, old ones, pubescent boy ones, ugly aunts, unmarried daughters, chunky cousin, skinny in-law; a hawk-nosed, dark-haired, keen-eyed gathering of the Gypsy clan. They eyed me coolly, a few over their shoulder, some with dislike, some disinterest, all polite. Obviously, the natural family conversation had subsided at my introduction into the small crowded parlor.

Chato was not home. I saw amongst the faces there, some echoes of his nose, his eyes, of that magnificence which made him heir apparent to head of the clan. But he was not yet chief. Flanked by that Gypsy gathering, sat his father: the king of Egypt, by his fearlessness, his nobility, and absolute reign in the room. The father was white-haired, voluble, warm. He was sitting in state awaiting the noon family meal. Wine had been passed. I was seated opposite him and handed a glass.

"Well, now," he began, blue eyes crinkling, "Amparo says you're married to a Gypsy. Do you like Gypsies?"

The gallery hushed. I had been challenged. The question was a Gypsy's trap to catch the hypocrite, the gypsophile, the sycophant, the slummer, the tourist, the promiscuous, the racist, the missionary, the weakling, the dope, the coward -- in a word, the Gachí. Did I merit the dignity of this Gypsy company even for one glass of wine? I felt the pull of piercing eyes upon me.

I looked him in that blueness and shrugged my shoulders and smiled, "How should I know if I like Gypsies. I like MINE."

He laughed his approval. With a few nods, faces softened, conversations began, wine glasses refreshed. An old woman brought a small dish of giblets stewed in wine. The father ceremoniously fed me his first forkful. The morsel tasted heavenly, so did the wine.

Their chicken dinner, for sure a bird killed and cleaned by them that morning, according to old Gypsy custom, was ready to serve. So we two dancers said goodbye.

તે તે તે   ન ન ન

Soon after that honor, my dancing mellowed. Amparo left for Seville, and my new black dancing dress was the sister of hers. Never was I more beautiful than in that black dress. Wearing it, my Soleá turned to art. Instead of repeating the same stiff dance I had learned years before in the Gachó's academy, I began to flow and recede with the music, to be fed by the cante, to merge into rhythm of the clan-hands behind me. My soul joined the cuadro.

In great blissful moments, nothing else existed but me and Flamenco. Flamenco, a creation of beauty, by souls united in anguish. United. For a precious while every evening, the abstract passions of the clan of man were mine. And I belonged.

అఅఅ ಆಆಆ

Shouting, stomping and clapping the tricky, wacky rhythm of Bulerías, everyone was on stage. It was the most alive moment of the evening, the closing group number of the third show at Los Rombos. Five dancers sat in motley Gypsy colors, scarves and bangles, sat with elbows akimbo, taunting the audience.

I sat amongst them on the edge of my chair, my feet apart and skirt bunched between them. My loose hair was a dark mane of energy, my eyes danced devilish. I gestured and grimaced in funky Gypsy fashion, all the while tapping a foot and clapping. Suddenly out of my seat, I drew menacingly up. I circled the floor audaciously, pacing to the beat with bragging toss of head. My weighted skirt of patched gingham strips swirled and billowed. Gold coins cascaded from my ears. Earrings and laughing eyes, I knew, caught the footlights and dazzled the people, as I flipped my skirt, turned in rhythm, stomped some counter rhythm with comical stops and starts ... Then, over my shoulder I shot a jeering glance at the crowd, and paused dead still for an impish instant. Scurrying back, I landed statue-still with a stop in the music, seated in my chair, grinning, as if I hadn't yet gotten up.

After each woman danced such a sampling, all came forward together, pounding out the foot rhythm. Accelerating like a cadre of snare drums, we turned, spinning skirts, then paced offstage in a squatting line, with mocking hand gestures, each with her own Bulerías burlesque of Flamenco.

Puffing and chortling, we dancers nudged each other through the green-room door, pattered up the stairs, flocked to the dressing rooms to undress.

"Oh-hoo, that guy at the front table claps constantly - could really throw you off compás."

"Lucky Chato's palmas can drown him out."

"Yeah, well Chato's palmas drowned out my footwork, too."

"Well, hey, just don't work so hard, you'll get paid the same."

We chattered as we changed, bumping into each other, handing over a hanger, loaning a hairclip. Amparo and the other girl, hair glued back with sweat, combed and dressed, headed for the bar. I stayed alone in my robe. Hanging my wet white dance bodice, I pondered again that insignificant encounter in Chato's house and I wondered why it was so engraved in my heart.

Suddenly, it came clear. I turned quickly to my image in the mirror. My hair still tossed from dancing, stood out like an electric shock around my high-voltage face, eyes deep and arrested, staring back at me. The awareness ripped through me. That had been my initiation.

I had stopped needing to belong, and so was accepted. I had stopped working for the approval of others, and began to approve of myself. Gypsies had drawn me by their autonomy. In that Gypsy home, I found my own.

Thirty-one

"*Le le le le lay* ..." Curro crooned with that voice which absolved him of all his sins. That voice which was my soul made sound.

Impaled by his song, I froze, while those on either side of me continued their palmas. I sat motionless, hand on knee, head lowered to charge. Chest forth, like an arched beast, I pulled out of my chair. I left the others seated clapping in that half-light, as Curro's voice lured me, skirts kicking ahead of me, downstage into my smouldering light, into my place alone on that stage.

The black suits behind me no longer intimidated me. They were kinfolk, the foundation of my dance. And I wore black too. Wrapped in my beloved new black dress tailored to my body like a glove, the long swing and sway of it pulled at my legs like surf. The arcs and swirls of my best fuchsia underskirts marked the compás. My conversion dress unleashed the fury of my depths, the power of my restraint. In mourning black, in stark photo black, in professional black, I became my Soleá.

Si al infierno que te vayas, me tendría que ir contigo
Pues quien fuera in tu compañá lleva la gloria consigo

If you went to hell, I'd have to go with you
Because in your company, I'd be in glory too

Gently, Curro sang. My dance emanated from his smokey voice, rather than from my own volition. Unfolding regal and lean, stretching, reaching towards the light, gathering it, pouring it over my head, I strained towards some invisible blessing, some unknown release.

With deft heft of knee, my skirts leapt into my waiting hands, to be held back for my footwork. I drummed simple underbeat to the beauty of the guitars' exquisite melodies. Then my feet pounded the signal to silence the music, inviting my husband to sing to me again.

Curro's cry, with the rage of a wounded creature, filled me. My body winced, writhed like a soul in torment or a lover in embrace. A yearning deep in my core flamed through my veins, undulating out through my fingertips. It burned too bad to cry -- I had to dance: to violate and caress, resign and beseech, surrender and triumph. How I resisted the throb of his song, how I revelled in it. The fusion of man's music and my soul. I embodied that wild sweet cry of Solea.

The best was the journey back to my seat, just a few feet but as treacherous as getting an animal back into her cage. I launched, then turned, stopped stiff-legged with a break in the music. My hair fell like laid-back ears of a wary beast, then worked into my face to be snarled away again in another turn. With Curro's final wail, I retreated to him, then turned abruptly again, pranced in a fury and flurry of fuchsia towards my chair, in high indignation, drawing it out, covering space in exquisite tension, arriving at a full stop just as Curro's song ended. We arrived as one.

In the silence, flooded with the power of that Soleá, I stood immobile at my chair. When the applause finally broke, I turned and sat. Dazed.

Re-entry was slow, after such intensity. The prodding elbows of the girls who flanked me, startled me to my feet to take my bows. I pushed wet hair off my face, grinning shy and vulnerable. My eyes met my husband's eyes across the stage. Curro nodded curtly back. This was it. Delicious. My grin opened into my grandest smile. I bowed.

Then I turned from the audience and reached back toward Curro. It seemed a polite gesture of acknowledgment. How could the people know how powerfully his voice drove me, how his cante was what tortured that beauty out of my body. I kept my back to the audience while they clapped. I merely walked back to my seat with my eyes on my man.

❧❧❧   ❦❦❦

He said it to me that night after work. It was not an intimate moment. He said it matter-of-factly while he hung up his suitpants. I was reaching under the bedcovers, as I did every night, to iron the sheets and heat the Spanish winter damp out of our bed. He said it then, with his husky wrung-out singer's voice.

"Chochete, tonight you danced the Soleá."

I laughed, thinking he was teasing me. "Yes, Curro, I've been dancing it for years." I parked the warm iron where my tired feet would soon rest.

But something new in his voice made me look up at the Gypsy in his shirttails who could spew his soul on the stage and lift dancers into greatness. He was solemn.

"No, woman, tonight you danced the Soleá."

Awash with awe, I had no response. That was the only word of praise Curro ever gave me; the highest word of praise he could possibly give.

I had danced the Soleá.

Thirty-two

"Goddammit!" glass shattered. In a rage, Curro deliberately dashed it to the kitchen floor. His little boy, silently eating watermelon, stopped mid-chew as the glass and his Papá's voice exploded simultaneously. The child spat his mouthful onto the table as his eyes jumped from the slivers of light on the linoleum to his father's scary face. While Curro stormed about the kitchen, Currito sat as still as a cornered creature.

The child refused to ever eat melon again. He began to prefer his mother's nearness, to shy away from his Papá. And he stopped obeying him. Could a man lose the respect of a three-year-old?

Curro's anger at the world was spilling over into his home. I never knew why he was mad. Once an eager little girl who struggled and failed to make my mommy happy, I now heaved blindly against my husband's misery.

The world irritated him, so he had the refuge of his own house. But he wasn't happy. People were against him, so his wife was loyal and adoring. But he wasn't happy. Lonely lifelong, so he had his own son. But he wasn't happy. Hunger frightened him, so he had a good job. But he wasn't happy. His brothers were launched, so his mother no longer burdened him. But he wasn't happy. Not yet admitting that this man might never be happy, I kept trying: dancing by night, and dancing my peculiar eggshell dance around him by day. Trying to keep the peace, desperate to keep our perfect life working. The more I tried, the more irritable he grew.

Curro's resentment smoldered, then erupted, then smoldered on. And maybe I was fatigued; maybe my diplomacy had grown thin. He used to say, "You know how to hit and hide your hand."

Perhaps it was the pressure of being together around the clock, at home and work. The pressure of fifteen volatile artistic personalities on one tiny stage -- eight shows a week, no rest, no break. We no longer laughed together. Perhaps Curro needed to carouse with buddies after work like he did in Barcelona, to release the work tension.

But carousing at dawn was not enough. Even in Barcelona I had heard Curro's chronic guitar complaint. Here in Mallorca, once again, he was complaining that the guitars were not giving him his "tones," the chordal changes he needed when singing. I never knew if it was due to a hearing loss, or if it was a guitarist's revenge on an obnoxious singer. I suspected that he would forget what to sing, and so graft in a verse from some other cante - an eclectic style in vogue then - and expect the guitar to switch modes mid-stream at inconvenient times.

Before a show, I would bring Curro a drink from the bar to the green-room where the men waited to go on; hoping to keep him from the bar. He complained that I brought too much ice, or the wrong soda. Gypsies minded their own business. But once Chato spoke up, "Hey man, slack off, she's a good woman." It startled me into noticing that not all men were hateful ingrates, that my situation was getting worse than I let myself believe.

It was more than alcohol, for he could be charming drunk, and nasty sober; mean drunk and happy sober. All Flamencos drank, but they weren't crazy. Maybe it was blood sugar gone awry or brain signals askew. The brain seizures of royalty ran through Gypsy families, too. I never knew.

ઉપ ઉપ ઉપ   ઉપ ઉપ ઉપ

Like a round of shots, palmas fired to open the Flamenco cuadro at Los Rombos. Black polka dots, the size of quarters, spilled over my knees, piled around my tapping black shoes. Flanking mine, blue and white and green and red knees jumped like keys on a player piano, as dancers' feet under mounds of ruffles pounded the downbeat. A row of clapping palmas machine-gunned. Castanets hung at cleavages. Painted mouths called and taunted.

Men stood at attention behind us, two male dancers in fitted long pants, and three suited singers with their somber Gypsy presence, all firing compás with feet and hands. The full cuadro of Los Rombos was clapping and chanting a jaleo. It was the opening number of the second show of the night.

A full house of tourists and Spaniards sat in shadow beyond hot stage lights and the raw wooden floor of the tablao. It was my tablao. This was the stage where my dancing ripened. This wooden stage, protected by lights and competent musicians, was my terrain. A seasoned dancer now, my solo would be one of the climaxes of the show.

Many of these beflowered cuadro girls flanking me were Pulpón's select from Seville. Smug girls, these Seville girls, in the finest of costumes, well-painted, and nicely shod. Amongst them, I held my own. My face was built for the stage. The curve of my cheek could be seen from any chair in the house, my masterfully-painted, expressive eyes drew all other eyes. I was aware of how I overshadowed those Seville girls on stage, how my candid delight, my avid lust for dancing, outshone their scornful style. But what mattered was that Curro praised me here. The only praise I ever treasured. Since then it sang in my heart like a hymn.

"Tonight you danced the Soleá."

As I clapped and shouted, Curro stood somewhere behind me, safely on stage working. My contentment on this stage nearly erased the Curro-worry, that chronic uneasiness he gave me. Soon he would be singing again for me to dance, carrying me away on his matchless cante, his tragic voice entering my marrow. Dancing to his cante provoked in me the joy of being alive and the relief of dying. My impossible Curro.

His brother, Rubio, stood clapping behind me, too. New to the stage, Rubio was learning quickly -- bright and able man that I always knew he was. Curro and I gave Rubio his life when we brought him out of Alcalá.

I sneaked a reassuring glance at Chato, the wise city Gypsy who led the cuadro. With sideburns like porkchops, Chato was engrossed in setting pace with his powerful hands.

Two guitarists draped waiting arms over mute upright guitars as though over the shoulders of sweethearts on their night off. The two guitars would soon be playing together, with that luxurious musical tinkling sound that was the mark of a superior Flamenco tablao.

Yes, this was my tablao. And my Curro sang for me here. All the diamonds, all the kingdoms, could not match this wealth.

A que sí, a que sí, los chugales se matan con flí
A que no, a que no, habichuelas, garbanzos y arroz
Yes, yes, lice are killed like this
No, no, no, beans, garbanzos and rice.

Like a jump rope rhyme, the girls chanted it, to the snap of their Bulerías palmas. Seated in my red wicker chair, to the popping of perfect palmas, I chanted with them:

Una vez que me embarqué, Mi barquito se fué a pique.
Y me dijo el capitán, 'Nada, Felipe, nada, Felipe'
Once when I embarked, My little boat capsized
And the captain told me, Swim, Philip, swim.

Then it happened.

Suddenly, into the center of my wooden tablao, just beyond my feet, from nowhere, a man hit the floor.

"Curro!"

I screamed in horror, hands over ears. Curro was face down in his tidy black suit, his arms and legs were flailing. Epileptic fit? Shot in the back? Dying? No, it was worse. Horrified, it dawned on me. Curro was swimming. Dismayed, I realized that my husband had dove to swim on the floor, to mime what the girls were chanting. Worse than dying, he was trying to be funny. His last Gypsy dignity died with that dive.

Shrieking, I ejected from my chair, mid-jaleo, and stumbled across the stage. I stepped on girls' skirts, pushed Chato aside. Without looking back at my man on his face in the lights, I left the stage.

Shot by shame, ashamed to death, I fled. I raced upstairs two at a time. I tore costumes, hangers and all, off the rack and stuffed them into the wicker trunk. Castanets, earrings, flowers, shawls. My bowels iced with indignation, I was all packed ready to leave Los Rombos, ready to leave the job of my life, ten minutes after the second show had begun.

I did not know where I was going nor why. But I knew I was getting out. I could never look at that stage again. With the raised hackles of a cornered animal, I would have climbed over anyone who tried to keep me at Los Rombos.

Curro found me standing alone in my empty dressing room, while everyone else was on stage.

"Woman, what is the matter ...?"

"Out!" I shrilled. "Getting out. I'm through. OUT!" I started tugging frantically on the wicker trunk. Obediently, Curro helped me heave and struggle it down the steps, out the back door. Unwieldy as a coffin, we carried it along the sidewalk and upstairs to our door. He left me there and returned to work.

I paid the sitter and told her not to come back. I checked the sleeping child and closed his door. I dragged my trunk down the long hallway to my bedroom, set it by the side of my bed. I washed off my stage face, then stared at the face in the bathroom mirror, at the dreary face of "a school teacher from Des Moines," with casualty eyes, stricken eyes, staring back at me. I pulled off my clothes, put on a T-shirt, turned out the light, and got into bed. For a performing dancer this was midday, and no time to be in bed. Undanced, unsleepy, I lay tense and cold.

And I stared at the dark. I watched it swell and spin. In that dark, I saw my Curro take that dive. I heard myself shrieking. I saw myself standing in that empty dressing room alone. Again he was on the floor and I was shrieking. I watched him flailing on the floor and my mind become one long shriek. What had I done? What urge from hell sent me out of my beloved red wicker chair? Stronger than the urge to reach air when drowning, was that urge to get off that stage where my husband lay face down. My mind boggled with the ruin of it all. Over and over I replayed it. His dive, my shriek, the dressing room stripped of my costumes. Over and over again. And again. I forgot where I was, as I watched the fatal scene spinning before me in the dark. I wondered if this were delirium and I soon would be cured. In fetal huddle, facing my trunk in the dark, totally numbed, I was barely breathing.

Then I heard Curro come in. I heard him lock the front door. I heard him urinate and flush, then rustle in our room. I listened to his shoes drop. Heard the click of the hanger as he hung up his suit. The bed tipped his way as he climbed in, and I bobbed and jiggled like a cadaver. Silence.

"Goddammit!" roared Curro, and the covers flew off of me. He stood up on the bed and marched to the foot and jumped off, causing me to bounce on the bed like a ball on a paddle.

White pain stabbed my unprepared eyes as he turned on the light. I whined involuntarily and covered my face with my arm.

"I can't sleep," he announced through clenched teeth. "And if I can't sleep, you're not sleeping either." He lay back down stiffly beside me, dressed in his socks and underwear.

"The Gachó fired me," my rabid husband snarled. "You quit, so the son of a bitch fired me, too." And he swore.

"Bitch, look at me," he growled. "Look at me," he demanded shrilly and fisted the bed. I turned toward him and squinted in the searing light.

"Don't you fall asleep. You are one ..." And he began to call me filthy things. He ranted and spun on the bed for hours, raving and swearing, lying stiffly by my side in that torturous white light. If I looked away, he pounded the bed until I returned my gaze to him. All night long.

At dawn he dozed off. Without any sleep, I arose to attend to the child.

Thirty-three

The three days and nights that followed were one endless, sleepless nightmare. Curro was so riled that he refused to let me sleep at all. His rage reached insanity as we waited for payday. Other years I would have made love with him to draw off his ire. Since that dive, I could no longer do it. And he was too enraged to be touched. So his tension mounted daily. Hate began.

"What am I doing in this hole? I can work anywhere in Spain. Pulpón will have jobs for me now," spewed Curro while dressing.

"Yes, Curro, we'll feel better back in our little house."

"We'll catch the boat, as soon as we're paid. You get everything packed," he ordered.

"Yes, I'm packing. But look. Currito was so sea sick coming. Curro, let's fly back. We can afford it."

"No flying. I say what goes, and we're going on the boat. You just pack up and shut up."

Secretly I packed our belongings in separate suitcases. I carefully washed my dance blouses, rearranged all my costumes in the wicker trunk. How many times had I packed, with pain and shame, after a job finished dishonorably. How many disappointments. Barcelona, Marbella,

Seville, now here in Mallorca. Grimly I packed, while the worried child looked on. My mind deadened, I held the little boy and reassured him automatically. I packed his things, peeled the black paper off his windows, sat with him on the beach staring out to sea. I pinched sand and watched it sift back, hour-glass back onto the beach, while my son poked the sand with his shovel.

I knew, without knowing why, that I was unable to work again on the same stage with Curro. And yet, if I left him and went to work elsewhere in Spain, he would charge after me like an enraged bull, pursue and persecute me.

From the restaurant I brought up some beef and potato stew to share with Currito. The child was no hungrier than I was. He studied my tormented expression with worried round eyes.

"Well, Chiqui, then here's flan." I removed the stew bowl and offered the golden custard, which the child ignored as well.

"Then, here's a bite for you," and I spooned it to him. "Good. Bite for me. Mmmmmmm." The burnt sugar slipped down my throat, tasteless, bitter.

Curro had been my only friend, and now he was lost to me. That dive had triggered an irreversible revulsion in me. But I was not yet aware of that. I had stood by him before and thought I could easily do it again, if he would just once more smile his sleepy sensual smile. If he would just hold and kiss his son, he still might be able to watch the child grow up.

But Curro stormed in and out of that beach apartment, always enraged, blaming, hateful. He made no move towards the child. Never allowed a smile. And at night he tormented his wife with the white light. Days bled into one another, with no sleep to distinguish them. Susana, who had been useful and beautiful, was now broken-off, useless. I no longer had purpose ... except to keep this child safe.

"*Mamá, mírame, mírame*. Lookee, Mommy, lookee me!" Currito whizzed down the narrow apartment hallway on his squeaking tricycle, free-wheeling with feet off the pedals once he had built up speed. The boy stopped cold as his father entered. Curro ignored the child, charged down the hall, began muttering and swearing in the bedroom. Clothes flew around the room.

"What do you want?" I rushed to the bedroom door to find him tearing apart the neatly packed suitcases.

"Your scissors. Where are those damned scissors!?"

"My sewing scissors?"

"Where are they? I need them now!"

"Hold on, Curro. I'll get them" I fished them out of a side pocket, handed them over quizzically.

"I'm going after that Gachó. It's all his fault and I'm going to get him."

"What's all his fault? What Gachó?"

"Everything. The owner of Los Rombos, Don Sebastian. He started it all, and I'm going after him. With these." He held up my fine little American sewing scissors, then pocketed them at his chest.

"Oh, Curro, listen. Please listen to me," I was actually wringing my hands -- lacing and squeezing my fingers. I begged with voice deep with pain, on the verge of wailing. "Currete, you are a very rich man. You have everything. You have a son. Look at him. He is your son."

Curro did not even glance at the child in the doorway on the tricycle.

"You have a loyal wife. You own a beautiful house with a lemon tree and an olive. You're a fine Flamenco singer. You can work anywhere. Curro, don't waste it all. Don't throw it away. You could lose everything you have. Don't waste it. Appreciate what you have." I was crying with gargoyle face. I felt my face lock into a grimace like a tragic mask, drooling.

He pushed me aside, stepped around the child without even a word, not one affectionate gesture, and stormed out.

From then on, Curro hung out around town, restlessly bragging that he would find opportunity to stab the Gachó. Cowardly talk, I knew, for he would even send me on payday. He would not face the man.

తతత ళళళ

"Sit down, Susana." Don Sebastian's voice brimmed with concern, so I obeyed. "How are you?" he asked, his eyes searching mine.

I could not answer. I had forgotten the handy little "Fine" one uses to stuff such moments.

The owner of Los Rombos was staring at me. I knew he

was trying to be sure that this haggard woman across his desk was the delightful dancer who graced his stage a week ago. Without my stage make-up I looked a different vintage. And after these days of torment, my face hung heavy.

"Well ... then," he counted out our severance pay and placed the cash in my open hand. I clutched it, but did not move to pocket it.

"Susana," there was pity in his eyes. I had seen it in Pulpón's eyes before. I held my head high.

"Yes."

"You are in trouble. That man of yours is crazy."

"I know." I studied the paperweight on his desk, a polished black rock. Figured it had a significance for him. It meant nothing to me. Everything meant nothing to me. Anymore. I felt as though I were recuperating from surgery. Someone had just removed my entire heart. "He'll be better once he gets home," I managed.

"Do you know a lawyer down there in Seville?"

"A lawyer ...?" A lawyer. I thought of CocaCola, of Joaquin, and nearly snickered. I did not even know anyone who pronounced the word.

"It's illegal for a woman to leave her husband. He can have you put in jail. That's the old Spanish law. I'm not sure ... It still might be in effect in the Province of Seville."

"Jesus." I stared at the man's brown tweed jacket. I avoided his eyes and my plight mirrored in them.

"Do you have money?"

"Only this." I held up the salaries he had just paid me. "And what we've saved here ..."

"Do you have people back home in America who can help you?"

"Yes ... my sister ..." I gazed sidelong at the black telephone on his desk. I had not seen many phones in Spain.

"Call her. Use this phone. Be my guest. Get her to send you a ticket out of here."

I hesitated, my eyes still on the phone.

"No. Thank you." I stood up very tall and looked down into his merciful brown eyes. "You are very kind," I said with dignity. "But you don't know Curro. We'll be fine."

I left. I could not risk it. If the Gachó mentioned that telephone call to someone and it got back to Curro, I would be dead.

❧❧❧ ❦❦❦

"Good! Just one more bite of egg!" I scraped the cup and spooned dregs into the child's open mouth. My gritty sleep-deprived eyes stretched wide, seeking lubrication, then folded back into bales of wrinkled lids. To my reeling mind, the sunlight from the kitchen window seemed sheer, tinny.

"Oh, look," I pointed out the window. The sparkling harbor glinted back up to us. "There goes your little blue boat. See it?"

The child with egg on face and bright morning eyes, searched.

"Chug-chug-chug. Taking Mommy and Papá and

Currito back home to Seville." The boy nodded with excitement as he chewed and clapped hands.

"Done? Good for you. Here's your orange juice and your banana." I froze. I heard the front door and Curro's strides the length of the corridor. He paused at the kitchen to announce, "I have to go to the police."

"The police! What for?!" I dropped the banana on the table and followed him to the bedroom, my robe flapping.

"The Gachó at Los Rombos turned me in. Son of a bitch. I told you he was a son of a bitch." Curro was pulling off his pants.

"Will they put you in jail?"

"No, stupid. I just have to report to them. At headquarters in Palma. I'll only be gone a few hours." He was wound tense, but somber. After days of ranting, Curro was in control of himself.

"Will you be all right?" I remembered the Guardia Civil's treatment of Gypsies.

"Yes, I'll be all right, woman. Shut up. Iron me a shirt."

I took one of his shirts out of the suitcase and ironed quickly on the open bed. The police. Worrisome word. In all of Curro's skirmishes, the police had never even been mentioned. He had never received a summons before. Was this the beginning? Was I going to raise this boy while his father was in and out of prison? Revulsion and terror curdled my stomach. I ironed and wrinkled and ironed out the wrinkles, then wrinkled again.

Finally I hung the shirt on the door. I was just straightening out the bed when Curro returned from shaving.

"Bitch, this shirt looks like shit." He threw it at me, and I got a cup of water from the kitchen and started over.

His black curls got a careful combing. He moved deliberately with a cold clarity. Maybe he was a little scared, maybe the threat of police just sobered him appropriately. Dressed in his best mohair suit, Curro prepared to leave.

Frightened for him, I followed him down the hall to the door. Sticky-eyed, and squinting, my exhausted mind moved in a stumbling distorted fashion. Strands of my uncombed hair blew wild when he opened the door of our high seaside home. He turned. Crazed eyes, like the eyes of a rearing horse, peered at me.

Suddenly my eyeballs exploded, my head snapped to the side with a bang that echoed down the hall of the windy corridor.

Curro had slapped me.

I leaned back against the wall, speechless. I watched him move to leave, then turn again. He glowered hate. Tiny transversal tensions pulled his eyes open, taut, like moth specimens. Just before slamming shut the door, he spit his promise, "And that's not the last time I hit you."

Thirty-four

It certainly was. He never hit me again because he never saw me again. That slap, like a lone sniper's shot out of nowhere, changed my history. The closing shot.

I looked back down the hall to see the child standing next to his dropped banana, mouth hanging, staring at his distraught, mindless mother.

I gathered him up, held him tight in the warmth of the kitchen window, summoning strength. Then while the frightened boy watched, my trembling hand managed to write three letters to Curro. One, I left in the apartment, telling Curro that I was flying with the boy to Seville. One, mailed to our empty house in Seville, instructing Curro to go to his mother's in Alcalá for another note. The one mailed to his mother's house, he would read with Coral nearby to console him. It told him that his wife and son had fled to America, never to return; and he was left with his own beautiful home in Seville, with a lemon tree and an olive.

I dressed quickly, closed suitcases, sent for a cab. Grabbing money, clothes, my wicker trunk full of costumes, and my three-year-old child, I left. The taxi jounced us to the airport. My stomach was iced by the fear that I had miscalculated my escape and Curro would catch up with me.

Child in arms at the airport counter, I asked for the next flight leaving Spain. Shivering, I glanced back at the entrance, watched the cabby wrestling with my trunk. Relief and grief dizzied me when they told me, "You're in luck, Señora. A plane leaves for London in twenty minutes."

෴෴෴ ෴෴෴

So there I was, alone again in London, this time fleeing a mad Gypsy, with his tiny stolen child.

Not one airport, London was a conglomerate of airports. How to get from one to the other, a distraught pedestrian in a vehicle's world? Huge pile of luggage toppled off my cart. Clumsy peasant wicker truck -- oh, where was my donkey - the "*borrico*" promised to this child? Black square-backed limousines rushing by from unexpected directions. I let go of the child at a busy curb to catch my falling load. I stepped out into oncoming cars. I pushed up ramps blindly, scream-ing in fright at the bewildered little boy who kept forgetting to hold on to my coattail. Into a maze of parking levels -- cars whooshing out at me.

I waited in London airport for two days, until my sister could manage to send me a ticket back to California. Like a river-bottom Gypsy, I camped next to my wicker trunk, a bed of stale costumes for my son, on the floor of London airport, a cruel hatchery of urgent matters, of emergency. The ceiling was too high. Alien, all artificial, not a speck of God's reassurance in sight - no tree, no loam, no splintery wooden siding.

I did not exist, but I was in a hurry. Anonymity. And endless waiting. Faces were all familiar - all somber or smiling, waiting, pacing, rushing faces, no more strange than the faces in my life.

My soul was so uneasy, so anxious, it seemed to leave me. My eyes went out of focus, my mind numb, my feet cold. My fidgety little boy would not let me sleep; my anguish would not let me awaken. I scolded my son and jerked his arm, and he studied me with burnt eyes. I held him and kissed the hair off his hot forehead, to avoid his eyes. His warmth against my belly comforted me. Something inside me was rotten, like the dark gut of a murderer who cannot tolerate the enormity of his crime.

In Spain, like a drowning person, I had grabbed at whatever was in reach - at Curro - to regain the surface of my life. Then I took away with me Curro's only treasure - his son, the sun of his sky. And I left behind my only treasure - that once upon a time Curro sang for me, and I danced the Soleá.

Closing my eyes to erase how lost and small I was in this dome of an airport, I waited in despair to go home.

Home?

Behind my lowered lids, the purple dark receded and I saw ugly Angelita dancing sublime against the careless sky. Home for Angelita? Home was from whence she raised her arms. Was something in the core of her. Deaf CaraEstaca, Gypsy machine -- his power came from his core. And Maruja's passion, and Manolito de Maria's simplicity, and Rubio's compassion, and Coral's whimsy. I had their bones, their power, their passion, compassion, whimsy, simplicity, in my core. When Curro sang, he got into where the pain was. Wrestling with his own soul, he tempered that pain into beauty of song. And that painful beauty knew how to spill from my body when I danced.

I took a long long breath.

Home was a place deep in my heart, my being. A decent place. A new place. A place that Flamenco showed me. A place all my own. A place that wrought my dance ... and my life ... and me.

I was waiting, in an airport going somewhere. And I was already home.

END

Epilogue

Huge Gypsy heads squint out from their posterboards over a cluster of students in the middle of a small gymnasium floor at UCLA. Susana stands lecturing at a podium.

"There are perhaps five million Gypsies living all over the world today. Gypsies tend to be nomads. They don't live very long in one place. There is no written history about Gypsies. A nomad is not going to pack a lot of books, so how can he maintain a history of himself? They don't talk about themselves. In the stacks of the UCLA library, I read every book there was on Gypsies, and I could carry all the books at once to the reading table. Half were inaccurate fantasy."

Stretch of spine, lift of head, tilt of face, mark Susana as a dancer. Her fluid arms reach towards a mounted map.

"The best theory on the origin of Gypsies, I think, comes from studying their language. Gypsies, no matter where they are in the world, speak a language called Romani. They all speak dialects of Romani mixed with the languages of the places where they have been living. And that's how their path can be traced. It is thought that Gypsies originated in India. Romani comes from Sanskrit, the mother language of India, and a dead language now.

Judging by the changes which have taken place in Sanskrit since 1000 A.D., Gypsies must have left India and started their migrations sometime around then. And there are some people in Northwestern India whose lifestyle and behavior still seem Gypsy.

"They slowly migrated through the Middle East, then forked. Some roamed all through northern Europe. Others came across North Africa and went over into Spain, where they settled in Andalucia. These Spanish Gypsies, then, created Flamenco in Andalucia. No other Gypsies anywhere else in the world do Flamenco. Why? That we will explore in this six-week extension class, as we learn what Flamenco really is."

Without her stage makeup, Susana's face is not beautiful. Arresting, perhaps, with shadowed cheekbone and large, lidded eyes. Ultimately expressive, her eyes might seem overcome with compassion, or with foreboding hostility, when she may be merely trying to remember your name. Her eyes are pouched prematurely, as though she has lived too hard. Susana's eyes dance eagerly now, as she lectures about her beloved Gypsy Flamenco.

"We trace the trail of the Gitanos, Spanish Gypsies, by the remnants of other languages which they have absorbed. They did not travel quickly. It took five hundred years to get from India to Spain -- time enough to adopt local languages along the way. Caló, the dialect of Gitanos, is a mixture of Spanish, Arabic, and Romani.

"I remember a break between shows at Los Rombos, a

Flamenco tablao where we worked outside of Palma, Mallorca. My husband, Curro, and I were at the bar, and I was translating for an English customer. The man was an English Gypsy. In order to prove it, he and Curro started pulling out all the Gypsy words they could remember to test on each other. They each recognized the words, but with difficulty, because they pronounced them so differently. They were pleased, for theirs was a kinship from centuries back, a special kinship that the rest of us don't share."

Enrapt, the thirty students sit on hardwood armed desks which they have pulled around her. Some are fans of hers who have watched her dance at El Cid or the Matador or the Lobero Theatre in Santa Barbara. Some are housewives with a dream; some, aspiring guitarists who want to learn to accompany dancing. She will teach Flamenco theory, which she has gleaned from thirteen years of experience. As she describes Gypsies, these people catch her zeal. Some are taking notes, some are recording on cassettes, all are engrossed.

"Gypsies have adopted customs, music, dress, names, even some racial characteristics, of the countries they travel through. So, English Gypsies are named Smith or Stanley; in Spain, Flores or Amaya. As you can see in these posters: here is an Indian Gypsy, cooking on the floor just like any Indian woman; here is an English Gypsy, blond and blue-eyed. This Spanish Gypsy looks like an Arab."

Susana's dance-heels click on the gym floor as she turns from the mounted posters to her notes at the podium. She moves like a river eddies, speaks with the conviction of any man in his element, and blushes with passion. She is very much a woman. Very much a human. Very self-assured.

"Gypsies all over the world share some common characteristics. Let's look at those. Gypsies are everywhere feared or mistrusted by non-Gypsies. People of fixed residency always regard nomads as dangerous, no matter what kind of nomads they are. Certainly Gypsies have their own special reasons for being especially disliked. Gypsies are bad, as judged by our Judeo-Christian ethics. They don't value labor. They don't have our sense of honor, of telling the truth, our sense of consistency and commitment. They have their own honor system. They are very elusive and exclusive. No matter where they are in the world, their sense of identity is primarily as a Gypsy, of the Gypsy "race", and separate from non-Gypsies. Gypsies tend to despise non-Gypsies and consider them inferior. They call them Gaché, which originally meant 'bumpkin' or 'sucker,' someone foolish enough to grunt and sweat in the fields. Gypsies maintain themselves in an aura of mystery, a fog, to keep the Gaché from knowing much about them. They use a lie. That is, they use the truth any way they want. They'll tell part of it, tell all of it, tell none of it. And you never know which. That is their camouflage, a fine protection against social injustice."

Indignation raises Susana's voice and sparks her eyes. She is speaking from much more than what she learned in the library stacks. Her words are pulled from something in her very core, something which is not being told. Some students are wondering whether they will hear her full story in this college gymnasium ...

"They tend to be very fine 'psychologists.' My mother-in-law, Coral, a Gitana, is ignorant and illiterate. But she can smell things, she has a knowing. The first day she met me, I had only known her son for a couple of weeks and later she told him, 'She's yours.' I wouldn't become intimate with him for many months yet, but she already knew. And she knew when I was expecting my son, weeks before I knew, by the look in my eyes. She had that sense. And most Gypsies I knew were that way. I think it is something about being outside of society, looking in. They just learn to read people by watching them rather than being involved with them. Look at it like this. A Gachó is a fool inside of society, so dependent upon acceptance that he cannot see clearly. A Gypsy is wise, outside of society with no social ambition to blind him.

"So of course, this perception, this instinct, aids Gypsies in one of their greatest sports."

She flips a note card on the podium. Her full woman's voice chokes and lofts in delight, as though on the verge of laughing or shouting. There is a quality of unshed tears crackling behind it, or perhaps uncontainable excitement. She is intense.

"Worldwide, throughout history, Gypsies love to gyp Gaché. It is a sport, a great art. It is a marvelous pastime, and it is their major livelihood. They also cheat each other, there is no honor among thieves. The more Gypsy you are, the harder it is for your fellow Gypsy to fathom you. It is a Gypsy status match.

"They fool us Gaché by exploiting our self-deceptions, our self-importance, our greed, our bureaucracy and hypocrisy. That happened in the 1500's and it happens today in America. They can outsmart computers. They were getting airline companies to send them tickets without a check, then cashing in the ticket for money. They con the police department. Some have two or three authentic driver's licenses, each with different names on them.

"During the Middle Ages, remember, the Moslems were not only in Spain, they were in the Holy Land. The European Christians were crusading East to free the Holy Land from the infidels. If you crusaded, you carried a letter from the Church stating that you were on this Crusade as penance, and the townspeople and monasteries were to give you food and shelter to help you along your road. The Gypsies found it a marvelous opportunity.

"They would go to the archbishops and obtain papal letters of protection. Fine way to get free room and board and a respite from persecution. They would use any story that worked, borrowing from local folklore. They got the name Gypsy from their story that they were Egyptians; that they were the lost tribes of Israel, descendants of Cain, under some sort of a curse and must travel the earth; that they had originally fabricated the nails that went into Christ's cross; or had been forced under torture by Moslems to deny Christ, and felt so badly about it, that they confessed and repented and could be forgiven if they would travel and not sleep in a bed for seven years!"

Susana chortles at the irreverence. "They hadn't slept in a bed for centuries," she pounds her podium, "but these poor suffering penitents were forsaking a bed for seven years!"

Her cheeks flex; and her words flow into laughter as smoothly as her body flows into another pose, leaning forward on the podium with hunched shoulders, then turning, skirts aswirl, to pace the room.

"Although the Church represented religious devotion, it was also the biggest business, the most powerful political body -- a conflict of interest which engendered some religious hypocrisy. And no matter what the century, Gypsies found ways of exploiting that hypocrisy. A Gypsy woman telling your fortune will pray and mix in religion constantly. They profess the religion of their surroundings. Gypsies arrived in Spain just as Moslems were being evicted by the Catholic Monarchs. So, of course, Gypsies would profess Catholicism. My husband, like all his fellows, was Catholic, but he never entered a church, except for a wedding or a baptism. His mother always wore her gold Virgin medallion. Theirs is a mixture of religion and superstition and convenience.

"They exploit our desire to get something for nothing. They invented most of our con-games. Like, 'we'll sew your dollar into this handkerchief and it will turn into a hundred dollars if you sleep with it under your pillow.' After whispered incantations, you get home and find paper sewn in place of money. Tricks like that have been going on for hundreds of years and are documented. We are vulnerable in these ways and Gypsies, so long discriminated against and ostracized, have got our number.

"They were great horse-traders. They'd find an old nag, paint her up, prop her up so that she somehow looked good -- there were all kinds of tricks for fixing her teeth -- then sell her back to her unsuspecting owner. They do that now with used cars. In the USA, Gypsies are often used car dealers. Or they will go around from house to house and do bodywork on cars. Another con game is roofing. They will fix the leaks in your roof, and in the next rain, the axle grease they used washes off. Or they'll 'blacktop' your driveway.

"They are quick-change artists, you know, thinking faster than a cashier and getting more than twenty dollars change for a twenty-dollar bill.

"Know that violence and prostitution are the exception amongst Gypsies, just as they are the exception amongst Gaché. If somebody hits you on the head and steals your money, that hurts. But a Gypsy has more style. You will actually thank him as he leaves, and later you find you have been tricked. That stings. Perhaps this is why people have always been enraged by Gypsies."

Susana admires the ways of these people. Their history lives within her. Is it possible she has lived many lifetimes before this one? Has she been a Gypsy? She feels a pride in

Gypsy audacity ... like a sense of vengeance, like the faint taste of blood. She declares,

"It is their shameless charm, their fearlessness, which fascinates. In Spain they are accustomed to *mangar*, to beg -- actually the art of friendly persuasion. They won't request money, they'll charm you. Gypsy women sell carnations at the fairs. You know the flower is not worth five bucks, and she really does not charge that. But with her beguiling manner, you just cannot help it, you have to give it to her. She has a flair about her, some honesty and mirth, and she is quick as a kaleidoscope. It is worth paying her five dollars just to watch her style."

Susana rakes back her dark mane. Fine golden hoops wag at her cheeks.

"Question!" An arm is up.

"Yes?"

"I'm just curious," the young man hesitates. "How would you describe the difference between a Gypsy and a Gachó?"

"You mean, bloodline and Flamenco aside? Their gestalt, so to speak?"

"Well ... yes."

"A Gypsy can be true to himself and lie to others. A Gachó can be dishonest with himself and profess truth to others."

"Which one are you?"

Susana blushes, then grins. "I've done both." Her brows pull up and mouth pulls down in a Gypsy shrug.

"There's another place to be: true to me and true to you. I'm working on that one."

She eyes the others. "More questions?"

"Yes, please." The woman is disconcerted. "Didn't Gypsies have any acceptable...well... legitimate, professions?"

"Yes, they did: Smithery. Selling of wares or services. Working with animals. Since ancient times in India, Gypsies were famous as metal workers. The forge, all through European history -- and its related professions such as blacksmith and locksmith -- has been feared. People thought that it was the work of the devil. They have been afraid, since heathen times, of the sparks flying off the forge. Gypsies have always worked with metal, and for that they were avoided. Gypsy tinkers in England were itinerant makers and menders of pots and pans, and generally unwelcome. 'Monger' in its various forms is a common Gypsy last name: it is Smith in English, -guero in Spanish. Today in Spain, common Gypsy professions are mining, metalwork, precious metal craft, copperware, auto-body work. The knife-sharpener who goes around from door to door in Spain is most likely a Gypsy. Horseshoeing, horsedealing, veterinary practice, racing, jockeying, working fairs, circus performing -- are customary Gypsy occupations."

"Bullfighting?"

"Yes, exactly. Not only the matador and his crew, but all those behind the scenes at a bullfight; those tending the bullring animals and running the business, number many Gypsies among them."

She flips her cards.

'Zincali' is an obsolete word for Gypsy. My husband calls himself a 'Calé' or 'Calorrí' and calls his language, 'Caló'. Perhaps 'Zincali' came from a Greek word which means 'untouchable.' When you think back about the castes in India, you wonder if it was the 'untouchables' who started wandering. We don't know why. Gypsies might have been Indian prisoners of war in Egypt in the beginning. Then, once you start going West and guys are on your heels, you keep going West. You keep offending people by doing what they disapprove of. You dance and make music when others consider it sinful. You tell fortunes which frightens people. Your con games annoy them, your iron-mongering prods deep superstitions. So you just have to keep on going."

She recalls her husband. He seemed driven by a relentless sense of persecution. He was not a migrant, but was always running ...

"As a culture, Gypsies have always been outcasts. They were given asylum only in Hungary, and so would forage out from there to make a living. That explains why a 'typical Gypsy costume' with full skirt and bandanna, was fashioned after the standard Hungarian peasant dress of those times. The word for Gypsy in most languages connotes 'foreigner' or 'heretic.'. In the Middle Ages there were outcast societies like Robinhood's, little communities of people living outside of society. They were robbers, soldiers, and crusaders. Gypsies were just another such community at that time, living outside of society.

"There have been occasional purges of those Gypsies. During the Spanish Inquisition, they slaughtered all the Gypsies they could find. In Hitler's Germany, over 400,000 Gypsies were exterminated. In Spain today, the Gypsy considers the Guardia Civil as his natural enemy. My husband would walk a wide berth to avoid a pair of Civiles. He had seen them beat a Gypsy to death for lack of anything else to do.

"When their migrations brought Gypsies to the West coasts of Europe, they stopped. They are noted for their dislike of water, their fear of the sea. I suspect it is because they don't want to get into somebody else's boat and be under somebody else's jurisdiction. Also," she grins, "you cannot fool the sea. There are Gypsies in the New World, but masses of them stopped in France, England, and Germany as well as in Spain. In Andalucia they became sedentary, merged into the Spanish culture, and gave Spain much of its spice."

"So then, Gypsies brought Flamenco with them from India?"

"No. Flamenco is Spanish." She checks her notes, then leaves the podium and slips deftly into an empty desk. She sits amongst them, fondly eyeing them, as if they were a flock of tousled kids. She glimpses a dab of eagerness here, some curiosity, some small desire towards freedom there, a pocket of yearning - but not one sends off the heat that burned in her, white as an alchemist's flame, for thirteen searing years. Susana has the humility and the dignity of a woman who knows her flaws and does not mind. She glows with a certain satisfaction. She is enjoying herself.

"Let's go back. Moors had ruled Spain for seven centuries. Moors? Moslem kings from North Africa. They had in Spain the most enlightened civilization on earth from the 8th to the 13th Centuries. They had street lights and surgery and baths and universities and silverware. Europeans were still in the Dark Ages, gnawing their meat off the bone and wiping their hands on their smelly clothes. Moors were refined. They brought fountains and tiled courtyards, elegant music and libraries, into Spain. Sephardic Jews were the wise men, the advisors to the Moorish kings. The Sephardim translated all the knowledge of classical Greece.

"When the Catholic Monarchs, Ferdinand and Isabella, pressed the Moors back down out of Spain, they established the Spanish Inquisition and sent Columbus to discover America. Just then the Gypsies were arriving. The Moors fled south to North Africa. The Sephardim fled east to Greece and Turkey. But many Moslems and Jews just 'headed for the hills' and became outlaws in the mountains of Andalucia. The Gypsies joined them there. The three outlaw cultures mingled — *moro, judío, gitano.* And Flamenco was engendered.

"Maybe that is why Flamencos often sing, 'I have the blood of kings running through the palm of my hand.'

"Today, if you go to a wedding in a Sephardic synagogue in Hollywood, the wedding songs might remind you of

Flamenco cante. If you listen to the evening prayers chanted from the Moslem mosque, you will think for a moment that you are hearing the nasal call of a Flamenco singer.

"Some Gitanos still live in caves on hillsides or under the ramparts of the Moorish castles in Andalucia. But they are sedentary and have become integrated into village life. Or they live in urban barrios in the cities, like in the 'Ramblas' of Barcelona, or in 'Triana' of Seville. My husband courted me in juergas in Triana. Flamenco doesn't come from caravans. It comes from the ghettos of Spain. Nowadays Gypsies are just more Spaniards, living everywhere - not much distinction."

"What is a 'juerga'?"

"A spontaneous jam session, where Flamencos gather and drink wine and do Flamenco together."

"Did you know Gypsies in caves?"

"I visited Gypsies living in caves around the Alhambra palace of Granada. Those tourist traps with 'typical' brassware and wicker chairs provided cynical Flamenco. The Gypsies in caves under the ramparts of the fortress in Alcalá de Guadaira, were still devoted to their cante. Alcalá was a large town, thirteen kilometers outside of Seville, on the Guadaira River, and was a hatchery of Flamenco. Other Flamenco hotspots were Utrera, Jerez, Triana in Seville. 'Curro' was a common Gypsy nickname. The Flamencos would distinguish between themselves using their hometown. There was a Curro from Utrera, a Curro from Jerez, a Curro from Triana, which also indicated which style of cante each man specialized in. My husband was known throughout the province as Curro from Alcalá. That became his stage name and was a true credential.

"Soon after I met my husband, he took me to Manolito de María's house. That is Manolito there," she points to a poster, "with the hat and the angelic look. Manolito de María was a master Flamenco singer. He sang the Alcalá style of Soleá, which my husband learned from him. Manolito was a poor man. His home was a cave...

Susana's voice is as quiet and distant as her eyes. She stops, then returns to her podium and flips to the last of her note cards.

"Gypsies are cultural rats. And cultures are contagious. Gypsies pick up what appeals to them from one country, make it their own, and take it somewhere else. Hindu dance stamps out barefoot rhythms and tells stories with hand postures. I believe that Flamenco's undulating hands and stomping feet and fast turns are Gypsy secular hand-me-downs from Hindu sacred dances. Some Indians worship a black goddess named Kali; and the Calé, the Gypsies of Triana, worship their black Virgin of Triana. Gypsies always sang and danced around the campfire. They were often heard before seen. The violin was already in Europe; they put their own Gypsy music on it. The guitar was already in Spain. Gypsies made it a percussive instrument, threshing out their own rhythms to back their odd dissonant chants. The flamenco Rumba, pride of Catalan Gypsies has been tossed back and forth between Barcelona and Cuba. My guess is the word 'rumba' is of African derivation.

"So. As it became safer for Gypsies to settle into villages and urban barrios of Andalucia, they brought their Flamenco out of the hills with them. In the 1800's 'senoritos,' upper class Gaché, took an interest. A Frenchman traveled to Seville and romanticized Gypsy life in a story called Carmen. And Flamenco became popular with the Gaché. Before the turn of this century, juergas were brought into taverns where Gaché paid to witness them. A raised platform of boards or 'tablas' was set up and called a 'tablao,' so that the Gaché, while meeting with their acquaintances in the local hangout, could see the Gypsies dance. On these tablaos the Gypsies could hear their own heel-work and that added a new dimension to their Flamenco performance. The dancer's feet were added to the ensemble of voice, clapping, and battered guitar. Dresses with polka-dotted ruffles and silk shawls with fringe were the fashion in Andalucia around the turn of the century. Gypsies kept it, and it became the signature of Flamenco dancers.

"On the professional stage, dancing became the focus of the Flamenco performance. The guitarist and the cantaor became the accompanists. A performance of that group of Flamencos - dancer, singer, guitarist, on that tablao, is called a cuadro or cadre and lasts maybe an hour."

A student asks, "On our vacation in Spain next fall, how can we find cuadros?"

"You can't miss them," Susana thumps her podium.

"One. Cuadros are found in tourist traps such as the

caves of Granada or the wineshops of Barcelona.

"Two. Cuadros are gathered for special occasions - provincial fairs, private parties, Flamenco festivals.

"Three. There are three or four cuadro performances nightly at the Flamenco nightclubs called 'tablaos flamencos'. Tablaos are found in cities all over Spain, especially in the South and along the coast.

"El Cid here in Hollywood is the best of all tablao stages. Big enough to move freely and be creative. Small enough for that intimacy, informality, improvisation, which turns Flamenco into fun.

"Four. Cuadro-like performances are offered by little dance companies in ordinary nightclubs or small town auditoriums. Usually by some male whosis and 'his troupe.'

"Five. There are some big Flamenco ballet companies for the concert stage, and they often have a group number imitating the intimacy and spontaneity of a cuadro. Mind you, any time two people are dancing alike, it is not improvised authentic Flamenco, it is a choreographed number. Which is fine for a big theatre. I love a concert stage - all that space to move. I love expanding and filling that magnitude. However, I prefer tablao work, where I can dance nightly, where I can do Flamenco as it is meant to be, improvised, fresh and daring. To do that, a dancer needs to see much dancing. She needs to be working amongst a variety of dancers, to keep replenishing her art. She needs to be recharged on the job nightly.

"Flamenco has been perishing in California, audiences

dwindling, clubs closing down. So, inspiration is skimpy here. In Spain, although the old Gypsies die away, new ones emerge. Flamenco is flourishing, evolving, breeding with other art forms, strengthening, enriching. For dancers, there seems to be constant Flamenco rebirth in Madrid, where masters in fine dance academies teach new material, new styles. They teach technique, as well as choreograph your numbers and tailor them for you. Not so in Andalucia where I learned. There I purchased basic choreography only. I trained my body with modern dance work which I had learned at Cal Berkeley, and built technique by daily drilling myself alone. Style, I developed on the job in cuadros all over Spain.

"If you are serious about performing Flamenco, you go to Spain frequently to collect your material, or keep finding young performers who have just returned to bring you fresh ideas. Flamenco dance is a live art form. It requires constant feeding."

"Question."

"Yes?"

"Are all Flamenco dancers Gypsies?"

"No. Not even the majority. Gypsies have the artistic advantage. But for reliability, the Gaché have the edge. Dancing is for everybody, even foreigners," she smiles. "However..."

She considers not saying this. Basically prejudicial and under dispute. But she cannot resist giving her opinion.

"Look. I'm a good Flamenco dancer. I'm a Gachí. A

Gypsy often has something beyond 'good.' It is a muse, a wildness, an unpredictability, a fearlessness. I don't know what it is. Gypsies call it 'angel.' They'll say, 'Tiene a'je.' A'je' belongs to them like 'soul' belongs to American Blacks. We're not talking competence here. A lousy beginner Gypsy dancer can have a'je. It is not something you learn, nor imitate, nor summon at will.

"I am wondering if this a'je comes from centuries of stoicism, from a spiritual detachment. From inner autonomy. Like Janis Joplin sang, 'Freedom's just another way to say you've nothing left to lose.' That freedom is the goal of a religious aspirant, of a spiritual seeker, of any monk. Is that what we see in Gypsies? Tiny mystical moments? That same intuition which produces great humor? In fact, whenever my husband laughed, 'Que a'je,' he would say."

Dickering with herself, she paces the gymnasium, circling the group of listeners, then asks,

"Are you with me here?.... Take an example of a Gypsy and a Gachó. I saw the two greatest bullfighters in Spain in the same week. Féria de Sevilla, 1965. All of Spain was divided into two camps of fans. Antonio Ordóñez, the Gachó, was a master. Every time he fought it was a great bullfight. Every time.

"Curro Romero, the Gypsy, was sometimes cowardly, ordinary. But when that a'je came, Romero was brilliant, divine. He so far surpassed Ordóñez, that I was forever spoiled." Susana halts. Motionless, her eyes search their faces.

"What is autonomy?" She solicits responses by beckoning with her fingertips. The students answer:

"Self-reliance?"

"Marching to your own drum."

"Doing what you damn well please."

"Detachment?"

"Yes!" Susana returns to the front, lifts a poster-board so they can all read it, and waits while they do:

WILD Gypsy: AUTONOMY OF FEARLESSNESS

STOIC Gypsy: AUTONOMY OF DESIRELESSNESS

Gypsy SWINDLE: AUTONOMY OF DISREGARD FOR REGARD

Gypsy IRREVERENCE: AUTONOMY OF SHEER HONESTY

Gypsy MIRTH: AUTONOMY OF DISDAIN FOR PAIN

Gypsy PASSION: AUTONOMY FROM THE BODY. FOR IN TRUE
    PASSION YOU LEAVE THE BODY AND FIND YOUR
    ECSTASY IN ANOTHER REALM.

"Autonomy," she repeats. And with each pronouncement, she thumps the board for emphasis. "I don't wait for the guitar to stop before I end my move." Thump. "Compas emanates from within me." Thump. "Compas is my truth." Thump. "I stop my dance with that inner truth, and the guitar and I will stop in perfect sync." She pauses, watching them, then lowers the board, and softens.

"Dance to your own beat. That is the spiritual graduate work of Flamenco. Your worth can never be stolen nor bestowed by anyone outside of yourself.

A hand wavers up and down, finally stretches high and Susana nods for the question.

"Do you have a'je?"

Susana laughs, head thrown back, "I don't know. I've never seen me dance."

"What did your Gypsy family think of your dancing?"

"I had my husband's approval. But, then, my wages went into our joint stash." She laughs again. "Most of his family never saw me dance."

"Why not?"

"Because I worked in distant cities, or in places that cost money, and they were very poor. I would never even clap in a private Gypsy juerga, let alone dance."

"Why not?"

"Well, let's say, you are really good on the ukulele. I mean you are the life of the party, and people love you for it. Would you take your ukulele to Carnegie Hall to play along with a Beethoven violin concerto?"

They laugh, and someone asks,

"You mean, a juerga is Carnegie Hall?"

"Yes, a juerga is Carnegie Hall." Imperious as a queen, she eyes them. Then gently, with a self-effacing smile, she adds,

"I just mean that I have respect. I'm a guest in Flamenco."

"Did your husband's family accept you?"

"My mother-in-law, Coral, accepted me because I loved her son. She was kind. She loved our son very much. She thought he was beautiful -- he was her first grandchild. She marveled at his white skin. Gypsies in Europe tend to be darker than other Europeans, even around the Mediterranean, and rejected for it.

"Was I accepted? Good question." She clears her throat, then swallows thoughtfully.

"I would never really belong. I was a foreigner, remember. I expected to stay there the rest of my life, comfortable in their lifestyle. But don't forget that they were not nomads. They lived in Alcalá, a town with stores and running water. They were, as my husband said, 'civilized Gypsies'.

"I saw some Gypsy nomads once. My husband called them 'Hungarians,' so I assume they were nomads from the European bunch. I remember some freckles and reddish hair. The poorest of country Gypsies he called 'Canasteros,''basket-weavers.' They camped along rivers and wove baskets from river reeds.

"Hmm. Accepted? I don't know ... I suppose his brothers were fond of me. We were family - so intimate that two of them potty-trained my son. My husband, the eldest, and I helped them launch out of their mother's home. We brought them out of Alcalá into the big city and got them their first jobs. So there was a sense that I brought well-being to the family. I was like the ugly stepsister. Never considered a Gypsy, but I was O.K. I had a sense of humor, I defended myself well, and I was loyal to their brother.

"I earned their respect as a dancer simply because I got

paid. Flamenco is an art form which is very lucrative. Spaniards fancy themselves connoisseurs of it. Tourists seek it. So you can 'get rich quick' with Flamenco nowadays, because it has become commercialized, just like boxing in America, or like the early Hollywood days of the movie industry. Bullfighting and Flamenco in Spain are big opportunities for a poor person.

"Accepted...? Gypsies accepted me more than Gaché did. Gypsies always feel like outsiders, and I was an outsider. Perhaps that was a bond. Nevertheless, they always called me a Gachí."

She tamps her note cards and bands them. Twisting to look over her shoulder at the clock behind her, she asks for further questions. A hand is raised.

"When you were living that exotic, romantic lifestyle, did you ..."

The question is convoluted and she misses it all.

"Wait, wait. I'm sorry, you've lost me here. I got stuck on the words 'exotic' and 'romantic.'"

She stares at their white, well-fed faces. She paces the silent hall, struggling with the disparity between her experience of Spain and their concept of it. Finally she turns to them and offers,

"You know... a Gypsy mother feels just as helpless when her child is incurably ill as an American mother does. And just as alarmed when her husband gets drunk. A cold winter damp chills your bones in a Gypsy ghetto in Alcalá just as much as it does in a London flat. Not enough money for food makes you as hungry in Barcelona as it does in L.A. A slug of cognac can be your best friend there, like a shot of whiskey can here. And laughter arises everywhere.

"It was not an exotic lifestyle. I just lived daily life, bickering with in-laws, hoping for a job, mending clothes, loving my man, hurting when he hurt. Life is life, even amongst Gypsies. Poverty is poverty, death is death, and ghetto humor soothes the same there as here. Life for a Spanish Gypsy in Andalucia is not romantic. I knew some well-to-do Gypsies. But they were not the majority. For most, life is drab and hard. Only one thing seems worth living for: the family/tribal bond, which manifests as Flamenco. Flamenco cante is condensed passion. If you took your life and stripped it of most comforts, most pleasures, most satisfactions, you would have the harsh, depressing life of a typical Gypsy. An overcast day they ironically call a 'Gypsy sun.' And if you took everything that you stripped away and rolled all those goodies together and extruded them into one night -- that is the exquisiteness of a Flamenco juerga.

"Mind you, there are plenty of grand parties where wealthy Spaniards cull great Flamenco because they treat Flamencos with due respect and generosity. And there are juergas where food and wine and pesetas are lavished by rich Gypsies themselves. But my experience of Alcalá and Seville, was of a simpler, more stoic, day-to-day life of poverty. Dignified, but not romantic, nor exotic."

Susana turns to the poster above her like a priest to an altar. "The juerga in this photo here could last a few hours, all night long, or even a few days. Look at it."

She studies the seated men in the picture, pauses on Curro. He is knuckling a beat on the table with distracted smile, drumming up a lyric he learned as a kid.

"It looks like a city council meeting. Nothing romantic. Even pleasure is harsh and bone-spare. The only exotic thing here is the music. Hallowed Flamenco music. Distilled human soul."

She turns on her audience, eyes aflame.

"There are no Gaché in this juerga. I am not in this photo. But this juerga is in me. Somehow Flamenco took on life in this willing gachí body of mine. I never became a Gypsy, never even tried. But I really dance Flamenco. And, like these Gypsies," her grin is infectious, "I no longer need applause." She glances back at the clock and closes with,

"Soon I will leave Flamenco. Taking my autonomy with me."

Glossary

NOTE: *The first use of each Spanish and Gypsy (Caló) word in this book will be in italics, which is an indication to the reader to refer to this glossary, if it is not immediately translated in the text. Thereafter, most of these words will be treated as part of the English text, especially those with no English equivalent.*

a'je (angel): The muse or inspiration or "soul" of Flamencos

Alegrías: A mode of Flamenco cante and dance, of 12 or 6 beats, in gay tempo and key

Andalucía: The Southernmost provinces of Spain, which include the province of Seville.

baile: Dance. bailaor, bailaora: Dancer.

bata de cola: A dress with ruffled train, used in stage Flamenco performances.

bodega: Winery, wine cellar, wine storeroom cum bar and restaurant.

bollos: Individual bread rolls.

bringar: To sop up grease or gravy. bringue: fat

Bulerías: A mode of Flamenco cante of the most rhythmically complex and fast tempo, 12 beat

Cale: Romani Gypsy. Word meaning Gypsy. Caló: meaning Gypsy language.

cantaor, cantaora: Flamenco singer, male, female

cante: Flamenco singing or song in general (as opposed to canción, an ordinary song). Also a specific Flamenco mode with its own characteristic rhythmic pattern, key, chordal sequence, mood, traditional lyrics, and corresponding dance structure. The cantes named in this book are Alegrías, Caracoles, Soleá, Rumba, Tientos, Fandango, Fandango de Huelva, Sequidillas, Bulerías, and Tarantos.

Caracoles: A less common derivative of Alegrías.

caramelo: Wrapped hard candies, also a nickname for marijuana.

chato: Pug-nosed or short-nosed, or the person who is.

chocho, chochete: Andalucian nickname for female genitalia, used as a term of endearment for a wife or daughter.

chulo: Pimp, a prostitute's mate.

churros: Spanish street donuts.

compás: The rhythmic pattern of accents and stops in Flamenco music.

coraje: Anger/courage -- a desirable quality in a Flamenco performer.

corrida: Bullfight

cuadro: A Flamenco floorshow, or the group of Flamencos performing a show.

Curro, Currete, Corillo, Currito: Nickname for Francisco, typical in Andalucía and among Gypsies.

duro: A five-peseta coin. "20 duros" being a 100 peseta bill.

Fandango, Fandangazo: A portentous cante, sung often without guitar and always without clapping or dancing.

Fandango de Huelva: A Flamenco cante and dance of 6-beat rhythm, light short verses, originating in the town of Huelva.

fino (fine): Fine wine, meaning dry Spanish sherry from Jerez. ("Sherry" was the English pronunciation of "Jerez").

Flamenco (Flemish): Music and dance of Spanish Gypsies, or the performers themselves. Also used for the Spanish Gypsies' culture or those of their culture, and thus in Spain, interchangeable with 'Gitano'.

Gachí, Gachó, Gaché: Romani Gypsy word for people who are not Gypsies (female, male, plural).

género: Cloth goods

Gitano, Gitana: A Gypsy, more specifically here, a Spanish Gypsy.

grifa: Marijuana

hija: Daughter -- a term of endearment used even when people are not related.

jaleo: Hubbub. Shouting in compás of Flamenco music to encourage and inspire the performers. "A jaleo" is a set chant spoken in a Flamenco compás, not sung, like a nursery rhyme.

juerga: A Flamenco party, or spontaneous jam session where authentic Flamenco singers and guitarists (occasionally dancers) improvise together.

Majara: A Gypsy word for "crazy", the Sanskrit origin meaning "saint".

Maricón: effeminate gay man, frequently the cuadro male dancer.

matador: The bullfighter who kills the bull after doing capework alone on foot with him.

meneo: Swaying; swinging or grinding of hips.

niña, niño: girl, boy

oh-hoo: Oh! or Wow!

ole: Hooray (Olé as spoken more commonly in Andalucía)

palmas: Clapping. Not applause, rather, the percussion instruments of a Flamenco performance.

Papá: Daddy

Paso doble: Two-step - a dance and its music, commonly played at bullfights by bands with primarily horn instruments.

pensión: Small inexpensive hotel rooms; often a family business in the home of the proprietor.

pila: Laundry sink with built-in corrugated washboard, usually of molded concrete.

pitillo: hand-rolled cigarette

plato del día: Daily special in a restaurant.

plazuela: Central plaza of a town.

preñá (preñada): Pregnant

primo, prima: cousin, affectionate term used by Gypsies for one another, whether related or not.

puchero: Andalucian stew of chicken breast, garbanzos and potatoes.

puta: Prostitute

rubio: Blond

Rumba Flamenca: Flamenco cante and dance, 4-beat and erotic. The only cante that is sometimes sung and danced by the same performer simultaneously.

rumbera: A woman who specializes in singing and dancing the Rumba

Sequidillas: A Flamenco cante -- somber 12-beat pattern which counts like 5's.

señorito, señorita: Upperclass (unmarried) gentleman or lady.

Sevillanas: Regional folkdance of Seville, of non-Flamenco origin. Four short gay dances of a set choreography, danced by couples, with castanets -also of regional, non-Flamenco origin.

Soleá (soledad) (Solitude): A Flamenco cante, sad slow, 12-beat compás.

sordas, sorditas: (deaf) Muted palmas, clapping palm to palm (as opposed to "fuertes", clapping fingers to palm).

tablao (tablado): Wooden platform or small stage where Flamencos dance. Also the nightclub which houses such a show.

tapas: Snacks served when a glass of wine is ordered at any bar in Seville.

Taranto: A Flamenco cante from mining country, the music actually reflects the dark depths of a mine.

Tientos: A Flamenco cante, 4-beat compás but somber.

tinto: Red table wine

viejo: Old man

vino tinto or tinto: Red table wine

vino fino or fino: (fine wine) Dry sherry

Acknowledgements

In deepest gratitude to

Nantz, who picked us up when we were down

The sculptors of this book: Wert Williams, Orilla Winfield, Barbara Deal, Wendy McCobb, Marti Blumenthal, Susan Steel, Pam Fox Kuhlken, Lila Youngs, and most of all

Ken Kuhlken whose mastery, loyalty, and generosity of spirit, blessed this story with life.

About
Susan Salguero

At age 14, Susan Salguero witnessed Carmen Amaya's flamenco fury. The experience inspired her to study Spanish cultural history at Cal-Berkeley, where she brought supplies to her activist friends as they left on freedom trains for the South and wondered why she lacked their conviction. Upon graduation, she embarked for Europe and discovered that her quest was defiant as theirs. But she protested through Flamenco, the audacious art of Spanish Gypsies.

Years later, she returned to California to finish out her dancing career at the El Cid on Sunset Blvd, the Matador on West Pico, the Santa Barbara Lobero Theatre, and to teach Flamenco theory for UCLA Extension, before changing careers. She became a bereavement and hospice counselor and a writer. Her subjects are her experiences and insights, which she has published in local newspapers as editorials and an in ongoing column of over fifty articles on counseling issues. *The GACHI* is Susan's first book.

About

Curro de Alcalá

He was born Francisco Salguero, in Utrera, province of Seville, during the Spanish Civil War. Life for most Gypsies in Southern Spain was austere and Curro grew up with a tragic sense of life and his own mortality, but with an indomitable sense of humor. Gypsies in Spain share those traits, address each other as "cousin," and tend to be all distantly related. Curro is a second cousin of Antonio Mairena, who has been considered the most recorded and most knowledgeable Flamenco singer in Spain.

In Utrera, Curro was raised with Fernanda and Bernarda and Gaspar de Utrera, all top recording Flamenco singers. As children they ran together, hung out with Perrate, esteemed cantaor. Part of that time Curro and his mother lived in Lebrija, in the house of La Perrata, a great unknown cantaora, sister of Perrate, and mother of the more famous Lebrijano. Curro learned the cantes of Lebrija from La Perrata.

He moved to Alcalá de Guadaira at the age of sixteen and went out on juergas with other youths, learning cante from the masters alive at that time. Joaquín de la Paula, his brother Juan Talegas, his nephew Manolito de María, and the guitarist Diego del Gastor -- all hallowed Flamencos --

were Curro's personal friends and juerga companions as a young man, and in the Flamenco tradition, therefore, his masters. Later he lived in the flamenco neighborhood of Seville, called Triana, and learned the cante styles of Triana. He sang with La Cochinita, La Burra, Tragapanes -- unknown geniuses of cante. He learned the cantes of Cordoba. Curro has been influenced by the cante of Chocolate, Terremoto, Lebrijano, Camarón de la Isla. He has worked with many of these great singers, and, among others, the famous Fosforito, Beni de Cádiz, Lole y Manuel.

Utrera, Lebrija, Triana, and Alcalá are all crucial birthplaces of flamenco cante. As Curro lived in these places, their cantes grew in him. His favorite cante is the Soleá of Alcalá. Most of the cante of Alcalá was developed by the people who lived in the "Castle," a gypsy ghetto, a cluster of caves in the hillside underneath the old moorish castle of Alcalá.

As a professional singer Curro has performed on many of the tablaos of Spain, with famous flamenco dancers, guitarists, and singers; and he has performed abroad (Japan, Israel, USA). However his origins are ever with him, and he can spin stories of those old Gypsies with affection and respect. And that is how he sings their Flamenco, his Flamenco.

9 780975 904794